**CONNECTING CHILDHOOD AND OLD AGE
IN POPULAR MEDIA**

CONNECTING CHILDHOOD AND OLD AGE IN POPULAR MEDIA

EDITED BY

VANESSA JOOSEN

University Press of Mississippi / Jackson

www.upress.state.ms.us

The University Press of Mississippi is a member of
the Association of American University Presses.

Copyright © 2018 by University Press of Mississippi
All rights reserved
Manufactured in the United States of America

First printing 2018

∞

Library of Congress Cataloging-in-Publication Data

Names: Joosen, Vanessa, 1977– editor.
Title: Connecting childhood and old age in popular media
/ edited by Vanessa Joosen.
Description: Jackson: University Press of Mississippi, 2018. |
Includes bibliographical references and index. |
Identifiers: LCCN 2017029439 (print) | LCCN 2017055374 (ebook) | ISBN
9781496815170 (epub single) | ISBN 9781496815187 (epub institutional) |
ISBN 9781496815194 (pdf single) | ISBN 9781496815200 (pdf institutional)
| ISBN 9781496815163 (cloth: alk. paper) | ISBN 1496815165 (cloth: alk. paper)
Subjects: LCSH: Intergenerational relations in mass media. |
Youth in mass media. | Older people in mass media.
Classification: LCC P96.I48 (ebook) | LCC P96.I48 .C66 2018 (print)
| DDC 305.2—dc23
LC record available at https://lccn.loc.gov/2017029439

British Library Cataloging-in-Publication Data available

CONTENTS

Acknowledgments   VII

Introduction   3
VANESSA JOOSEN

1. United by God and Nature
   Johanna Spyri's Heidi and Her Relationship with the Elderly   26
   INGRID TOMKOWIAK

2. Happily Ever After for the Old in Japanese Fairy Tales   43
   MAYAKO MURAI

3. Vitalizing Childhood through Old Age in Hector Malot's *Sans famille*
   An Intersectional Perspective   61
   ELISABETH WESSELING

4. The Right to Self-Determination
   Ageism in Two Dutch Children's Books on the Voluntary Death of Elderly People   76
   HELMA VAN LIEROP-DEBRAUWER

5. Extremely Close Generations
   Childhood and Old Age in Jonathan Safran Foer's Novel   93
   VANESSA JOOSEN

6. The "Strawberry Generation"
   Two Views on Intergenerational Relations in Post–Cold War Taiwan   108
   EMILY MURPHY

7. Intergenerational Bonding in Recent Films from South Korea   128
   SUNG-AE LEE

8. Mischief and Mayhem
   A Cultural History of the Relationship between Children and Old People in the Contemporary Family Film   146
   LINCOLN GERAGHTY

9. Grandparents and Grandchildren in *The Simpsons*
   Intergenerational Rupture and Prefigurative Culture   168
   MARIANO NARODOWSKI AND VERÓNICA GOTTAU

10. Sustaining and Transgressing Borders
    The Relationship between Children and the Elderly in Mad Men   184
    CECILIA LINDGREN AND JOHANNA SJÖBERG

11. Representations of Intergenerational Relationships in Children's Television in Turkey
    Inquiries and Propositions   207
    GÖKÇE ELİF BAYKAL AND ILGIM VERYERİ ALACA

12. "It's Disgusting!"
    Children Enacting Mixed-Age Differences in Advertising   228
    ANNA SPARRMAN

    Notes on Contributors   247

    Index   251

ACKNOWLEDGMENTS

This volume results from a workshop held at the University of Antwerp in May 2015. It was the fourth workshop of the Platform for a Cultural History of Children's Media (PLACIM) that is hosted by Maastricht University, coordinated by Elisabeth Wesseling, and funded by the Dutch Research Council NWO. The Department of Literature at the University of Antwerp provided additional funding for the organization of the event. I would like to express my gratitude to all the institutional partners and funding organizations involved in PLACIM for supporting this inspiring network.

The authors who have contributed chapters to this volume were exceptionally pleasant to work with, and I want to thank them for the rewarding experience of editing their work. In addition, I extend my gratitude to those participants of the PLACIM network and the workshop in Antwerp who did not contribute a chapter but provided valuable feedback: Bahar Gürsel, Bettina Kümmerling-Meibauer, Bengt Sandin, and Helle Strandgaard Jensen. We have also benefited greatly from the feedback of two anonymous peer reviewers, who offered an encouraging combination of supportive comments and useful suggestions.

My own work on this volume was made possible by a VENI postdoctoral grant awarded by NWO, and by the institutional support of Tilburg University and the University of Antwerp. John Foster, my Fulbright English Teaching Assistant at the University of Antwerp, provided invaluable help in the copy editing of two chapters. I would like to use this opportunity to express my appreciation for my former colleagues at Tilburg University (Helma van Lierop-Debrauwer, Sara Van Den Bossche, and Odile Heynders in particular), my colleagues at the University of Antwerp (Bart Eeckhout, Luc Herman, Geert Lernout, and Dirk Van Hulle, and their PhD students and postdocs, as well as my own PhD student Frauke Pauwels) and PLACIM's driving force Elisabeth Wesseling. Thank you all for your unwavering support.

CONNECTING CHILDHOOD AND OLD AGE
IN POPULAR MEDIA

Introduction

VANESSA JOOSEN

In the final week of June 2016, when the electorate of the United Kingdom spoke out in favor of leaving the European Union, the first analyses of voting behavior revealed a striking age bias in those who had supported Brexit and those who had opted for "Remain." A mere few hours after the tight results of the referendum had become clear, a chart published on social media showed that sixty-four percent of the eighteen-to-twenty-four-year-old Britons had voted "Remain," while in the over-sixty-five category, "Leave" had won, with fifty-eight percent of the votes. The chart was matched with a "life expectancy" column, showing that the youngest age cohort scored highest in the "average number of years they have to live with the decision" that most voters in this age group had opposed (Elgot). In the days that followed, various young voters testified to feeling betrayed by their parents and grandparents (Cosslett). Brexit makes clear that the United Kingdom is in crisis—not just in terms of finances or politics, but also in terms of intergenerational support. As the heading of a column by Ben Chu in the *Independent* suggests, the intergenerational strife that resulted from the referendum is symptomatic of a broader intergenerational tension: "Brexit is one more example of the older generation financially bankrupting the young." Members of different generations are thus staged as competitors for scarce means, rather than as supportive allies striving for the same goal. In this atmosphere of crisis, the old are cast as selfish usurpers of the means that younger generations should be entitled to.

One could argue that the Brexit age chart and the ensuing debate are marked by ageism, suggesting that old people have less of a right to vote or that they are less entitled to social benefits because of their shorter life expectancy. Yet few critics picked up on that idea. After all, ageism is one of the most naturalized sets of prejudices in Western society. The poem that the former British Children's Laureate Michael Rosen published on his website is one instance where the ageist dimension in the response to the Brexit surfaces. Rosen parodies the hostile stance that the Leave camp took on refugees by applying it to the older generation that supported Brexit in such high numbers. Rosen begins by stating that "there are too many people in Britain today," then gives a litany of "wrongs" committed:

> they're putting pressure on our public services,
> they're forcing wages down through doing low-paid jobs
> and volunteering all over the place;
> they're hanging about on street corners
> talking to each other in their own odd ways (Rosen)

In the stanzas following this quote, the poem suggests that the measures that "Leave" raised for refugees should be applied to the elderly, taking away their benefits and then locking them in camps. The poem mimics the rational stance that marks not only the discourse used by UKIP, the right-wing United Kingdom Independence Party, but is also reminiscent of Nazi Germany's justification of the Holocaust. The title of Rosen's poem, "Time to cull old people," dehumanizes the elderly by using a term that refers to methods of selecting and killing animals. While "Time to cull old people" seems to be meant first and foremost as a parody of UKIP's discourse on refugees and migration from Eastern Europe, its irony also backfires on the "Remain" voters who reproduced age stereotypes uncritically in the aftermath of the referendum.

 The idea of the old preying on the young is neither new nor exclusive to the West. Yet, in light of the global phenomenon of greying societies in which the elderly take up an ever-growing percentage of the population, and—as the Brexit debate has made clear—the electorate, a better understanding of intergenerational relationships and the cultural associations attached to old age has gained new urgency. In the media and political discourse, the ageing population is usually cast as posing an impending threat, which calls for unpopular measures, such as raising the age at which workers recently entering the workforce will be eligible for retirement benefits or cutting pensions and other forms of social welfare (Watt, Wintour, and Elliott). This discourse fosters a sense of competition and sometimes even jealousy between generations (see, among others, Swinford; McVeigh and Helm; "New Zealand's Hidden Shame"). The so-called baby boomers in particular, as a large group with a high life expectancy that is currently retiring, are envied and seen as a threat to the prosperity of younger generations (Grant; Green 166)—both in financial and in political terms. The need to become "agewise," to use a term popularized by Margaret Morganroth Gullette, is urgent: age critics stress the impact that age and discourses about age have on people's daily lives and try to foster more awareness about this impact. The current volume hopes to cater to that need by shedding light on one type of intergenerational relationship in particular: the link between childhood and old age.

All the authors in this book explore cultural narratives that connect young and elderly characters, reflect on the nature of this connection, and situate it in its socio-historical and cultural context. Media narratives in popular culture often ascribe interchangeable characteristics to childhood and old age—the nature of these characteristics is extensive, ranging from physical weakness and the need for care or education, to wisdom and moral superiority. In the manner of George Lakoff and Mark Johnson's *Metaphors We Live By* (1980/2003), this volume envisions the presumed semblance between children and the elderly ("children are like old people" and vice versa) as a root metaphor. It explores the recurrent use of this root metaphor in literature and media from the mid-nineteenth century to the present, focusing on the late twentieth century. The authors demonstrate how it shapes and is reinforced by a spectrum of media products from Western and East Asian countries. Their cultural traditions in viewing childhood and old age, while clearly distinct, are regularly blended when stories travel and are adapted across continents, as is the case for several of the narratives we discuss. The equation of childhood and old age always has implications for the generations in between, which are often characterized in contrast to the young and the old. By exploring the various ways in which characters of different ages can be linked and opposed to each other, this collection offers ways to think about intergenerational relationships beyond clichés, prejudices, and cheap sentimentalism, recognizing instead the multifaceted nature of each stage of life, and the complexity of relationships across age groups.

Historical Perspectives

The tradition of connecting youth and senescence goes back a long way.[1] Already in the fifth century BC, the Greek philosopher Aristophanes called old age a "second childhood" (Hockey and James 3). In late antiquity, the link between youth and senescence became manifest in the so-called literary *puer senex* trope, a "literary motif which telescoped old age and childhood in a single figure" (Carp 737). Classical Latin authors, such as Ovid, Valerius

Maximus, and Pliny, described characters—both old and young in terms of their numerical age, both male and female—that united maturity and features of youth, so that "by the beginning of the second century the *puer senilis* had established itself as a topos" (Curtius 99).[2] Given that Ernst Robert Curtius also traced this motif in various biblical texts, it is not surprising that Teresa Carp finds it in several medieval hagiographies, where "certain children were characterized as having traits appropriate to persons of very advanced years; and conversely, aged persons were sometimes endowed with the attributes of children such as innocence and even a juvenile appearance" (737).

Most of the texts that Curtius and Carp refer to describe the connection of youth and old age in positive terms, with precocious children who have already acquired the maturity and wisdom of old age, and vital elderly figures who have retained the strength of youth. In several of Shakespeare's plays, by contrast, the comparison is made on less favorable terms. In *King Lear*, Goneril refuses to take her father seriously after she has acquired her part of his inheritance, claiming that "old fools are babes again / And must be used with checks as flatteries when / They are seen abused" (I.3, lines 20–23). In his famous speech on the seven ages of man in Shakespeare's *As You Like It*, Jacques too draws on childhood to describe old age: "Last scene of all, / That ends this strange eventful history, / Is second childishness and mere oblivion, / Sans teeth, sans eyes, sans taste, sans everything" (II.7, lines 163–166, Shakespeare 1649). In both Goneril's and Jacques's comparisons, childhood and old age are cast as periods of foolishness and want. Both characters, moreover, make generalized, negative statements about old age (and childhood, for that matter) that qualify as ageism.

A similar, uniform development of the life course is implied in the so-called *Lebenstreppen*, or stages of life (Figure 1.1). From the sixteenth century onward, these visual depictions of the various life stages on an ascending and then descending staircase, became popular (Lucke, Lucke, and Gogol 132). They equate childhood and senescence visually: on top stands a man (and, from the seventeenth century onward, sometimes also a woman) at the age of fifty, which suggests that middle age is the summit of human life. Infancy, childhood, and old age are depicted on the lowest steps of the staircase, at opposite ends. One is close to birth, the other to the grave. As in Shakespeare's plays, the image of the double staircase functions somewhat differently from the *puer senex* trope as it is understood by Curtius and Carp. Youth and old age are not so much combined in the same person but are, rather, cast as comparable stages in the life course. From the way the staircases are constructed, those similarities seem to reside in biology

Figure 1.1. *The Ten Ages of Man* by Jörg Breu (1540).

and social status. What Gullette, in *Aged by Culture*, calls the "decline narrative" that dominates Western thinking about old age is here matched with a view of growing up as a form of physical and social ascension. The titles and accompanying rhymes of some *Lebenstreppen* make that view explicit. Abraham Aubry's depiction of the steps of life is, for example, called "Auff und Nidergang deß Männlichen Alters" (Rise and fall of man's age; Lucke, Lucke, and Gogol 135). The accompanying text that describes "The Ages of Man" shows that being on the same level did not necessarily foster respect and understanding between certain stages in life. The age of "90 years" is accompanied with the line "the scorn of children" (Botelho 119).

Affectionate relationships did exist, though. As Lynn Botelho points out, people in the seventeenth century "clearly did live long enough to know their grandchildren" (171), and some contemporary art shows the young and the old enjoying each other's company. Christian van der Passe's *The Seasons and Ages of Man*, for example, depicts an old man and a smiling child warming their hands by a fire, while Rembrandt draws a smiling elderly woman who teaches a young child how to walk (Figure 1.2), and in one of his family paintings, Jan Steen includes a prominent image of an old woman playing with a smiling toddler. At the end of the seventeenth century, Botelho (172)

Figure 1.2. Sketch by Rembrandt (1646).

notes, "spoil-the-child" grandparents appeared, while the old would also act as substitute parents to their grandchildren when their own children were in need or deceased. She warns, though, "While these relationships could be warm and loving, as well as mutually rewarding, they were not quite the sentimental relationships of the modern West" (172).

The sentimentalization of the connection between childhood and old age, rather, appears to be an eighteenth-century legacy, when the spoiling grandparent becomes a recurrent trope: "Whether in memoir or fiction, grandparents began to loom large in the world of children" (Troyanski 180). David Troyanski points out that autonomy was an important ideal for the elderly of the eighteenth century, who often cared for their children, rather than vice versa (182), even if reflections on the weakness and detriments of old age were also numerous. Competing discourses about old age thus existed side by side, as they still do today, with the elderly functioning as "allegorical figures, representing grief, suspicion, malice, parsimony and calamity, but also wisdom, experience and penitence" (Troyanski 200). In art the elderly were often depicted with children, yet this affectionate image of the old and the young interacting was countered by narratives about "old people as blocking the progress of youth" (Troyanski 204) by preying on a family's resources or even on the vitality of the young.

Lebenstreppen remained popular in the eighteenth and nineteenth centuries, as did the trope of the *puer senex*. Yet this ambivalent figure was also subject to change. About the poetry of Charles Lamb, for example, Judith

Plotz writes that his "old men are habitually childlike" (114), evoking the *puer senex* trope. The association with childhood can be revitalizing, as Plotz refers to the old schoolmasters in Lamb's works who have retained their childhood's studiousness. Yet the metaphorical childhood that these seniors relive can also be based on perceived mental decline, for instance, when it refers to a man "who sank into senile reversion to boyhood memories" (Plotz 115). Lamb even "deepens the connection between extreme youth and extreme age" by conceiving the idea of "superfoetation," comparing the old men to fetuses who will never be born (Plotz 115). This tragic image is countered by his alternative view of history, which allows for the recapitulation of childhood in old age: "By conflating old and young, Lamb plays games with normal sequence and turns the past into the future" (115–116). As often happens in later children's books, such as Guus Kuijer's *The Book of Everything* (see Joosen), Lamb connects the young and old in his "Dream Children" via stories: "Children love to listen to stories about their elders, when *they* were children" (Lamb cited in Plotz 116). In the dream that Lamb evokes, children and the elderly coexist in what Plotz calls a "stretched imagination" where age categories become particularly fluid and reversible (116).

Connecting childhood and old age remained a literary and artistic trope in the nineteenth century, as Elisabeth Wesseling's and Ingrid Tomkowiak's contributions to this volume show, and as Claudia Nelson points out in *Precocious Children and Childish Adults*. Victorian literature "sometimes showed youth and age as interdependent allies against a more powerful mainstream," yet did so on ambivalent terms: "the aged might be perceived as preying on, exploiting, or projecting their own weaknesses onto children" (Nelson 2). At the turn of the twentieth century, when social welfare and education systems were gradually established in various countries, the old and the young were joined in a discourse on their weakness and need for protection. In the course of the twentieth century, taking care of children and the elderly increasingly became a responsibility for the state rather than the family, and the development of laws and funds for this care often ran parallel for the young and the old (Sandin, "Ages"; Sandin, "Child Labor").

Although *Lebenstreppen* have gone out of fashion, recent practices still draw on related ageist prejudices. In *Growing Up and Growing Old* (1993), Jenny Hockey and Allison James stress the similar social conditions in which children and the elderly dwell. In residential homes, the old are frequently subjected to infantilizing treatment. Their study yielded that through "overt and hidden social practices, whether of caring control or controlling care, both elderly people and young children were being denied full personhood," in particular when it came to "autonomy, self-determination and choice" (3). Several of the chapters in this book address the treatment of the elderly as children in residential homes—either as established practice, as in *The Simpsons* (discussed by Mariano Narodowski and Verónica Gottau), or as a dreaded prospect in *De regels van drie* (*The Rules of Three*, a Dutch children's book analyzed by Helma van Lierop-Debrauwer). On a more positive note, international sociological research by David Blanchflower and Andrew Oswald (2007) indicated that the relationship between age and happiness follows a U-shape, with a dip between the mid-thirties and late forties, when stress levels peak. This means that children and old people generally have a higher sense of well-being than do the generations in between. In fact, the U-shape in their statistics inverses the ascending and descending movement in the life course suggested by the *Lebenstreppen*. In current narratives that link childhood and old age, various models of growing up and growing old compete with each other and are sometimes blended.

The Connection between Childhood and Old Age as a Root Metaphor

Curtius (1948) finds the recurrence of the *puer senex* trope so pervasive that he calls it "an archetype" that should be understood as a manifestation of the unconscious (101). In this book, rather than opting for a Jungian, psychoanalytic approach, we treat the connection between childhood and old age as a root metaphor, drawing on George Lakoff and Mark Johnson's *Metaphors We Live By* and their conviction that "metaphor is pervasive in everyday life, not just in language but in thought and action" (ch. 1). There is some overlap between what they consider a root metaphor and Max Black's description of an archetype as "a systematic repertoire of ideas by means of which a given thinker describes, by *analogical extension,* some domain to which those ideas do not immediately and literally apply" (241). In our case, ideas about childhood are mapped onto old age, and vice versa. Hockey and James's findings on the similar treatment of children and elderly people in care illustrates how metaphorical associations affect not only our language but also our thinking and consequent behavior. The chapters in this book make clear how metaphors related to childhood and old age influence and are in turn influenced by narratives in various media. The current volume is the third in a series of studies of metaphors related to childhood in various media, developed by the Platform for a Cultural History of Children's Media (PLACIM, see www.placim.org). The first volume focused on the repeated association of children and "savages" (Elisabeth Wesseling's *The Child Savage, 1890–2010*), and the second explored metaphors related to childhood nostalgia (Elisabeth Wesseling's *Reinventing Childhood Nostalgia*). As the title of the current volume suggests, the root metaphor "childhood is like old age" is not just manifest in linguistic expressions (most notably in the English expression "second childhood" or the Dutch "kinds" that are used for old-age dementia) but also in the popular imagination and narratives about the old and the young. While the connection of the two stages in life can be witnessed since antiquity, the basis on which childhood and old age are considered comparable differs, as do the concrete manifestations and effects of the connection.

Given the fact that childhood and old age are two stages in life, all the contributions in this volume draw on the interdisciplinary field of age studies, which includes life course theories. One of the central tenets of this booming field is Gullette's credo that people are "aged by culture," as the title of one of her books reads. The meaning that people attach to biological, numerical age—even the mere fact that we calculate a numerical age—is culturally determined, as is the way that people "act their age," that is, how they let their age influence their behavior. The authors in this volume thus consider age as performative, with characters enacting certain age roles rather than merely being a given age. In her investigation of children's responses to age, Anna Sparrman, for example, contrasts the concept of numerical age with functional age (based on skills), insisting that age is always enacted and made up in and through situated practices. For example, age is not gendered in itself but rather made gendered. The intersection between age and other social categories is explored in depth in Elisabeth Wesseling's chapter on Hector Malot's *Sans famille*.

In addition, all the chapters in this book deal with fiction—whether in the form of literature, film, television, animation, or advertising. As a result, the construction of age that we analyze relies on narrative strategies, which are in turn determined by the medium in which a narrative is developed. The attribution of a certain age to a character, for example, will differ according to the medium in which the character is presented. In literature, the reader will rely on textual clues provided by the narrator and characters, and a numerical age may be spelled out (as it often is for child characters); but, as Anna Sparrman shows in her contribution, in a verbally sparse medium such as advertising, viewers have to interpret a series of visual and contextual clues to figure out whether a depicted person is old or young. When Gökçe Elif Baykal and Ilgım Veryeri Alaca question the stereotypical representation of the elderly in Turkish television cartoons, they also recognize that certain signs of old age function as a formulaic shorthand to assign a character to a certain category. Acknowledging the function of stereotypes, however, does not mean that they cannot be criticized.

Regardless of the medium, features that are attached to age may serve a certain narrative function, and we should not treat them as a straightforward reflection of reality. For example, in children's books, parents often fail to take care of their children, who are then put in the care of elderly characters as substitute parents. The failure of the parents and the lack of rigorous control exerted by the elderly frequently serve a plot-related motive: they provide the circumstances necessary for the children to start an adventure without strict adult supervision (see also Shavit 95). As Elisabeth Wesseling shows in her discussion of Hector Malot's *Sans famille* (1878, *Nobody's Boy*), the death of the traveling musician Vitalis should not be interpreted as a manifestation of a decline narrative that culminates in death, but rather contextualized in the genre of naturalist melodrama, which often uses sudden tragic events to elicit an emotional response from its audience. Mayako Murai advances the hypothesis that old characters feature so prominently in Japanese fairy tales because they may be better suited than the young to explore the human psyche symbolically, as they are no longer tied up in processes of maturation or finding a partner for life. When age is constructed in fiction, generic conventions, style, plot, humor and intended audience play a significant part. Moreover, the scale on which media products are created and distributed also determines how age is performed. There is a political economy behind the production of stories, especially for products that are intended for an international market.

Defining Childhood and Old Age

Age and the life stages are negotiated, relational concepts. When considering age in a historical, international, and intermedial context, as the authors in this volume are, the relativity of age norms becomes apparent. The labels "young" and "old" can be matched to a variety of numerical ages, depending, among things, on the historical period, culture, and the age of the person who assigns it. According to Lorraine Green's categorization of life stages, old age is reserved for people over sixty (5–9). To a child, however, someone in their forties may already appear quite old, and in some gay communities in the 1980s, the benchmark for old age was lowered to forty or even thirty-five years of age—mostly due to the devastating effects of AIDS (Goltz 7). As Sparrman's contribution shows, even within a group of children with similar ages and backgrounds, age norms may raise debate. Finally, Baykal and Alaca's chapter illustrates how Turkish grandparents' perception of their stage of life differs substantially from their grandchildren's.

If we extend our concept of age beyond the numerical, a person can be argued to have various ages at the same time. In *Understanding the Life Course,* Green (2010) lists a number of "non-chronological age variables" according to which one and the same person can have different ages

> These include one's *subjective* age, which may be older or younger than your chronological age ("you're as old as you feel"); or how others perceive you: *other-perceived age; social age,* the extent a person's roles and behavior parallel social expectations regarding someone their age; *functional age* which is comparative and is a judgment about whether someone's bodily systems, such as heart and lungs, intellectuality or dexterity, compare to similar-aged peers; and *biological age* which relates to potential life span. Therefore, a fit fifty-five-year old may have a lower biological age than an unfit and unhealthy forty-year-old. (Green 29)

For pragmatic reasons, most authors in this volume work with broad labels to refer to certain stages in life (young and old, child, elderly, middle age). When the narratives themselves are more specific about the life stage to which certain characters belong, these broad labels can be further refined. Green (5–9) distinguishes among the following life stages: infancy and childhood, adolescence (from the early teenage years to early adulthood), young adulthood (eighteen to forty years), middle adulthood, and old age (sixty and above). While she mentions age ranges for the various stages in life, she also notes that the stages are rather defined by key experiences, such as physical and intellectual development for puberty, or the empty nest syndrome and midlife crisis for middle adulthood.

The life stages that Green outlines are influenced by other nonchronological variables. Given the focus on intergenerational relationships in this volume, rather than life stages in a personal context, some authors have chosen to depart from Green's classification of life stages, especially when it comes to young adulthood and middle adulthood. The generation of parents that is staged in some of the narratives under discussion often spreads over these two stages. Emily Murphy, for example, uses the term "middle generation" to speak about the generation of parents (in contrast to that of children and grandparents) in two Taiwanese novels. A similar issue arises with grandparenthood. Some people (especially men) still have children after the age of sixty, but many become grandparents before the age of sixty. A study by Orit Taubman-Ben-Ari et al. (2012) on first-time Jewish grandfathers found participants to be in a broad age range, from forty-five to sixty-seven years old. In 2005, the average age at which British grandparents had their first grandchild was reported to be forty-nine (Womack)—an age at which they are still likely to be part of the workforce.[3] Nevertheless, in the narratives under study in this book, having grandchildren is usually equated with old age and retirement, and the grandparents' actual age is rarely made explicit. It is interesting to see how the intergenerational dynamics change when not two or three, but four generations are included in one story. Van Lierop-Debrauwer's discussion of Marjolijn Hof's *De regels van drie,* which features two grandchildren, a mother, a grandmother and a great-grandfather, underscores the way age norms are related to a person's position within a family's generational composition.

In addition to the mere numerical age and experiences that we associate with certain periods in the life course, the affective dimensions of a given age may differ immensely. These variable sentiments are well documented for childhood. Various studies on historically and culturally variable images of childhood exist (see, among others, Sánchez-Eppler, Natov, Shavit). Often, child characters are a complex amalgam of different features that adults attribute to the young. Ingrid Tomkowiak, for example, discusses how both enlightened and romantic images of childhood informed the character of Heidi in Johanna Spyri's *Heidi* (1880). With the increasing importance of age studies as a field, the ideologies and sentiments associated with various other stages in the life course are becoming better documented. This volume in turn wants to contribute to that understanding, exploring in detail the affective dimension in the connection between childhood and old age.

Affinity, Conflict, and Complementarity

The chapters in this book all study cultural products in which childhood and old age are somehow linked. All consider narratives in which child characters and old characters interact. In several stories, moreover, we also find manifestations of the *puer senex* trope as Curtius and Carp describe it, that is, a character who unites features of youth and senescence. What those features are exactly varies from story to story. In some of the fairy tales that Mayako Murai analyzes, the vitality of youth is retained in the elderly characters. Van Lierop-Debrauwer discusses the figure of great-grandfather Grampy Kas, who claims to have preserved the independent mind that he already had as a young boy: nobody will tell him what to do. In narratives that rely on the fantastic, such as *Cocoon*, discussed in Lincoln Geraghty's chapter, elderly characters can be transformed back into their younger selves without giving up the knowledge and experience they have gathered in life.

In addition to the *puer senex* trope, three basic patterns emerge in the ways that childhood and adulthood are linked: affinity, conflict, and complementarity. Affinity between the old and the young is constructed on the basis of perceived strengths as well as weaknesses (which in turn can be both physical and mental), and on concomitant shared values, beliefs, and experiences. Both childhood and old age can and have been romanticized and colonized. In *De regels van drie*, the Dutch novel that Van Lierop-Debrauwer discusses in the light of the Dutch debates on euthanasia, a boy is the first to sympathize with his great-grandfather's struggle for the right to self-determination, because both are patronized and marginalized by the younger adults. In stories that adopt a more romantic discourse, nature appears as a recurrent and strong connecting force. It proves to be the preferred setting where the old and the young connect, as Tomkowiak shows for Johanna Spyri's influential classic *Heidi* and Van Lierop-Debrauwer for the more recent *De regels van drie*. Yet nature is also associated with stasis, for instance, in Malot's *Sans famille*, where the old man Vitalis twice removes the young boy Rémi from a gratifying natural setting to ensure that his character can further develop. Moreover, organic discourse is also used to "naturalize" the decline narrative and the end of life, or to devalue too close a relationship between the old and the young as "unnatural," as Sparrman shows in children's reactions to advertisements that suggest a sexual relationship between a young and an elderly person.

Whereas nature has been a constant factor in connecting childhood and old age since romanticism, other shared values and beliefs seem to be more historically and/or culturally specific. A closeness to or interest in the transcendental is an aspect that is shared by children and the old in various narratives. In the medieval Japanese collection *Tales of Times Now Past*, which is influenced by Taoism and mentioned by Murai in her chapter, childhood and old age are considered to be closer to the sacred realm and hence envied by Buddhist ascetics who are in between those stages. In *Heidi*, God acts as a unifying force that transcends polarizations between all classes, settings, and generations, as Tomkowiak shows, yet God serves in the novel in particular to strengthen the ties between children and elderly characters. Although this religious basis is less strong in contemporary children's books, some titles are still available where the old and the young share an interest in God or the spiritual, such as Guus Kuijer's *Polleke* series or Sjoerd Kuyper's *Robin en God* (Van Lierop-Debrauwer).

Affinity can lie at the basis of a good relationship, yet so can difference. In that case, the young and the old become complementary, and their mutual relationship makes them stronger. In the older texts under discussion, Spyri's *Heidi* and Malot's *Sans famille*, the old characters provide not only moral lessons for the young but also more elementary schooling, teaching them literacy. This direct form of teaching is no longer prevalent in the more contemporary texts and media products discussed here. Usually, the elderly bring to the relationship their wisdom and independence as adults, which means that they can care for the young in a meaningful way. The young in turn can enrich the relationship with the elderly by their mere youth, revitalizing the old and giving them a purpose in life, as Geraghty shows for two family films: Tim Burton's *Charlie and the Chocolate Factory* and Paul King's *Paddington*. This process is boosted if the child characters prove to be not only young and in need of adult guidance but also cheerful, loving, and grateful.

In their analysis of two episodes from the American television series *Mad Men*, Cecilia Lindgren and Johanna Sjöberg show how elderly figures can act as gatekeepers or enablers in their interaction with children. Gatekeepers make sure that adult knowledge is kept from the young, while enablers facilitate children's access to knowledge and skills. Lindgren and Sjöberg demonstrate that the elderly in *Mad Men* are more willing than the middle generation to act as enablers. This also holds for some elderly figures discussed in other chapters too: Grampy Kas in *De regels van drie*, for example, does not refrain from telling his great-grandchildren about his various love affairs, nor does he hide his naked body from them. In the case of this novel, the enabling function of the elderly figure extends to the implied child reader, albeit mediated by an adult author of the middle generation. In Jonathan Safran Foer's *Extremely Loud and Incredibly Close*, a novel for adults, the enabling function of Oskar Schell's grandmother is ambiguous. Even more candidly than Grampy Kas, she includes in a letter to her grandson intimate, painful details about having sex with her husband —yet it is unlikely that he will ever read her confessions, so that her function as an enabler remains ambivalent.

Similarity can lead to affinity, yet it can also create conflict. "The grumpy old man/woman next door" is a popular antagonist to the young protagonist in narratives for children. Mr. Curry, Paddington's neighbor in King's film, provides a good example of this stereotype, as Geraghty shows. Yet conflict can also take various other forms, from the exploitation of children in Malot to the disdain and envy that are implied in the label "Strawberry Generation" for Taiwanese youth who are supposed to be "easily bruised" because they grew up without hardship—prejudices about youth that Murphy also finds in China, Japan, and Singapore. In times of social change, or when means are scarce, the old and the young are more likely to be cast as rivals. The Brexit debate with which this introduction opened also proves that point. Both Murphy and Wesseling refer to Viviana Zelizer's *Pricing the Priceless Child* (1985), which discusses the attribution of economic and emotional value to children in a historical context, to contrast the value of children in societies facing great poverty and economic turmoil (nineteenth-century France and late-twentieth-century Taiwan respectively) with more affluent communities, such as the contemporary West. In the former, intergenerational competition becomes particularly fierce, and children are more likely to be exploited (and even sold) by members of older generations. Yet, as Wesseling shows for Hector Malot, some narratives suggest that competition in poverty mainly affects the intergenerational relationships between youth and middle age, producing new, mutually reinforcing partnerships between the young and the old.

Adulthood, when it is used for grown-up characters who are not constructed as old, but as a sort of mid-generation, may appear at first sight to function as a neutral, self-evident category, as an "empty signifier." Yet, as the analyses show, it is filled with meanings when compared to the construction of childhood and old age, and often these connotations are quite negative. In my article "Second Childhoods and Intergenerational Dialogues," I use the term "seesaw effect" to describe the frequent dismissal of middle adulthood in narratives that depict a strong connection between children and elderly characters. I borrow the metaphor from Anna Altmann's discussion of feminist fairy tales, where she shows how the promotion of previously downgraded groups (in her case, women) often goes at the cost of others (men)—if one goes up, the other goes down. Altmann problematizes this practice in feminist fairy-tale rewritings because it perpetuates the very gender dichotomy that these texts seek to problematize. While she is writing about gender, a similar dynamic occurs with age: narratives that give agency to children and elderly characters frequently cast a negative picture of the generations in between. In this volume we see this not only in Wesseling's discussion of Malot but also in Heidi's antagonist, Fräulein Rottenmeier, who is a strict educator lacking humor and fantasy, or in *De regels van drie*, where a mother and grandmother are oblivious to a boy's and his great-grandfather's needs, putting their own narrow-minded concerns first. The prevalence of the seesaw effect is all the more striking because an overwhelming number of media products on childhood and old age are not developed by people in these life phases, but rather by adults belonging to the generations in between. Critics like Jacqueline Rose and Susan Neiman argue that the romantic construction of childhood stems from adult fantasies. "Having failed to create societies that our young want to grow into, we idealize the stages of youth," Neiman argues (Introduction). Does the same hold for old age when it is envisaged by those who have not yet reached this life stage? That would imply a sentiment similar to nostalgia but one that actually holds promise for the future. Is old age constructed as a future arcadia for those who "survive" adulthood?

A few considerations complicate the picture. First, in narratives aimed at children, the elderly may be included first and foremost as props to the narrative, mainly there to support the young rather than being fully developed characters. Tomkowiak's analysis of *Heidi* addresses this narrative function of the selfless wise old man or woman, which Sylvia Henneberg characterizes as a form of ageism. Second, John Stephens and Maria Nikolajeva interpret children's literature as a carnivalesque genre. Stephens argues that children's books "offer the characters 'time out' from the habitual constraints of society but incorporate a safe return to social normality" (121). Nikolajeva adds that in these narratives, "children are allowed [. . .] to become strong, brave, rich, powerful, and independent—*on certain conditions and for a limited time*" (Nikolajeva 10, emphasis in the original). Carnival implies a reversal of power structures. With regard to age, upgrading the young typically means downgrading those who traditionally hold the highest status and power: adults who are not yet considered old.[4] Elderly characters may be implicated in this carnivalesque dynamic, sharing with the young the empowerment that children and the old lack in real life. As with all carnivalesque texts, one could argue that the reversals ultimately serve to maintain rather than overthrow existing power structures, even if they may have a subversive effect that lingers.

Especially in recent narratives, the negative image of what Green calls young and especially middle adulthood ties in with concerns that Neiman elaborates on in *Why Grow Up?* Neiman identifies J. M. Barrie's Peter Pan—the boy who does not want to grow up—as an emblem of our times, not just in the West but, as Murphy shows, also in countries like Taiwan. As mentioned above, Neiman believes that adulthood is currently being perceived as a time of resignation, where you have to settle for less. She identifies a decline narrative that is reminiscent of Gullette's: "By describing life as a downhill process, we prepare young people to expect—and demand—very little from it" (Neiman, "Introduction"). While Gullette has old age in mind when she criticizes the decline narrative, Neiman applies it to the transition from youth to adulthood. Narratives that display a seesaw effect are complicit in this process, even though they do predict some light at the end of the tunnel for those who can endure young and middle adulthood until they reach old age, thus endorsing Blanchflower and Oswald's view that the relationship between age and happiness follows a U-shape.

Another alternative to the decline narrative, whether it is situated in old age or middle age, is offered by Nick Lee in *Childhood and Society*, a book on which various contributors in this volume draw. As Lee argues, "there are no 'human beings,'" only "potentially unlimited numbers of ways of 'becoming human'" (2). The dynamic nature traditionally associated with childhood is increasingly mapped onto adulthood, which is understood as neither fixed nor stable. Rather than seeing this as a loss of adult certainties, viewing adults as human "becomings" rather than human beings endows every stage of life with the potential of change. This is a powerful alternative to the decline narrative. Lee describes the aim of his book mostly in relation to childhood: "to give a positive alternative to age-based discrimination by maximizing our acknowledgement of human variation and by showing that there are many ways to 'become human,' some more and some less available to children" (3). Several of our authors show how stressing the potential for change at all ages also helps to endow the elderly with more agency. In most of the narratives analyzed here— from Spyri's *Heidi* to Foer's *Extremely Loud and Incredibly Close* —the process of "becoming" in an elderly character is either inspired by or runs parallel to a child's.

A Transnational Perspective on the Connection between Childhood and Old Age

The connection between childhood and old age is unmistakably influenced by the socio-political situation of a given culture, and in this volume, we juxtapose Western and East Asian narratives to expose shared as well as distinct tropes in connecting childhood and old age. In their exploration of practices in care for the young and the old, Hockey and James stress that the "Western framing of such dependency as 'childish' is just one version, just one vision of old age" (5), suggesting that other cultures may treat the old with more respect for their adult status. That the elderly function as protagonists in Japanese folktales, as Murai shows, at least suggests that their position in society raises more interest in other generations than in the West, where the old get to play mainly supporting roles in fairy tales. Japanese tales show the aged to be more fully embedded in society, to which they keep contributing with work and which does not treat them with disdain or pity. Nevertheless, Murai, Sung-Ae Lee, and Murphy reveal the respect for the elderly that the West often ascribes to East Asian countries as an orientalizing myth. Japanese fairy tales present a varied picture of old age, which includes wise but also evil and silly elderly characters. Murphy and Lee also locate narratives of decline and intergenerational conflict between the old and the young in East Asian countries. The nuanced pictures that they paint strongly argue against generalizations about old age within a certain cultural context. Murphy's consideration of intergenerational relationships in YA literature and family films produced in Taiwan, illustrates that within one culture and one time frame, the picture can be quite varied. While Chang Ta-Chun's *Wild Child* (1996) thematizes both envy and supportive bonding between the old and the young, the film version of Jimmy Liao's *Starry Starry Night* (2011) highlights the role of the elderly in preserving childhood innocence and fostering the imagination of the young. Some symbols and scripts are culturally specific—Lee refers to the A-frame, among others, as metonymic of tales about the abandonment of the old—various others (for example, the *puer senex*) can be found in both Western and East Asian traditions. Several of the more recent narratives discussed in this book have, moreover, been adapted across continents, which further complicates their national identity.

Overview

As this introduction has made clear, the current volume brings together researchers from a variety of disciplines (anthropology, sociology, childhood studies, pedagogy, media studies, film studies, literary studies), covering a range of media, historical periods, and cultural contexts. The chapters are organized in clusters around certain media to facilitate transitions and comparisons. The first three chapters deal with classic children's stories that have been particularly influential in constructing a connection between childhood and old age, and that are still being read and adapted to the present day: Johanna Spyri's Swiss classic *Heidi* (Ingrid Tomkowiak), the Brothers Grimm's fairy tales and Japanese folktales (Mayako Murai), and Hector Malot's *Sans famille* (Elisabeth Wesseling). The subsequent two chapters deal with more recent literature. Helma van Lierop-Debrauwer's exploration of two Dutch children's books about euthanasia forms a contrast with Vanessa Joosen's discussion of the connection of youth and senescence in Jonathan Safran Foer's *Extremely Loud and Incredibly Close*, showing how the implied audience of a book affects the representation of this connection.

The next cluster revolves around film (including film adaptations of novels). The first two chapters explore intergenerational tensions in societies in change in East Asia, with Emily Murphy discussing a selection of Taiwanese post–Cold War narratives, and Sung-Ae Lee analyzing three South Korean films. While the novels and film in Murphy's chapter counter the elderly's dismissal of the young (the so-called Strawberry Generation) as spoiled and lazy, the South Korean films offer a biting critique of the misery that society inflicts on the elderly. Lee frames this analysis most productively by making use of cognitive theory. These two chapters form an interesting contrast with Lincoln Geraghty's analysis of the Western family films *Charlie and the Chocolate Factory* and *Paddington*. He situates the nurturing relationships between young and old and the more optimistic future perspectives for the old in the historical context and generic features of the family film, illustrating how genre and audience influence the construction of intergenerational relationships.

The final cluster in the volume revolves around television—a popular and powerful medium when it comes to shaping and criticizing discourses about age for young and older viewers. Mariano Narodowski and Verónica Gottau reveal the ambivalence with regard to old age in the popular American TV series *The Simpsons*, referring to Margaret Mead's anthropological findings about intergenerational relationships in pre-and post-figurative societies. Cecilia Lindgren and Johanna Sjöberg analyze the ambivalent role of grandparent figures as "enablers" and "gatekeepers" in the American television series *Mad Men*. With their reception study of grandparents in contemporary Turkish television cartoons, Gökçe Elif Baykal and Ilgım Veryeri Alaca make a bridge to the final chapter, in which Anna Sparrman presents an empirical research project on children's responses to age in a sexually suggestive advertising campaign.

Read side by side, these chapters make clear how age is always enacted and acquires meaning in interdependence with other stages in life. Patterns of affinity and complementarity between childhood and senescence dominate narratives for young and dual audiences—while some are rooted in romanticism and sentimentalism, various others cast the young and old as allies in societies that are groaning under political or economic pressure. Narratives as varied in origin as *Heidi*, *Sans famille*, *Starry Starry Night*, *Cherry Tomato*, and *De regels van drie* stage a competition with the young and the old on the one hand, and the professionally active generations in between on the other. The implied wish to make children "agewise"—in the sense that narratives shed light onto various aspects of senescence—can often be deduced, although it could be argued that an "agewise" narrative should involve a nuanced reflection on all stages in life. That being said, the connection between childhood and old age is dynamic and may shift even within one narrative. In *De regels van drie*, for example, a young character's view of old age evolves from ageist prejudice to understanding and respect. In *Mad Men*, grandparent figures switch roles, sometimes acting as gatekeepers, and sometimes as enablers. As Geraghty articulates particularly well, various narratives cast both children and old characters as involved in the process of "becoming" that Nick Lee describes as an alternative to human "being." Films like *Paddington* and *Charlie and the Chocolate Factory* suggest that growth and change are possible at any age. In contrast, narratives that do not allow for this dynamic view of enacting age, such as the Turkish cartoons discussed by Baykal and Alaca, meet with resistance from agewise audiences. Humor and plot conventions often complicate the understanding of old age and intergenerational relationships—what to think of the hyperbolic ageism in nine-year-old Oskar Schell's narrative in Foer's novel, the countless jokes at Grampa Simpson's expense, or the weirdness of *Mad Men*'s Grandpa Eugene? As the chapters on these narratives, as well as Sparrman's reception research, make clear, enacting age always requires an audience's active involvement, complying with, questioning or resisting constructions of age.

Notes

1. While some sociologists reserve the term "youth" for adolescence, we follow its more common use for a period that includes both childhood and adolescence (see Green 6).

2. Curtius uses *puer senex* and *puer senilis* as synonyms (99).

3. As a result, great-grandparents are more frequently taking on active roles in the care of young children. Kevin Kinsella calls this phenomenon "the great-grandparent boom" (Rosenbloom).

4. See, for example, an article in the Belgian newspaper *De Standaard* (2016) on the power of middle-aged adults in making decisions on behalf of the young (Tegenbos).

Works Cited

Altmann, Anna E. "Parody and Poesis in Feminist Fairy Tales." *Canadian Children's Literature* 73 (1994): 22–31.
Black, Max. *Models and Metaphors: Studies in Language and Philosophy*. Ithaca: Cornell University Press, 1962.
Blanchflower, David G., and Andrew J. Oswald. "Is Well-Being U-Shaped over the Life Cycle?" *Warwick Economic Research Papers* 826 (2007): 1–36.
Botelho, Lynn. "The 17th Century." *A History of Old Age*. Ed. Pat Thane. London: Thames & Hudson, 2005. 113–173.
Carp, Teresa C. "*Puer senex* in Roman and Medieval Thought." *Latomus* 39.3 (1980): 736–739.
Chu, Ben. "Brexit Is One More Example of the Older Generation Financially Bankrupting the Young." *Independent* (29 June 2016). http://www.independent.co.uk/voices/brexit-eu-referendum-financial-economic-impact-older-generation-bankrupting-young-a7107666.html. Accessed on 29 June 2016.
Cosslett, Rhiannon Lucy. "Family Rifts over Brexit: 'I Can Barely Look at My Parents.'" *Guardian* (27 June 2016). https://www.theguardian.com/lifeandstyle/2016/jun/27/brexit-family-rifts-parents-referendum-conflict-betrayal. Accessed on 29 June 2016.
Curtius, Ernst Robert. 1948. *European Literature and the Late Middle Ages*. Trans. Willard D. Trask. London: Routledge, 1953.
Elgot, Jessica. "Young Remain Voters Came Out in Force, but Were Outgunned." *Guardian* (24 June 2016). http://www.theguardian.com/politics/2016/jun/24/young-remain-voters-came-out-in-force-but-were-outgunned. Accessed on 29 June 2016.
Goltz, Dustin Bradley. *Queer Temporalities in Gay Male Representation: Tragedy, Normativity, and Futurity*. New York: Routledge, 2010.
Grant, Linda. "Don't Blame All Babyboomers for Brexit." *Guardian* (27 June 2016). https://www.theguardian.com/commentisfree/2016/jun/27/dont-blame-babyboomers-brexit-generation-voted. Accessed on 4 July 2016.
Green, Lorraine. *Understanding the Life Course: Sociological and Psychological Perspectives*. Cambridge: Polity, 2010.
Gullette, Margaret Morganroth. *Aged by Culture*. Chicago: University of Chicago Press, 2004.
Gullette, Margaret Morganroth. *Agewise: Fighting the New Ageism in America*. Chicago: University of Chicago Press, 2011.
Henneberg, Sylvia B. "Of Creative Crones and Poetry: Developing Age Studies through Literature." *NWSA Journal* 18.1 (2006): 106–125.
Hockey, Jenny, and Allison James. *Growing Up and Growing Old: Ageing and Dependency in the Life Course*. London: Sage, 1993.
Joosen, Vanessa: "Second Childhoods and Intergenerational Dialogues: How Children's Literature Studies and Age Studies Can Supplement Each Other." *Children's Literature Association Quarterly* 40.2 (2015): 126–140.
Kuijer, Guus. *Polleke*. Amsterdam: Querido, 2012.
Kuyper, Sjoerd. *Robin en God*. Amsterdam: Leopold, 1996.
Lakoff, George, and Mark Johnson. 1980. *Metaphors We Live By*. Chicago: University of Chicago Press, 2003. Kindle ed.

Lee, Nick. *Childhood and Society: Growing Up in an Age of Uncertainty*. Buckingham: Open University Press, 2001. https://www.mheducation.co.uk/openup/chapters/0335206085.pdf. Accessed on 4 July 2016.

Lucke, Christoph, Margot Lucke, and Manfred Gogol. "Lebenstreppen—oder wie man den Alternsprozess über die Jahrhunderte gesehen hat." *European Journal of Geriatrics* 11.3–4 (2009): 132-140.

McVeigh, Tracy, and Toby Helm. "UK 'Failing Its Young' as Gulf Grows between Generations." *Guardian* (11 July 2015). https://www.theguardian.com/society/2015/jul/11/uk-young-fairness-george-osborne-budget. Accessed on 5 July 2016.

Natov, Rani. *The Poetics of Childhood*. New York: Routledge, 2003.

Neiman, Susan. *Why Grow Up?* London: Penguin, 2014. Kindle ed.

Nelson, Claudia. *Precocious Children and Childish Adults: Age Inversion in Victorian Literature*. Baltimore: Johns Hopkins University Press, 2012.

"New Zealand's Hidden Shame." *Sunday Star Times* (17 March 2013): D6.

Nikolajeva, Maria. *Power, Voice and Subjectivity in Literature for Young Readers*. New York: Routledge, 2010.

Plotz, Judith. *Romanticism and the Vocation of Childhood*. New York: Palgrave, 2001.

Rose, Jacqueline. 1984. *The Case of Peter Pan, or the Impossibility of Children's Fiction*. Philadelphia: University of Pennsylvania Press, 1993.

Rosen, Michael. "Time to Cull Old People." http://michaelrosenblog.blogspot.nl/2016/06/time-to-cull-old-people.html. Accessed on 29 June 2016.

Rosenbloom, Stephanie. "Here Come the Great-Grandparents." *New York Times* (2 November 2006). http://www.nytimes.com/2006/11/02/fashion/02parents.html. Accessed on 17 January 2017.

Sánchez-Eppler, Karen. "Childhood." *Keywords for Children's Literature*. Eds. Lissa Paul and Philip Nell. New York: New York University Press, 2011. 35–41.

Sandin, Bengt. "Ages of Man, Childhood and Old Age: Imagery and Social Change." Paper presented at the PLACIM workshop in Antwerpen, 21–22 May 2015.

Sandin, Bengt. "Coming to Terms with Child Labor: History of Child Welfare." *The World of Child Labor: An Historical and Regional Survey*. Ed. Hugh D. Hindman. London: Routledge, 2009. 53–56.

Shakespeare, William. *The Norton Shakespeare*. Ed. Stephen Greenblatt et al. 3rd ed. New York: Norton, 2016.

Shavit, Zohar. *Poetics of Children's Literature*. Athens: University of Georgia Press, 1986.

Stephens, John. *Language and Ideology in Children's Fiction*. London: Longman, 1992.

Swinford, Steven. "Ed Miliband's Tuition Fees Pledge Risks 'Intergenerational Envy.'" *Telegraph* (25 February 2015). http://www.telegraph.co.uk/news/politics/ed-miliband/11435516/Ed-Milibands-tuition-fees-pledge-risks-intergenerational-envy.html. Accessed on 5 July 2016.

Taubman-Ben-Ari, Orit, Liora Findler, and Shirley Ben Shlomo. "Personal Growth and the Transition to Grandfatherhood." *International Journal of Aging and Human Development* 74.4 (2012): 265–285.

Tegenbos, Guy. "De middelbare leeftijd regeert het land." *De Standaard* (20 April 2016). http://www.standaard.be/cnt/dmf20160419_02246812. Accessed on 20 April 2016.

Troyanski, David G. "The 18th Century." *A History of Old Age*. Ed. Pat Thane. London: Thames & Hudson, 2005. 174–209.

Van Lierop-Debrauwer, Helma. "The Power of Dialogue: Religion in Contemporary Dutch Novels for Children." *International Research in Children's Literature* 2.1 (2009): 115–127.

Watt, Nicholas, Patrick Wintour, and Larry Elliott. "State Pension Age to Be Raised to 70 for Today's Young Workers." *Guardian* (5 December 2013). https://www.theguardian.com/uk-news/2013/dec/05/state-pension-age-raised-to-70-autumn-statement. Accessed on 5 July 2016.

Wesseling, Elisabeth, ed. *The Child Savage, 1890–2010: From Comics to Games*. Farnham: Ashgate, 2016.

Wesseling, Elisabeth, ed. *Reinventing Childhood Nostalgia*. Farnham: Ashgate, 2016.

Womack, Sarah. "Average Age of the First-Time Grandparent Is Now under 50." *Telegraph* (28 July 2005). http://www.telegraph.co.uk/news/uknews/1494949/Average-age-of-the-first-time-grandparent-is-now-under-50.html. Accessed on 17 January 2017.

Zelizer, Viviana. 1985. *Pricing the Priceless Child: The Changing Social Value of Children*. Princeton: Princeton University Press, 1994.

-1-

United by God and Nature

Johanna Spyri's Heidi and Her Relationship with the Elderly

INGRID TOMKOWIAK

In the light of the international resilience of Johanna Spyri's novel *Heidi* (1880), the American scholar Michael Hearn remarks that "Heidi is tougher than she looks" (179). Spyri's heroine manages to win almost everyone's heart, heal her grandfather's and Dr. Classen's wounded souls, cure her friend Klara's paralyzed legs, educate Peter the goatherd, and help his poor, blind grandmother. Jürg Winkler stresses the novel's innovative—even revolutionary—character (26): with *Heidi*, an author was daring to put herself wholly on the side of the child instead of, as was customary, aligning herself with authoritarian adults! Spyri (1827–1901) played a pioneering role in children's literature by propagating respect for the child as a child. In order to do so, the author chose a plot and setting where the main character, Heidi, who stands in the romantic tradition of the divine child, has to interact with the elderly. She takes a liking to several people from her grandfather's generation, and they in turn are very fond of her. It could be argued that these same people use and even exploit Heidi for their own benefit rather than hers. In this chapter I relate this paradox to the images of the child and old age as they are constructed by the author. I will show how the elderly in *Heidi* respond to this child of nature and how they quasi interact in synergism to promote Heidi's development, with each representing his or her own educational approaches and worldviews. With the exception of Grandfather, whom Spyri draws as a round character, these figures remain flat, pictured solely in the role they play in relation to Heidi. Spyri demonstrates that different styles of education can ultimately work together to foster a child's personality.

The first volume, *Heidis Lehr-und Wanderjahre*, was first published by the German company Perthes of Gotha in 1880 and translated into English by

Helen B. Dole as *Heidi's Years of Learning and Travel*. At first glance the story is simple. Aunt Dete leaves her niece Heidi, a five-year-old orphan, to find a home with her grandfather, high up in the Swiss Alps. He has been leading a solitary existence; it is rumored in the village that he is a sinful and unsociable man. Heidi, an open-minded and trusting child, soon wins his heart, and the girl also makes friends with Peter the goatherd and his blind grandmother. Heidi becomes acquainted with the animals, flowers, trees, meadows, brooks, and mountains and comes to love them with all her heart. When Heidi is eight years old, Aunt Dete takes her to Frankfurt-am-Main, where she is to live with a well-to-do family, the Sesemanns, and act as a companion to their disabled daughter Klara. While Klara and Heidi are immediately fond of each other, the housekeeper, Fräulein Rottenmeier, constantly spurns Heidi. Offering little understanding for Heidi's character, she strives hard to teach her bourgeois virtues and manners. By contrast, Klara's grandmother, Grandmamma Sesemann, takes Heidi into her care, teaching her to read and explaining to her the importance of religion. Nevertheless, the big city makes Heidi homesick, and she is eventually sent back to her grandfather. She is now able to read hymns to Peter's blind grandmother and manages to persuade Grandfather to return to the church and the people in the village.

In the second volume, *Heidi kann brauchen, was es gelernt hat* (1881, translated as Heidi makes use of what she has learned), Heidi's experiences and the knowledge she has acquired in the city increasingly make their mark on the life in the alpine village and the mountains. Heidi works hard, keeping house for Grandfather, and even manages to teach the uncooperative Peter to read. Dr. Classen and Klara pay them a visit. With the help of Heidi, Grandfather, and the doctor, Klara learns to walk again. Dr. Classen becomes so fond of Heidi that he wants to keep her by his side. He finally buys a house in the village, where he will allow Heidi and Grandfather to live in winter, and makes legal provisions for Heidi to ensure she has a secure future after his and Grandfather's deaths. With her story about orphan Heidi, who, after many trials and tribulations, finds happiness in a simple life in the Swiss mountains, Johanna Spyri catered to contemporary literary tastes in Germany, where the book became at once a resounding success.[1]

Polarities in Heidi

As an author influenced by Pietism, Spyri conveys a simple yet striking picture of the world, which is strongly characterized by polarities (Küpfer 7–31;

Leimgruber 172–183). The contrast between the Swiss Alps and the German city of Frankfurt is further associated with the polarization of nature and culture, tradition and modernity, home and away, the familiar and the unfamiliar, health and sickness, Christian piety and paganism, young and old. Heidi always acts as a go-between in relation to such poles, and functions as what Walter Leimgruber calls a reparative figure (175).

When Heidi goes to live with her grandfather, she first has to discover the magnificent yet unfamiliar world of the Alps. With her contrast between the idealized, beautiful highlands and the city, Spyri picked up on the hostile attitude toward urban life at the time. As Gisela Wilkending has demonstrated, the polarization of town and country also implied a contrast between rich and poor, and between the educated and uneducated ("Heidi" 192). For Verena Rutschmann, the mountain alp in *Heidi* is above all free from constraint. With this setting Spyri created her own personal paradise—a world where the artificial and ridiculous etiquette of the city can be dropped, granting space and scope instead for natural feelings and talents. As the author constitutes the mountain world as a place of education in accordance with Jean-Jacques Rousseau's pedagogical views, she adds a utopian element that raises the story above the level of a domestic idyll. In *Heidi* the landscape of the Alps not only offers relief from the constraints of society but is furthermore a place where mind and soul can develop freely (Rutschmann 34). Peter Skrine states that the ascent from Maienfeld to Grandfather's hut can be seen as a structural element of transition in the story. The alp is the setting where everything ultimately turns out well. The ascent up the mountain is associated with liberation from personal misfortune and with the power of nature to heal physical, psychological, and emotional wounds. Characters of various ages—the children Heidi and Klara, the adults Herr Sesemann and Dr. Classen—have that experience, while the self-assured Grandmamma Sesemann's admiration for the "glorious" (294) mountains seems to grow in the course of her visit.

The antithesis to the Swiss Alps is the German city of Frankfurt. First of all, it stands for unfamiliarity, a lack of orientation and an oppressive claustrophobia as perceived by Heidi in the house of the Sesemann family. Unlike in the mountains, in Frankfurt Heidi spends most of her time inside the house, which suffocates her despite its substantial physical size. Her desperate attempt to open a window in the hope of seeing the mountains calls up the image of a bird trying to escape from a cage. As Escher argues, however, the city is not condemned as a place of moral and cultural decline (285). Criticism is most readily apparent in Spyri's descriptions of the strict table manners and rules of behavior prevailing in the Sesemann household. Here, Simon Bunke speaks of the disciplinary confines of Frankfurt (550). Although Fräulein Rottenmeier's rigid educational methods initially have only limited effect on Heidi, in the second volume the girl takes along these rules to the rural world of the alp, together with other standards of urban culture. In this regard, Heidi's stay in Frankfurt functions as an initiation rite, covering the typical steps of being torn out of one's natural environment, feeling forsaken and finding one's way back in enlightenment. The personal development that the figure of Heidi experiences ultimately also entails social change and productive interaction between town and country, the modern world and tradition (Domenig 158–160).

Heidi—The Child

With Heidi, Spyri created an archetypical figure who went beyond the book (Schindler, *Spyri* 105). Heidi represents what is good and noble in humanity: she is selfless and compassionate, she stands for a healthy life in harmony with nature, and she embodies freedom, authenticity, and unspoiled purity.[2] The novel thus appeals to the reader's longing for *Heimat* (home), security, intactness, and genuineness. Telling for the characterization of the child Heidi is the image that Fräulein Rottenmeier has in mind when she is looking for a girl to act as a companion to the sick Klara:

> I fixed my mind on a young Swiss girl, expecting to see such a person appear as I had often read about—one who sprung up in the pure mountain air, so to speak; goes through life without touching the earth. [. . .] I mean one of those well-known forms living in the pure mountain regions, and which pass by us like an ideal breath. (Spyri, *Heidi: Little* Swiss 127–128).

The picture Fräulein Rottenmeier paints here inevitably conjures up an image of the divine child as it emerged in early romanticism (see Alefeld, *Göttliche Kinder*). It has little to do with the lived experience of childhood at the time but is rather a glorifying construct. The child becomes a symbolic figure for the qualities desired by the adult: harmony, innocence, purity, artlessness, and proximity to one's origins. The harmony of children, their being at one with nature, contrasts with the inner conflict of the worldly adult, who is alienated from true reality and, as Vanessa Joosen points out, downgraded in symbolic value (130–133, 137). In 1797 Ludwig Tieck stated that children, with their wisdom and sublime mysterious earnestness, are able to put to shame even the very old (who are generally the ones labelled as wise, see Woodward 205–206). Tieck considered children as truly serious-minded and lofty because they are so close to the divine source of radiance, which becomes ever fainter as it moves further away with the passing of time (Ewers, "Dieser Ätherschimmer" 61).

The divine child—a concept that was highly influential in the further development of children's literature—featured first in Tieck's *Die Elfen* (1812, The elves) and then in E.T.A. Hoffmann's *Das fremde Kind* (1816/17, The strange child; see Ewers, "E.T.A. Hoffmann" 77). Heidi strongly resembles this child genius, in particular when she is in the mountains. A key scene in this regard can be found right at the beginning of the book, when Heidi and Aunt Dete are en route to Grandfather's house:

> Suddenly the child sat down on the ground and in great haste pulled off her shoes and stockings; then she stood up again, took off her thick, red neckerchief, unfastened her Sunday frock, quickly took that off, and began to unhook her everyday dress. This she wore under the other, to save her Aunt Dete the trouble of carrying it. Quick as lightning came off also the everyday frock, and there the child stood in her light underclothes with delight, stretching her bare arms out of her short chemise sleeves. Then she laid them all in a neat little pile, and jumped and climbed after the goats by Peter's side, as easily as any in the whole company. (Spyri, *Heidi: Little Swiss* 12)

Heidi thus not only divests herself here of the only luggage she is bearing, worn in layers over her body, but simultaneously casts off all the baggage of civilization, becoming, as Christophe Gros puts it, a little mountain deity (115). Lois Keith interprets the fragment along similar lines: "Like the goats and the birds, the flowers and the insects, Johanna Spyri's child is a part of nature. Heidi gambols around like a little strong, brown goat, she eats good, simple food and grows and blossoms like the flowers" (103). For Ernst Halter, Heidi is even more than that: the personification of a supra-individual, indeed a superhuman principle—the love of God on earth (25).

Spyri's evocation of childhood, however, draws not only on the romantic tradition of the mystical, divine child but also on the cultural anthropological reflections of Rousseau and Johann Gottfried von Herder, which are rooted in the Enlightenment. According to this view, childhood is a revocation of the state of nature and the childlike state of humankind (a theory better known as "ontophylogenesis," as explored in Elisabeth Wesseling's volume *The Child Savage*). For Rousseau, who in *Emile ou de L'Education* (1762, Emile, Or on Education) advocated the idea of a natural system of education, children may have bodily strength and physical-manual dexterity, but their intellectual abilities are barely developed. According to Rousseau, the savage man and the "true" child share the following qualities: a keen power of observation with regard to the outside world, a few elemental feelings (such as self-love and compassion), and a strong and independent, indeed autarkic character, deeply solitary in nature. Children find themselves in perfect harmony with their lack of ability (Ewers, "Romantik" 100). For Herder, in contrast, a child is in need of family. In his view, children are affectionate, willing to submit and fit in, trusting in authority, highly impressionable, receptive and eager to learn—in other words, the exact opposite of Rousseau's independent and solitary child. As Hans-Heino Ewers points out, some ten years after the publication of *Emile*, all elements of the romantic image of childhood were already present in Herder's anthropological view of the child. It is marked by intense emotions, an active faculty of imagination and exuberant fantasy, a lack of sobriety, and a poor sense of reality, an animistic view of the world and of nature, an attachment to society and a sense of authority, gullibility, and a high level of impressionability ("Romantik" 101).

No matter how diametrically opposed the positions of Rousseau and Herder may be in certain aspects, Spyri is perfectly able to reconcile both in the figure of Heidi. While Heidi enjoys a model of natural education in the mountains, guided by her grandfather, in accordance with Rousseau, and generally explores her environment by running and jumping through it, she also develops a sense of religion, which, at the beginning, tends to be oriented toward her intense experiences of nature in an all-embracing manner. According to Regine Schindler, nature is the expression of a divine presence, of godly omnipotence. She suggests the term "natural piety" for a type of reverence of the heavens and the world of the mountains, rather than adhering to a strict theological doctrine ("Form und Funktion" 189). Hansjürgen Kiepe also argues that God manifests himself in Heidi's experiences of the landscape, which is imbued with the familiar features of home and has its own inherent value. Despite not being specifically named, God is nonetheless present in the depiction of such deep-felt experiences, with

Heidi's innocent, childlike love for the countryside and the feeling of security it offers her. The animistic landscape bends towards the child Heidi and lovingly enfolds her as God the Father does with his children (427).

However, once Grandmamma Sesemann has instilled in Heidi a belief in God and read with her the parable of the prodigal son, her devotion to him is expressed far more directly. On her return to the alp:

> The grass all around on the Alm was golden; from all the crags it glimmered and gleamed down, and below, the far-reaching valley swam in a golden vapor.
>
> Heidi stood in the midst of all this glory, and bright tears of joy and rapture ran down her cheeks, and she had to fold her hands, and, looking up to Heaven, thank the dear Lord aloud that he had brought her back home again, and that everything, everything was still so beautiful, and even more beautiful than she had thought, and that it all was hers once more. And Heidi felt so happy and so rich in the great glory that she could not find words to express her thankfulness to the dear Lord. (Spyri, *Heidi: Little Swiss* 190)

In Skrine's view, this passage testifies to a religious fervor that is almost baroque in nature (159). The early romantic topos of the divine child is merged with the late romantic motif of the devout child. It is now only logical that what has been learned is swiftly followed by its practical application: with the conversion of Grandfather, now using the parable of the prodigal son herself, Heidi acts as a missionary.

Ewers observes that the more the romantic view of childhood became established in the course of the nineteenth century, the more evidently the purportedly "true," authentic and "false," fabricated childhoods were confronted in realist children's fiction; in the mid-nineteenth century, it emerged as a contrast between urban and rural childhood, and in this context Ewers explicitly mentions *Heidi* ("E.T.A. Hoffmann" 80). While Winfred Kaminski attributes to Spyri a simplified version of Rousseauism (447), Wilkending points out that toward the end of the nineteenth century, when alpine farmers were increasingly exploited and impoverished through the encroachment of capitalism on every distant corner of the Alps, a new response to Rousseau's theories and romantic, idealized pictures of childhood can be witnessed. Wilkending sees Heidi as a sentimental "sister" to Rousseau's Emile, a child that is endowed with healing powers but also capable of suffering ("Mädchenliteratur" 245).

In appearance, Heidi is described as a physically delicate girl, with black hair and black eyes. "She is certainly not wanting in intelligence" (Spyri, *Heidi: Little Swiss* 301), Grandfather says to himself on Heidi's arrival. Heidi's great alertness, independence, and highly original solutions to problems, which result from a combination of tenacity and naïveté, lead to a sort of felt omnipotence (Wissmer 54). Through her lively character this little girl radiates a strong lust for life and a tremendous ability to empathize with others. She generally acts in an intuitive and spontaneous manner, sustained by courage and kindness. She is also very trusting and obedient—once she has acquired literacy, she swiftly assumes that everything she reads must be true.

Spyri's protagonist was the subject of controversy (Leimgruber 182): on the one hand, Heidi is seen as a strong, undisciplined girl who wants things to go her way, and Heidi repeatedly manages to achieve her goals. Thanks to her communication skills, she is able to persuade, motivate, and reconcile other people: all who come into contact with Heidi develop further and are released from their isolation. On the other hand, Heidi has also been considered a weak, obedient, and conformist figure, who puts others' needs first and fails to stand up for herself. When she returns from Frankfurt and goes back to live with Grandfather, she more or less takes over the household. This obviously delights the old man, but whether Heidi is in fact disregarding her own needs is debatable. The question seems to arise from a modern viewpoint, oriented toward female emancipation.

Heidi's relationship with other characters may raise similar questions. She offers Peter's grandmother so much physical and emotional support that the old lady always wants to have the girl around. So, Heidi's willingness to help and her good nature are also exploited. Adopting a psychoanalytical viewpoint, Jana and Andreas Benz-Conzen note that almost all the relationships that Heidi maintains are with people who are elderly, sick or social outcasts, backward in their development or suffering from hunger. She offers comfort, helps them re-integrate in the community or provides them with instruction or food. The Benz-Conzens claim that fear of abandonment compels Heidi to consistently adopt the position of giver and helper in relation to adults and to always place their needs before her own. They consider Heidi pays for this approach by becoming stunted in her personal development (124).[3]

Heidi's relationship with Peter is less altruistic. He functions as a negative example of a child of nature who is not willing to learn but prefers to enjoy the freedom that nature offers. In the first volume, Heidi is perfectly happy with what she learns from him and her grandfather. Face to face with Grandmamma Sesemann, Heidi even uses Peter as a role model and a pretext to refrain from learning to read. However, when she herself is teaching him in the second volume, she uses rigid methods reminiscent of Fräulein Rottenmeier's educational principle based on the threat of punishment:

> If A, B, C, you do not know, Before the school board you will go. [...] D, E, F, G, must smoothly fly, Or else misfortune will be nigh. [...] If now you fail to know the W, There hangs a stick and it will trouble you. [...] If you the letter X forget, For you no supper will be set. [...] Who hesitates upon the Z, With the Hottentots shall be. (Spyri, *Heidi: Little Swiss* 270–274)

Gerhard Härle divides Heidi's psychological development into three stages: Heidi is first depicted as an androgynous child of nature, who then develops a hysterical character trait in Frankfurt and finally becomes a desexualized child-woman (69, 80). During all these stages, she eagerly serves others. One blatant example is Dr. Classen's request to Heidi at the end of his visit to the mountains: "If I am ever sick and alone, will you come to me then and stay with me? Can I think that then someone will care for me and love me?" (250–251). Heidi is willing to accompany him to Frankfurt at once, as she loves him nearly as much as Grandfather. At the very end of the book the doctor's claim to Heidi is once again formulated in an explicit manner: "So I have also my right in our Heidi, and can hope that she will care for me in my old age and stay with me; this is my greatest desire" (362–363). Jean Villain speaks here of the arrogance with which a woman's entire life is ruled by someone else: the supposed happy end to the story, if we take it to its conclusion, becomes the menacing curse of a woman's unfulfilled life (80).

Grandfather, Grandmother, and Grandmamma Sesemann

Heidi's development takes place in a sphere in which Grandfather, Peter's blind grandmother, and Grandmamma Sesemann interact in synergism. The three representatives of Grandfather's generation, on which I will focus in the rest of this chapter, each deal with Heidi in a very different manner and so contribute to the further development of her personality in their own unique ways. One of the villagers sketches a rather negative picture of Grandfather's character to Dete:

He will have nothing to do with a living soul; from one end of the year to the other he never sets foot in a church; and if once in a twelve-month he comes down with his thick staff, everyone keeps out of his way and is afraid of him. With his heavy gray eyebrows and his tremendous beard he looks like a heathen and a savage, and people are glad enough not to meet him alone. (4)

As an outsider with a discreditable past, the old man does not initially seem the ideal person to whom to entrust the care of a child. The figure of Grandfather is strongly characterized by guilt. In the village he is said to have led a sinful and possibly even criminal life. His wife died early on in their marriage, and their son, Tobias, was killed in an accident. Tobias's wife also died shortly afterward, leaving Heidi as an orphan. Aunt Dete takes advantage of Grandfather's history to hand over the responsibility for Heidi to him, reminding him of the family obligations he neglected in the past. While he does not care about the people in the village, he apparently knows exactly what Heidi needs to be happy. After initial difficulties he lovingly cares for Heidi and becomes the father figure the little girl has always lacked.

Grandfather is modeled on the romantic figure of a guardian who intentionally refrains from acting as an educator (Ewers, "E.T.A. Hoffmann" 79): if the enlightened children's friend of the eighteenth century was a person who accompanied them on their entry into the world of adults, the ideal adult companion of the romantics is someone who is privy to the secrets of childhood and protects its world from assaults by modern (education-based) society. In contrast to the enlightened children's friend, the romantic figure is an outsider to the world of adults: how could he otherwise be an accomplice to childhood, which is diametrically opposed to the principles of modern-day life?

When Heidi first goes to live with Grandfather in the mountains, he is still very brusque and shows little interest in the child. However, as the narrator informs the reader, he observes her closely, helps where necessary, and rejoices in her independence. They are soon in agreement, each engaging with and responding to the other, avoiding conflict. Grandfather provides Heidi with food and care. He also tells Heidi everything she wants to know about nature and mountain life. According to Gros, he represents the wise old man of the mountains, who passes on his knowledge about animals, herbs, and the stars to his granddaughter (127).

In keeping with Rousseau and his younger contemporary Johann Heinrich Pestalozzi, who stated that education should be based on the child's personal rhythm and allow the young to make their own discoveries and experiences (Bertlein), Grandfather considers it important to protect little Heidi from external influences that might accelerate or advance the natural process of her development. He is thus not keen on the idea of Heidi attending school, learning to read, or receiving a bourgeois education in Frankfurt. He has quickly become fond of Heidi and is hit all the harder by her loss when Dete takes Heidi to Frankfurt. As a consequence, Grandfather becomes even more embittered and no longer speaks to anyone in the village until Heidi comes back. She induces him to return to the church, God's loving embrace, and the village community, both with the parable of the prodigal son and with her childlike innocence and devotion. Grandfather can now also rejoice in what Heidi has learned in Frankfurt and makes no further objection to her attending school.

As Jean-Michel Wissmer observes, the relationship between Heidi and her grandfather can be attributed to the topos of the intuitive understanding between children and the elderly, which is frequently found in romantic literature: a common experience, as both the very young and the very old live on the fringes of active society (49). The orphan and the lonely old man, writes Schindler, belong together not just through their family ties: both have something elemental and savage about them (Schindler, *Spyri* 112). Regarding the ageist tropes that Joosen (132) distinguishes in children's literature, Grandfather seems to be a prototype of the wise old mentor. But it is not as simple as that. He is also an angry and stubborn old man, ranting and raving, suffering from "emotional perturbations" (Woodward 195) and finally, assisted by Heidi, willing to reinvent himself.

Religion is central to the role that both grandmothers play. For Heidi they are important moral authorities. Grandmamma Sesemann is a comforting figure in the cold and alien environment of Frankfurt. She is a person of authority who is respected by all, a source of wisdom and piety who lovingly leads Heidi toward education. Sagacious and prudent, yet very firm at the same time, she takes Heidi seriously as a child and as an individual, considering all the girl's personal abilities and inclinations. Grandmamma's successful approach is reminiscent of progressive educational methods. She inspires in Heidi the wish to be able to read by reminding her of her daily life in the mountains with the help of an illustrated children's Bible. She deals with Heidi's despair by talking to her about God and helps her make the transition from a magical understanding of God to pietism: God knows the right moment to come to the help of those who pray to him. If you abandon God, he will abandon you too.

As Sylvia B. Henneberg points out, Grandmamma Sesemann is a modern version of the elderly fairy godmother:

> At first sight Clara's "Grandmamma," Frau Sesemann, seems like an exception because she is a strong and self-assured presence. Ultimately, however, she is no more than a means to an end, the good fairy godmother who makes life and happiness possible for the young. [...] Though in the most positive way imaginable, she merely reacts to those around her, never once acting on her own behalf, never once revealing a need of her own. [...] As deeply involved as Grandmamma is in the lives of her loved ones, she has withdrawn from her own life. For all the fictional girls (and the reader) can tell, she has no history before them and no life apart from them. (130)

While Henneberg mainly aims to draw attention to Grandmamma Sesemann's self-sacrificing nature and the way her character is constructed in the novel, her account also makes clear that Heidi is not just a giver, but also a recipient of attention, comfort, and education, and that others also serve her needs.

A third elderly character who plays a prominent role in Heidi's life is Peter's grandmother. Like Grandfather, she lives on the fringes of society. She is a victim of the arduous mountain life, characterized by poverty and sickness. In her case the depiction of old age follows another of the ageist tropes that Joosen distinguishes in several children's books (133): the decline narrative that tells of weakness and approaching death. In Heidi, the grandmother's infirmity above all evokes pity and deep-felt compassion. Heidi becomes her one and all. Her presence makes Grandmother happy, and she sees her as a gift from God. After she complains to Heidi about being blind, cold, and hungry, the girl aids her with practical assistance and reads hymns to her. In line with Heidi's transition from a piety rooted in nature to a Christian belief in God, Spyri selected for the German version of the book a baroque poem by the hymn writer Paul Gerhardt, which is a eulogy to nature as a magnificent work of God. The reading transforms Grandmother, filling her with joy as she turns her blind gaze to heaven. From her Heidi learns—without noticing it—yet another, different form of worship: praise, gratitude, the expression of hope and lamentation, but well articulated and based on rhetoric (Schindler, *Spyri* 98). In a conversation that Grandmamma Sesemann and Peter's grandmother have right before the end of the novel, God is, moreover, presented as the equalizer of all classes and ages: "How is it possible that there are such good people who trouble themselves about a poor old woman," says Grandmother to Heidi. "There is nothing that can so strengthen one's belief in a good Father in heaven who will not forget even the lowliest" (359). At this, Grandmamma Sesemann, as a voice of authority, retorts: "My good grandmother, [...] before our Father in heaven we all are equally poor" (360), thereby also suggesting that God does not make a difference between the old and the young. The novel closes with a hymn that Heidi speaks to express the characters' gratitude to God. He appears as the ultimate connection between people of all generations.

Conclusion

As my discussion of Heidi's relationship with the three elderly characters in Spyri's novel makes clear, considering Heidi's character as someone who only adopts the position of the giver and ignores her own needs is too limited a perspective. Spyri's novel, rather, suggests that Heidi both gives and takes from her intergenerational friendships with her grandfather, Grandmamma Sesemann, and Peter's grandmother, making their relationship complementary rather than exploitative. That Henneberg considers Grandmamma Sesemann as an all-giving figure underscores that Heidi is not only on the giving but also on the receiving end.

Each connection between Heidi and the three elderly figures is based on different traits—which all lead to a mutually reinforcing "exchange" of goods, knowledge, virtues, and/or acts of care. The connection between Heidi and Grandfather arises, perhaps even more than from their blood ties, from a shared love of nature and the appreciation of a simple lifestyle. He provides her with food and shelter and offers her the temporary isolation from urban life that allows her to thrive in nature freely and carelessly as she grows up from a toddler to a young child. In her turn, Heidi reinstills in Grandfather an interest in other human beings, and ultimately in God, fulfilling the role of a child redeemer who pulls the old man out of his social isolation and spiritual dearth.

From Grandmamma Sesemann, Heidi receives not only the comfort of kind company but also the gifts of literacy and Christianity. From her repeated invitations, it can be derived that the old lady enjoys Heidi's company (in contrast to that of the strict Fräulein Rottenmeier, who is another companion of Frau Sesemann's). Moreover, the text spells out that Grandmamma Sesemann is "laughing with satisfaction" (145) at being complimented on

Heidi's progress in reading. The successful teaching experience is thus presented as equally rewarding for the elderly tutor and the learning child. Moreover, thanks to Heidi, Grandmamma Sesemann can also rejoice in the natural beauty of the Alps when she visits her former pupil together with Klara. Like Heidi upon her arrival in the Alps, Grandmamma Sesemann is described as being immediately impressed by the beauty of the mountain surroundings (292) and the simple life in the Alps. Her enjoyment seems to increase steadily in the course of the visit:

> The grandmamma was perfectly enchanted at this dining-room, from which one could see so far, far down into the valley and above all the mountains into the blue sky. A cool, mild breeze gently fanned the faces of the guests and rustled as pleasantly in the fir trees as if it had been especially ordered music for the feast.
> "Nothing like this has ever happened to me. It is really glorious!" exclaimed the grandmamma again and again. (294)

Here, Grandmamma Sesemann is not so much a fairy-tale enchantress, as Henneberg suggests, as "enchanted" herself. The experience draws from the otherwise so composed figure of the grandmamma a reaction that also puts into perspective her wisdom as an elderly tutor. She is, after all, not too old for new experiences herself—and her delight in the new experience resembles Heidi's childlike enthusiasm at seeing the world with fresh eyes. Finally, Grandmamma is described as rejoicing in the progress of Klara's health and the daily letters that the two girls write to her to keep her up to date on the progress (310, 336–337), reinforcing once again the impression that both the children and the elderly lady are rewarded by their friendship. Moreover, Grandmamma Sesemann offers a powerful counterbalance to the decline narrative that is suggested by the illness of Peter's grandmother. Although the text does acknowledge the limits of Grandmamma's physical ability, for instance, in her inability to climb the mountain on a regular basis, it mostly stresses the authority that she holds and the joy that she derives from new experiences and friendship.

The relationship between Heidi and Grandmamma seems to be mirrored in the way that Heidi cares and provides comfort for Peter's grandmother, who is alienated from society through her illness. It is in this relationship that a sense of entitlement becomes most pronounced, and that Heidi adopts the position of a giver more obviously than in the relationship with Grandfather or Grandmamma. Yet from Peter's blind grandmother Heidi discovers the comfort offered by religious literature. In this moment, her experience of literacy (learned from Grandmamma Sesemann) and her adoration of nature (as taught by Grandfather) converge, and the task of Heidi's education is fulfilled.

Notes

1. Irma Hildebrandt (18) suggests that Spyri was in fact writing with a German audience in mind. From an imagological perspective, as developed for children's literature by Emer O'Sullivan (2011), a child living in the mountains is a stereotype associated with a healthy life, light and air, goat's cheese and herbs. The Swiss people were embarrassed to be seen abroad as country bumpkins who sleep in hay, look after goats, and think nothing of progress (Morkowska; Hentschel; Paul 206–217). Although cultural aspects linked to the city also enter the mountains with Heidi's return and with the Sesemann family's visit, the novel suggests a striking contrast between Germany and its cultured environment and the natural setting of Switzerland. Spyri's story relies on an image of the Alps and Swiss mountain life that had been common abroad from the eighteenth century onward (Escher 281). In the dynamics between "those images which characterize the Other (hetero-images) and those which characterize one's own domestic identity (self-images or auto-images)" (Leerssen 27), Spyri created a text based on a hetero-image of Switzerland that was first held by foreign visitors tourists and that finally also crept into the Swiss self-image.

2. According to Skrine, there is no doubt that Spyri was familiar with the works of J. W. Goethe, who is acknowledged in the title: "By calling it *Heidi's Lehr-und Wanderjahre*, Spyri makes clear and explicit reference to the major example of the novel genre in German, Goethe's *Wilhelm Meister*, which its author worked at from 1777 to 1829 and which consists of two vast and almost self-contained novels respectively entitled *Wilhelm Meisters Lehrjahre* and *Wilhelm Meisters Wanderjahre*" (149). Bettina Hurrelmann describes Heidi as "Mignons erlöste Schwester" (Mignon's redeemed sister), Mignon being Wilhelm Meister's love interest in Goethe's novels.

3. See also Nelson (71–134) on women as girls and girls as women in Victorian literature.

Works Cited

Alefeld, Yvonne-Patricia. *Göttliche Kinder: Die Kindheitsideologie in der Romantik*. Paderborn: Schöningh, 1996.

Benz-Conzen, Jana, and Andreas Benz-Conzen. "Heidi: Ein Kind hilft Erwachsenen." *Jahrbuch der Kindheit: Kinderleben in Geschichte und Gegenwart 1*. Eds. Christian Büttner and Aurel Ende. Weinheim: Beltz, 1984. 123–130.

Bertlein, Hermann. "Pestalozzi, Johann Heinrich." *Lexikon der Kinder-und Jugendliteratur*. Ed. Klaus Doderer. Vol. 3. Weinheim: Beltz, 1979. 20–21.

Bunke, Simon. *Heimweh: Studien zur Kultur-und Literaturgeschichte einer tödlichen Krankheit*. Freiburg im Breisgau: Rombach, 2009.

Domenig, Aya. "'Cute Heidi': Zur Rezeption von Heidi in Japan." *Heidi: Karrieren einer Figur.* Ed. Ernst Halter. Zurich: Offizin, 2001. 149–165.

Escher, Georg. "'Berge heissen nicht': Geographische, soziale und ästhetische Räume im 'Heidi'-Roman." *Heidi: Karrieren einer Figur.* Ed. Ernst Halter. Zurich: Offizin, 2001. 277–289.

Ewers, Hans-Heino. "'Dieser Ätherschimmer, diese Erinnerungen der Engelswelt': Anmerkungen zum Kindheitsbild der deutschen Romantik." *Der rote Wunderschirm: Kinderbücher der Sammlung Seifert von der Frühaufklärung bis zum Nationalsozialismus.* Ed. Wolfgang Wangerin. Göttingen: Wallstein, 2011. 59–63.

Ewers, Hans-Heino. "E.T.A. Hoffmann, *Das fremde Kind* (1816/1817)." *Unter dem roten Wunderschirm: Lesarten klassischer Kinder-und Jugendliteratur.* Ed. Christoph Bräuer and Wolfgang Wangerin. Göttingen: Wallstein, 2013. 75–83.

Ewers, Hans-Heino. "Romantik." *Geschichte der deutschen Kinder-und Jugendliteratur.* Ed. Reiner Wild. Stuttgart: Metzler, 1990. 99–138.

Gros, Christophe. "Heidi—die kleine Berggottheit." *Heidi: Karrieren einer Figur.* Ed. Ernst Halter. Zurich: Offizin, 2001. 115–129.

Halter, Ernst. "Johanna Spyri, Marlitt und ihr verwaistes Jahrhundert." *Heidi: Karrieren einer Figur.* Ed. Ernst Halter. Zurich: Offizin, 2001. 9–27.

Härle, Gerhard. "Die Alm als pädagogische Provinz—oder: Versuch über Johanna Spyris Heidi." *Erfolgreiche Kinder-und Jugendbücher. Was macht Lust auf Lesen?* Ed. Bernhard Rank. Baltmannsweiler: Schneider-Verlag Hohengehren, 1999. 59–86.

Hearn, Michael. "Heidi Goes to America." *Johanna Spyri und ihr Werk—Lesarten.* Ed. Schweizerisches Institut für Kinder-und Jugendmedien. Zurich: Chronos, 2004. 163–181.

Henneberg, Sylvia B. "Moms Do Badly, but Grandmas Do Worse: The Nexus of Sexism and Ageism in Children's Classics." *Journal of Aging Studies* 24 (2010): 125–134.

Hentschel, Uwe. "Faszination Schweiz: Zum deutschen literarischen Philhelvetismus des 18. Jahrhunderts." *Schweizerisches Archiv für Volkskunde* 96 (2000): 29–53.

Hildebrandt, Irma. *Mutige Schweizerinnen: 18 Porträts von Johanna Spyri bis Liselotte Pulver.* Kreuzlingen: Hugendubel, 2006. 11–24.

Hurrelmann, Bettina. "Heidi—Mignons erlöste Schwester." *Neue Sammlung* 33.3 (1993): 347–363.

Joosen, Vanessa. "Second Childhoods and Intergenerational Dialogues: How Children's Literature Studies and Age Studies Can Supplement Each Other." *Children's Literature Association Quarterly* 40.2 (2015): 126–140.

Kaminski, Winfred. "Spyri, Johanna." *Lexikon der Kinder-und Jugendliteratur.* Ed. Klaus Doderer. Vol. 3. Weinheim and Basel: Beltz, 1979. 446–448.

Keith, Lois. *Take Up Thy Bed and Walk: Death, Disability and Cure in Classic Fiction for Girls.* London: Women's Press, 2001.

Kiepe, Hansjürgen. "Landschaft Gottes: Zur Rolle der Verbzusätze in Johanna Spyris 'Heidi.'" *Wirkendes Wort* 17 (1967): 410–429.

Küpfer, Romana. *Immer wieder neu?! Film-und Fernsehadaptionen von Johanna Spyris Heidi.* Unpublished master's thesis, University of Zurich, 2007.

Leerssen, Joep. "Imagology: History and Method." *Imagology: The Cultural Construction and Literary Representation of National Characters.* Eds. Manfred Beller and Joep Leerssen. Amsterdam: Rodopi, 2007. 17–32.

Leimgruber, Walter. "Heidi: Wesen und Wandel eines medialen Erfolges." *Heidi: Karrieren einer Figur.* Ed. Ernst Halter. Zurich: Offizin, 2001. 167–185.

Morkowska, Marysia. *Vom Stiefkind zum Liebling: Die Entwicklung und Funktion des europäischen Schweizbildes bis zur Französischen Revolution.* Zürich: Chronos, 1997.

Nelson, Claudia. *Precocious Children and Childish Adults: Age Inversion in Victorian Literature.* Baltimore: Johns Hopkins University Press, 2012.

O'Sullivan, Emer: "Imagology Meets Children's Literature." *International Research in Children's Literature* 4.1 (2011): 1–14.

Paul, Ina Ulrike. "'Wache auf und lies . . .' Zur Tradierung von Nationalstereotypen in europäischen Enzyklopädien des 18. Jahrhunderts." *Populäre Enzyklopädien: Von der Auswahl, Ordnung und Vermittlung des Wissens.* Ed. Ingrid Tomkowiak. Zurich: Chronos, 2002. 197–220.

Rutschmann, Verena. "Natur und Zivilisation oder Fortschritt und Heimweh in der Schweizer Kinder-und Jugendliteratur." *Naturkind, Landkind, Stadtkind: Literarische Bilderwelten kindlicher Umwelt.* Ed. Ulrich Nassen and Arbeitsgemeinschaft Kinder-und Jugendliteraturforschung. Munich: Fink, 1995. 25–44.

Schindler, Regine. "Form und Funktion religiöser Elemente in Johanna Spyris Werken." *Der Anteil der Schweiz an der deutschsprachigen Kinder-und Jugendliteratur.* Ed. Schweizerisches Jugendbuch-Institut. Zurich: Chronos, 1999. 173–199.

Schindler, Regine. *Johanna Spyri (1827–1901): Neue Entdeckungen und unbekannte Briefe.* Ed. Salome Schoeck. Zurich: Neue Zürcher Zeitung, 2015.

Skrine, Peter. "Johanna Spyri's *Heidi*." *Bulletin of the John Rylands University Library of Manchester* 76.3 (1994): 145–164.

Spyri, Johanna. *Heidi kann brauchen, was es gelernt hat: Eine Geschichte für Kinder und auch für Solche, welche die Kinder lieb haben.* Gotha: Friedrich Andreas Perthes, 1881. http://www.e-rara.ch/doi/10.3931/e-rara-16913. Accessed on 15 October 2015.

Spyri, Johanna. *Heidi's Lehr-und Wanderjahre. Eine Geschichte für Kinder und auch für Solche, welche die Kinder lieb haben.* Gotha: Friedrich Andreas Perthes, 1880. http://www.e-rara.ch/doi/10.3931/e-rara-16704. Accessed on 15 October 2015.

Villain, Jean. "Johannas früh erwachter Sinn fürs Medizinische." *Heidi: Karrieren einer Figur.* Ed. Ernst Halter. Zurich: Offizin, 2001. 65–81.

Wesseling, Elisabeth, ed. *The Child Savage, 1890–2010: From Comics to Games.* Burlington: Ashgate, 2016.

Wilkending, Gisela. "Heidi: Rückkehr aus einer kranken Welt." *Kinder-und Jugendbuch.* Ed. Gisela Wilkending. Bamberg: Buchners, 1988. 191–202.

Wilkending, Gisela. "Mädchenliteratur von der Mitte des 19. Jahrhunderts bis zum Ersten Weltkrieg." *Geschichte der deutschen Kinder-und Jugendliteratur.* Ed. Reiner Wild. Stuttgart: Metzler, 1990. 220–250.

Wissmer, Jean-Michel. *Heidi: Ein Schweizer Mythos erobert die Welt.* Basel: Schwabe, 2014.

Woodward, Kathleen. "Against Wisdom: The Social Politics of Anger and Aging." *Cultural Critique* 51 (2002): 186–218.

- 2 -

Happily Ever After for the Old in Japanese Fairy Tales

MAYAKO MURAI

Compared with canonical Western fairy tales such as those of the Brothers Grimm, Japanese fairy tales abound with aged heroes and heroines.[1] The most typical beginning reads: "Once upon a time, there lived an old man and an old woman." Unlike old people in Western fairy tales, who generally play a supporting role for young characters, old women and men are often the protagonists in Japanese tales and, at the end of the narrative, bring the story to an equilibrium that is different from the idea of happily ever after in Western fairy tales. In many stories, such as "The Old Man Who Made Flowers Bloom" and "The Tongue-Cut Sparrow," the aged protagonists themselves undergo adventures and perform difficult tasks. In some stories, a long-childless couple finds a child in a magical situation, but even in these tales, the narrative tends to focus on the fate of the old couple rather than that of the child that goes on to have adventures. The reward they receive for their good conduct is not a royal marriage but the recognition of their kindness by the magical foundling they adopt. The absence or the marginality of characters in the middle generation in these tales builds a contrast with the focus on the process of coming of age in Western fairy tales.

This old-age-oriented tendency is also reflected in contemporary children's media drawing on traditional fairy tales. A popular TV series called *Manga Nippon mukashibanashi* (Manga Japanese folktales) was broadcast every Saturday evening in primetime for nearly twenty years (1975–1994) and featured adaptations of 1,474 Japanese folktales.[2] In this animation series, not only are the narration and all character voices provided by older actors, one male and one female, but aged heroes and heroines also predominate in the stories. The series began as a program intended for Japanese families living abroad but soon became very popular inside Japan; in 1980 it reached a viewing rate of nearly 40 percent in western Japan. Since production finished in 1994, it has been rebroadcast several times and inspired similar anime folktale adaptations that are equally old-age-oriented. The Japanese audience, therefore, has been simultaneously exposed to two different fairy-tale cultures: the globalized canon formed largely by Grimm's tales and Walt Disney animation films on the one hand, and, on the other, the Japanese canon formed by the printed fairy-tale collections disseminated widely since the seventeenth century, as well as by contemporary popular media which draw on traditional Japanese tales in the form of TV animation series, manga, and picture books.

In this chapter, I first consider the marginalized place allocated to the elderly in the Grimms' tales, which have been canonized in Western as well as many non-Western cultures. I then examine the link between old age and children in traditional Japanese fairy tales by focusing on tales about aged protagonists who adopt magical children, particularly "The Tale of the Bamboo Cutter" and its recent Studio Ghibli adaptation *The Tale of the Princess Kaguya* (2013), directed and coscripted by Isao Takahata. I argue that Takahata's film reflects the cultural dilemma that Japanese fairy-tale adaptations are facing now, divided between the two different narrative traditions. Through this cross-cultural analysis, I hope to offer a new perspective on the link between old age and children in the fairy tale, a genre that gives many children their first contact with literature and can therefore have a formative impact on people's understanding of their life trajectories.

The Marginalization of the Old in Western Fairy Tales

Fairy tales abound with old people. In both the complete collection of the Grimms' tales (242 tales)[3] and in the Japanese collection edited by Keigo Seki (160 tales that are categorized as fairy tales), about 40 percent include explicit depictions of the elderly. As I stated at the beginning of this chapter, however, the most noticeable difference is that in Japanese tales old couples often play the central part throughout the story, whereas in Grimm's tales old people, whether they are good or evil, tend to play a supporting role. Hans Christian Andersen, in contrast, wrote fairy tales featuring old protagonists, such as "Grandmother," "The Old Bachelor's Nightcap," and "The Old House." In one sense Andersen's stories can be considered more old-age-oriented than the Brothers Grimm's tales; however, old heroes and heroines in Andersen's stories are generally depicted as isolated figures who are about to die and whose present lives are sustained only by the happy memories of their youth. This contrasts with the old protagonists in Japanese fairy tales, who neither live in the past nor die in the story. Moreover, unlike his stories about young characters, such as "The Little Mermaid" and "The Ugly Duckling," Andersen's stories with old protagonists have not entered the international fairy-tale canon.

In the Brothers Grimm's tales, old people are often associated with supernatural power, whether benevolent or malevolent, and they tend to live isolated from society in such liminal spaces as cottages in the woods. Although old characters with magical power such as witches and wise crones often bring about pivotal changes in young protagonists' lives, their status within the stories remains marginal. When they do not possess supernatural power or authority, they tend to be portrayed as poor, feeble, or simple-minded (for example, the father in "Thumbling's Travels") and play a role even more minor than that of their magical aged counterparts. In other words, whether they are cast as helpers or adversaries, as supernatural creatures or ordinary human beings, old people in Grimm's tales usually do not figure as protagonists themselves; their fate is not the central concern of many stories, which instead focus on the progress of young protagonists. The young in these tales are characterized by their boldness, beauty, or strength and judged by their actions or inborn physical characteristics (for instance, the protagonists in "The Brave Little Tailor" and "Cinderella" respectively).

The marginalization of old age in canonical Western fairy tales is also reflected in the literary tradition of the Bildungsroman, a type of novel that traces the moral and psychological growth of the protagonist from childhood to adulthood. The coming-of-age plot of such novels usually devalues aging by seeing it as physical, psychological, or social decline. In *Safe at Last in the Middle Years: The Invention of the Midlife Progress Novel*, Margaret Morganroth Gullette argues that the plot of "systematic disillusionment" in realist novels serves to inculcate the reader with the "decline theory of life" that equates aging with downfall (xviii). Traditional fairy tales such as "Snow White" and "Hansel and Gretel" share this standard emplotment that sees aging as a downhill trajectory and relegates old people to the margins not only of the story but also of society.

In this respect it is interesting to consider the exceptionally lively crone in the Grimms' "The Goose Girl at the Spring," which offers potential for a different emplotment for the aged heroine. The story begins with a description of "a very old woman who lived with a flock of geese in a lonely place on a mountain" (695). Although she hobbles on her crutch, she can perform her everyday chores in the woods as energetically as many much younger people, gathering grass and wild fruit and carrying the heavy load home on her back while greeting people along the way. People are suspicious of her vigor and believe that she is a witch. Then the story shifts its focus to the ugly maiden living in her house, who turns out to be a beautiful princess in disguise and who marries a handsome young count with the help of the crone. At the end of the story, the old woman magically vanishes after turning her little house into a splendid palace with many servants. In the epilogue the narrator confides that the old woman was "a wise woman who meant well" (704), thus typecasting her in the role of a wise crone (similar to the fairy godmother in Charles Perrault's version of "Cinderella") and subsuming her into a conventional plot that focuses on the young. As this story illustrates, old women in the Grimms' tales tend to be polarized into two stereotypes, the witch and the wise crone, neither of whom belongs to the human sphere or performs the role of protagonist in the story-world she inhabits.

Unlike old women, old men do sometimes figure as protagonists in the Grimms' tales, for example, in "Faithful Johannes" or "Old Sultan." Importantly, these aged male characters possess no extraordinary powers. While Faithful old Johannes completes extraordinary acts of loyalty toward the late king without any magical assistance, Old Sultan, a dog depicted as possessing human feelings, escapes his predicament with the help of his friends. It is telling that these two tales, neither of which has entered the fairy-tale canon in the West, were among the most-often translated Grimm's tales in Japan at the end of the nineteenth century. "Old Sultan," as I discuss below, was even incorporated into the Japanese oral storytelling tradition.

The Centrality of the Old in Japanese Fairy Tales

The predominance of aged protagonists in Japanese tales may strike foreign readers as characteristically Japanese. For example, the Swiss folklorist Rudolph Schenda, in his brief essay on a collection of Japanese folktales edited and translated into German by Toshio Ozawa in 1976, notes that "it is worthy of attention that so many Japanese folktales feature aged people, especially aged couples" (Schenda 112).[4] Schenda, however, does not dwell on the significance of this characteristic but immediately shifts his attention to the moral point made in such stories. As he notes, the kind and humble old people are often contrasted with their evil and greedy neighbors who try to imitate the former's conduct that has brought them good fortune, and they end up being severely punished for their greed. This type of tale, usually referred to as "the old man next door," can be found throughout Japan and occupies a major place in the folktale canon, along with the "animal bride/bridegroom" tale type. The contrast between good and evil, of course, is a common theme in fairy tales all over the world, but, outside Japan, it is generally cast as sibling rivalry between young characters or as a conflict between a child and a parent or a step-parent. The Grimms' "Mother Holle" and "Cinderella" could serve as Western examples here.

In the rest of this chapter, I focus on how old age functions in Japanese tales, a topic that folktale researchers both in and outside Japan have neglected. That the tales featuring aged protagonists are characterized as "the old man next door" tale type creates a misleading emphasis on the moralistic contrast between the good old man and his greedy neighbor at the very end of the story, as we have seen in Schenda's response. In fact, however, the episode about the greedy neighbor is sometimes omitted altogether, as the folklorist Koji Inada notes (Ozawa 181), indicating that it is not an essential part of the story. The same misleading emphasis can be also found in Western collections including Japanese tales, such as Andrew Lang's *Violet Fairy Book* (1901), which includes the Japanese tale "The Old Man Who Made Flowers Bloom" under the title "The Envious Neighbor."

The centrality of the old in Japanese fairy tales becomes apparent if we look at the so-called Five Great Fairy Tales, namely, "The Old Man Who Made Flowers Bloom," "The Tongue-Cut Sparrow," "Kachi Kachi Mountain," "The Peach Boy," and "The Monkey and the Crab."[5] The first three have aged protagonists, and "The Peach Boy" can be considered to focus more on the fate of the old couple than on that of the eponymous boy they adopt, even though the latter half of the tale is devoted to his adventures. In "The Old Man Who Made Flowers Bloom," "The Tongue-Cut Sparrow," and "The Peach Boy," the main characters are a poor, old, childless couple, and the story begins when they come across a child or a small animal in a magical setting—respectively, a puppy, a child sparrow, both of whom can speak, and a boy born from a peach. They decide to adopt this helpless creature. Importantly, the child characters in these stories are born with some power or wisdom greater than the foster parents' and they do not develop psychologically, even if they physically grow up; neither do these stories mention the young characters' marriage at the end. In other words, these tales are not driven by the coming-of-age plot that is central to many Western fairy tales.

Another significant feature of Japanese fairy tales is that aged characters are depicted as people performing daily chores and that, even when the elderly are cast in the central role, old age itself is not the main focus of the narrative. The beginning of "The Peach Boy" is typical: "This was long ago. In a certain place lived an old man and his wife. One day the old man went to the mountains to cut wood, and the old woman went to the river to do her washing" (Seki 41). The opening lines of "The Old Man Who Made Flowers Bloom" and "The Tongue-Cut Sparrow" are almost exactly the same. The couple are indeed old and often poor, but, unlike the bedridden grandmother in "Little Red Cap," they are generally depicted as healthy, even if not vigorous, and independent. In these tales, therefore, old age itself does not necessarily lead to exclusion from everyday activities. Also important is that old characters, whether good or evil, rarely possess special power or knowledge as in the Grimms' fairy tales. Their ordinariness confirms their status within human society, rather than in the other world.

In this respect, it is interesting to look at the translation and adaptation of "The Bremen Town Musicians" in Japan. It is one of the few tales in the Grimm collection that features the adventures of old protagonists—in this case, anthropomorphized animals. "The Bremen Town Musicians" was the second-most frequently translated tale from the Grimm collection during the early years of its reception in late-nineteenth-century Japan—it was as popular as "Snow White," ranked just after "The Wolf and Seven Little Goats," and still remains one of the most beloved fairy tales in Japan. Also, it is one of the Western tales that were incorporated into the Japanese oral storytelling tradition. In "Where Do the Animals Go?" Kayo Kubo compares "The Bremen Town Musicians" in the Grimm collection's seventh edition (1857) with its early Japanese translations as well as with its oral adaptations in Japan. She pays special attention to the way in which the master treats the old donkey and notes that the Japanese translators "seem to have found it difficult to treat him coldly just because he has become old and useless" (Kubo 159). The translators' changes vary, but they do alleviate the master's cold treatment of the aged animal by adding details such as the master's regret for discharging the donkey and the animal voluntarily leaving the master to find a new job. Kubo also notes that the Japanese translators seem to have hesitated to accept the ending in which the animals live in a hut in the forest happily ever after without doing any work (160). In three out of the nine early translations, the aged animals follow their initial idea to play music in Bremen to earn some money while living in the forest, just as aged people in Japanese fairy tales continue to perform their workaday chores.

A group of Japanese oral tales called "The Tale of the Horse, the Dog, the Cat, and the Chicken" was apparently derived from the Grimms' "The

Bremen Town Musicians." Kubo points out that, in the process of oral transmission, the German text has generally been transformed into a tale about aged animals who were once ejected from their homes but are readmitted in the end when they repay their masters by bringing back some money or doing something useful. This altered ending, which reincorporates the aged characters into the community, recalls "Old Sultan," another tale from the Grimms' *Kinder-und Hausmärchen* (*Children's and Household Tales*), which was adopted by the Japanese oral storytelling tradition. This tale was transformed into a parable emphasizing the motif of loyalty toward one's master. In either case, rather than finding their happiness in a utopian space far away from society, aged characters are readmitted by the community and live happily ever after.

The Japanized endings where the animals return home show a way of accommodating old age in a fairy-tale narrative that is different from the Grimm tales. In *Disability, Deformity, and Disease in the Grimms' Fairy Tales*, Ann Schmiesing analyzes "The Bremen Town Musicians" as follows:

> While the animals create their own social utopia, the dystopic world they left behind remains. A more overarching social utopia, in which the masters would accept and value the aging animals as they are instead of slating them for death when they are no longer physically fit, does not appear. Dystopia also remains in "Old Sultan," where the dog escapes being killed by his master only because he successfully pretended to be of greater physical utility to the household than he actually is. (177)

As discussed above, some of the early Japanese translations of "The Bremen Town Musicians" alter this dystopian dimension by not banishing the animals to a space outside society but rather giving them a role in society. Also, the oral adaptations of this tale often end with the master's recognition of the good nature of the aged animals who have served him for a long time; the old animals need only to remind their master of their gratitude, rather than tricking him into believing that they are physically younger than they actually are, as the dog tries in the Grimms' "Old Sultan." These aged animals are accepted for what they are in the end, in a world that may not be a perfect utopia but is at least less dystopian than before.

The reason for the predominance of old protagonists in Japanese fairy tales as well as for the reevaluation of the old in Japanese adaptations of Western tales is sometimes ascribed to the Asian cultural tradition that regards the elderly as superior beings closer to the sacred realm. However, the elderly in Japanese fairy tales are not necessarily any wiser than the young, nor do they possess any supernatural power; there are as many silly, greedy, or evil old people as kind, grateful, and humble ones. The view that regards the centrality of the old in Japanese tales as a direct reflection of the Confucian principle of treating the elderly with the utmost respect does not hold in many cases. Neither can the Taoist archetype of the holy old man living alone high up on a mountain be applied to many old protagonists. Adopting these views may reinforce an orientalizing gaze on a non-Western culture by mystifying the image of old age in Japanese tales as a premodern alternative for the modern construction of old age in Western society. Erdman B. Palmore's *The Honorable Elders Revisited* shows that old people in Japan tend to be healthier, more integrated with society, and more satisfied with life than their American counterparts, and he attributes the positive aging in Japan to the Confucian respect for the elderly. It is true that the image of Japan as a Confucian society that regards aging as an empowering process may have held true at least partly until the 1970s. However, with significant sociocultural and demographic shifts, family values and attitudes toward the elderly have also changed since then, and, as the sociologist Yoshiko Someya observes, intergenerational bonding within the family has become "even weaker than in America" (186).[6] Since the 1980s Japan has been facing the same social problems as other economically developed countries, including the alienation of the elderly from family structures. One of the most serious problems is the sharp increase in the number of people aged sixty-five and up living alone.[7]

A more valid explanation for the old-age orientation still discernible in today's Japanese fairy-tale culture may come from taking into consideration the use of symbols in the fairy-tale narrative. The elderly, placed outside the social spheres of production and reproduction, can then be regarded as more suitable characters than the younger generations for the symbolic exploration of the human psyche and human beings' relationship with the world. The ideas of good and evil can be played out in aged characters in a more abstract way than in younger characters, whose good conduct tends to lead to maturity symbolized by marriage. Their attributes are different from those that usually characterize young protagonists, such as exceptional beauty in female characters and great strength or wit in male characters. Less spectacular qualities such as kindness, perseverance, and honesty are valued in aged characters; although these qualities also characterize some of the younger, often female, protagonists such as Cinderella and other so-called innocent persecuted heroines, their beautiful appearance is what ultimately brings them happiness. The Japanese fairy tale's preference for aged protagonists seems to derive not only from the Asian cultural tradition that honors old age but also from their symbolic quality that calls for a form of well-being other than royal marriage.

Although stereotyping the elderly as people devoid of sexual, social, and material desires can be considered ageist, the stories' focus on the oldest generation in society does allow storytellers to explore narrative developments other than those based on the model of growth and progress culminating in fairy-tale marriage. From an early age, the Japanese learn to cultivate their narrative expectations in line with the old-age-oriented plot, identifying themselves with aged heroes and heroines while at the same time being accustomed to the globalized canon of fairy tales represented by the Grimms' tales and Disney's filmic adaptations. These two kinds of fairy-tale narratives have coexisted without annulling each other and, as I argue below, have begun to interact and compete with each other in recent fairy-tale adaptations in Japan.

The Link between the Old and Children in Japanese Fairy Tales

In the final part of this chapter, I consider the link between old people and children in the story-world of Japanese fairy tales. As I suggested, old protagonists serve to create a story-world that is rooted in real life but separated from the concerns of the productive and reproductive activities of society. In "The Old Man Who Made Flowers Bloom," "The Tongue-Cut Sparrow" and "The Peach Boy," the senior couple's kindness toward the vulnerable creature seems all the more disinterested on account of their childless old age. Their reward comes when their kindness and affection are acknowledged by their otherworldly adoptees.

There is an old saying in Japan that children under the age of seven are still in the gods' hands. They are regarded as intermediary beings straddling this world and the world of gods, spirits, and the dead. This image of the child as half sacred is linked with the image of the wise man in the ancient Taoist philosophy, who is at once an old man and a little child. In this philosophical tradition, the child symbolizes the primordial life force and a unity with the world uncontaminated by rationalization, which the wise old man can reattain. In his study of the image of old men in traditional Japanese culture, Tetsuo Yamaori points out that the influence of this Chinese notion equating the old man and the child in their proximity to the sacred realm can be found in the medieval Japanese collection *Tales of Times Now Past*. Here, some old men and children are represented as possessing bodies devoid of worldly desires and needs—an ideal state aspired to by Buddhist ascetics who fall between the two opposite bordering stages of life. Within this tradition, the images of the old man and the child are superimposed on each other, and these "old children" are characterized by their ambivalent nature bearing both mature profundity and childlike innocence. However, although this Taoist archetype may apply to the magical foundling, as I stated earlier, it does not explain the ordinariness of the majority of old folktale protagonists, who are equipped with no special power or wisdom.

It is interesting to note that this Confucian influence can be found in a group of stories known as Ubasute-yama, literally meaning "a mountain for abandoning old women," a variant of the tale type about abandoning aged parents found throughout Asia. In Japanese variants, at the end of the story, the younger generation is led either to recognize the value of old people they once intended to abandon or to gain an understanding of the life cycle of which everybody is a part, when their children remind them that their turn will eventually come. Interestingly, whereas the allegedly once common custom of abandoning old people in mountains is generally claimed to be historically unfounded, the practice of infanticide, widely performed among poor peasants until the nineteenth century, did not enter the folktale canon in Japan. This reversal shows the complex relation between historical facts and folktales and makes clear that the depictions of the elderly and children do not directly reflect historical reality, but rather the roles these two age groups are expected to play in certain narratives.[8]

Exploring the link between old people and children in Japanese folktales from a Jungian perspective, Hayao Kawai argues that the psychological state of old people in Japanese fairy tales represents the Japanese psyche. He contrasts the "senex consciousness" found in Japanese tales with Erich Neumann's notion of "hero consciousness," which is considered to represent the Western psyche (153). In support of his point, Kawai focuses on the tale "The Dragon Palace Boy," in which a man is invited to a palace under the sea, where he meets a dignified old man and a beautiful young woman. Upon leaving, the woman gives him an ugly boy, who brings him fortune. In the end, the man grows poor again due to the greed or impatience of himself or his family. Kawai sees the three inhabitants of the underwater world, the old man with white hair, the beautiful maiden, and the ugly boy, as representing the triad of grandfather, mother, and son, and argues that "the Japanese ego can sometimes express itself as senex consciousness, or as female consciousness, or as puer consciousness or a mixture" (165). The problem with Kawai's triad is that these three kinds of consciousness seem to represent the repressed aspects of the hero, who alone represents the conscious ego. The child consciousness can be compared to the Freudian notion of the id, the part of the self governed by instinctual impulses and drives; the ugly boy in "The Dragon Palace Boy" is usually depicted as dirty and unkempt. The female consciousness seems to represent the Jungian archetype of the anima, the unconscious feminine qualities in men. The senex consciousness shares some characteristics with the superego that supervises the ego. By relegating the old, women, and children to the realm of the unconscious deep under the sea, this view replicates and reinforces the male-oriented and adult-oriented metaphor linking old age, femininity, and childhood as marginal figures who play only a therapeutic role in the hero's spiritual quest.

My exploration of the link between old age and childhood takes a different approach from Kawai's, which marginalizes the old and children as representing the repressed part of the adult male protagonist. For my analysis, I focus on the tenth-century literary fairy tale "The Tale of the Bamboo Cutter," also called "Princess Kaguya." In this tale a poor old bamboo cutter finds a shining baby the size of his thumb in a bamboo stalk and brings her home. He and his wife suddenly become rich, while she grows up into a beautiful woman at a magical speed. After rejecting many royal suitors, including the emperor, she tells her foster parents that she comes from the moon. At the end of the story, she returns to the moon with great reluctance, leaving the old couple in tears.

This tale shares the motif of the old couple who adopt a magical child with the three folktales discussed above. It can be said that, in all of these narratives, the old couple's goodness is mirrored in the magical child's beauty, innocence, and wholesomeness; the elderly and the child are thematically connected. This is not to say that the magical child is a projection of the old couple's aspirations that they had to give up as they grew old; the adoptive children seem to see things from the perspective of the old, rather than the young, and do not act to achieve social success for themselves. The moon in "The Tale of the Bamboo Cutter" seems to symbolize the idealized image of a childlike innocence that never fades. Unlike the three other folktales, however, "The Tale of the Bamboo Cutter" does have a marriage plot, albeit one that is eventually thwarted. This difference seems to derive from the literary aspect of the tale's origins; although it draws on the oral tradition, the oldest extant text from the sixteenth century includes many details about royal customs and has the characteristics of the courtly narrative literature that developed in Japan from the tenth century onward. Like the literary fairy tales created by Madame d'Aulnoy and other writers of the seventeenth-century French salons, "The Tale of the Bamboo Cutter" is a literary fairy tale combining the characteristics of both folk narrative tradition and courtly literature.

The Studio Ghibli adaptation *The Tale of the Princess Kaguya* focuses, despite the title, on the aging man's progress, rather than the princess's. The most prominent change made to the traditional tale is the characterization of the bamboo cutter as an old man who still tries to hold on to his social ambitions; he is a combination of the good old man and his greedy neighbor in folktales. In the film the old bamboo cutter gradually loses his connection with his adoptive daughter, a pure and free spirit, and fails to recognize her true value, which leads to the tragic separation at the end of the story. The old man's obsession with the bamboo child, whom he calls "the princess," is repeatedly depicted throughout the film. For example, in a scene in the early part of the film, he tries to make the little girl toddle toward him; when she does not oblige, he continues to insist and raises his voice in desperation. When she grows up, he moves to the capital with his family to find a high-ranking husband for her, hoping also for his own social promotion. He becomes an impatient tyrant craving power and money and completely disregards his adoptive daughter's feelings despite his wife's attempt to dissuade him. As is often the case with Ghibli films, the motherly character is depicted as Mother Earth, a benevolent woman who nurtures, loves, and accepts those close to her for what they are. In contrast, his old age does not liberate the bamboo cutter from worldly desires, and the magical child becomes a means of achieving his social ambitions. When the princess leaves the earth, the old man finally has a moral awakening. In this way, Takahata creates a satirical portrait of contemporary Japanese society that tends to be driven more by the masculine desire for self-aggrandizement than by the maternal principle associated with traditional Japanese values.

A second change made to the traditional tale is the insertion of the episode in which the princess is momentarily reunited with the handsome young man who was her childhood playmate and her first love. Her love interest, a poor countryman who cuts wood and makes wooden bowls for a living, seems to stand for the old bamboo cutter's previous self that was free from avarice and more in tune with nature. The young lovers' reunion, however, is framed as a daydream; at the end of the film, the princess goes back to the moon, thanking her adoptive parents and forgiving the old man's foolishness. The romantic plot of the film, apparently an attempt at conforming to Disney's fairy-tale formula, is thus aborted by the traditional Japanese ending that emphasizes the gratification afforded to the old couple when their kindness is recognized by their adoptive child, who remains innocent and selfless. This ending, however, does not fulfill either plot, falling between the partially fulfilled marriage plot and the lost connection between old age and childhood.

This convoluted merging of the two traditions in Takahata's film seems to account for the confusion among audiences over its narrative implications. In Japan the film has received unanimous praise for its visual innovations, but its narrative revisions have invited mixed responses. This confusion is exemplified by the fact that the initial publicity slogan for the film, "The Crime and Punishment of Princess Kaguya," which was chosen by the producer and which Takahata found too "sensationalistic" (Takahata 73), was later replaced by "Ah, How Heartless!" which is the Japanese title of Victor Hugo's *Les Misérables*. The original slogan seems to be intended as a reference to the age-old theme of female curiosity punished (as in Perrault's "Bluebeard"), rather than to Dostoyevsky's *Crime and Punishment*. Towards the end of the film, the princess confesses that she was sent down as a punishment for being curious about the Earth. This confession does not make much sense in terms of moral integrity, nor does it bear any impact on the development of the story, as there is no further explanation about the nature of her crime or punishment. Hugo's novel about Jean Valjean, an ex-convict who lives in repentance and finds fulfillment in loving his adoptive daughter Cosette, seems closer to Takahata's narrative, which dramatizes the old bamboo cutter's excessive attachment to the innocent, beautiful girl. In this sense Takahata's film can be interpreted as a story of an old man's becoming, depicting the process of his misconstrued pursuit of worldly desires followed by his moral awakening. In contrast, the princess does not go through any moral development and remains pure and free from avarice throughout the story. Whereas her happiness derives from the positive aspect of earthly matters such as the beauty of nature, familial affections and romantic love (which, the story tells us, do not exist on the moon), his move from the world of bamboos to the world of power and money symbolizes the negative aspect of earthly affairs. The young countryman's name, Sutemaru, which contains *sute*, or "to discard," seems to refer to the act of discarding worldly attachments that is required of the old man. Seen from this perspective, the main narrative force of Takahata's film derives from the plot of the old bamboo cutter's awakening, rather than from the tragic fate of the strong-minded but

Figure 2.1. *The Tale of the Princess Kaguya*, directed by Isao Takahata (2013).

powerless princess, and approaches the plot of disillusionment in the Western tradition of realist novels discussed earlier in that the bamboo cutter comes to realize the foolishness of his aspirations after going through adventures.

The film seems to capture the cultural dilemma that Japanese fairy-tale adaptations are facing now, divided between the plot of progress and romance on the one hand and the desire for a moral and aesthetic balance on the other. Takahata's film reflects this conflict between different narrative traditions on multiple levels. The soundtrack, for example, shows the disjuncture between the portentous background score played by an orchestra and the simple, childlike optimism of the end credit tune sung by a young woman and accompanied by the piano. Also, the ingenious animation technique used for depicting the princess's frustrations distinguishes her stylistically from the other characters, whose features do not express much emotion, indicating visually that her selfhood as a modern, Westernized individualist does not blend in with the values of a traditional Japanese community (Figures 2.1. and 2.2.). The dissemination of Ghibli animation films outside Japan may invite the reconsideration and the reconfiguration of the Disneyfied happily-ever-after as a concept, offering new narrative potentials that will lead to innovation in the fairy-tale culture globalized by Disney's adaptations. Takahata's rendering of a Japanese fairy tale decenters the youth-centered narrative of Grimm tales, which has been reinforced by Disney and shows an alternative way of telling a story that does not marginalize old age. The film tries to achieve an aesthetic as well as emotional fulfillment by repeatedly evoking the blissful and mutually reinvigorating interaction between the old couple

Figure 2.2. *The Tale of the Princess Kaguya*, directed by Isao Takahata (2013).

and the magical child that takes place early in the film. The un-Disney-like happy ending, a curious fusion of the Buddhist belief in the Pure Land and the hippie ideal of an ecological paradise, arrives when everybody lets go of worldly attachments. Many of the English-speaking reviews appreciate this narrative twist. For example, the *Observer* film critic Mark Kermode states: "as the narrative takes flight and worlds collide, we find ourselves hoping against hope for a Disneyfied 'happy' ending. What we get is something altogether more elegiac—a cosmic conclusion of operatic proportions that somehow manages to sit organically among the feet-in-the-mud frolics that have gone before it."

The problem with Takahata's "cosmic conclusion," however, as in many of the Studio Ghibli productions, lies in the characterization of the princess as a conflation of the eternally innocent girl and the all-embracing mother who is expected to redeem the world, or men's world, from corruption.[9] The Feminine as transcendental signifier can be used for explaining and resolving problems in the world from a male perspective but leaves women fixed in a state devoid of opportunities for their own inner transformations. It is telling that Takahata states in an interview that his initial idea was to open the film with a scene where the princess's father, the emperor of the moon, reproves her for wishing to know about the Earth, a land forbidden to the inhabitants of the moon, before sending her there (Takahata 71–72); in other words, his retelling presupposes that the princess's father is the ultimate lawgiver. While the traditional story mentions but does not explain the princess's crime on the moon, Takahata speculates that she was punished for her curiosity about the earth, which she will inevitably find corrupted (72–73). This idea, however, is not developed in the film, which, together with the film's initial slogan "The Crime and Punishment of Princess Kaguya," has confused the Japanese. Despite the critics' unanimous praise for its visual aesthetics, the film has not attracted as large an audience in Japan as the producer expected.[10] Many English-language reviews claim that the film is more suitable for adult than young viewers, mainly because of its emphasis on visual experiments, rather than on the story's progress. Despite being an animation film based on a fairy tale, a genre usually categorized as a children's or family film, it was offered in Britain and America in both a Japanese-language version with subtitles for adults, in the evening, and a dubbed version for families with children during the day. From my discussion above, the centrality of the old couple can be seen as an additional element that may frustrate young Western audiences who are accustomed to Disney's focus on the fate of the princess. It is likely that Takahata's reimagining of "The Tale of the Bamboo Cutter" was made more accessible for Western audiences, because it was marketed primarily as the story of a beautiful, exotic princess who maintains her pure love despite all the corrupting influences of the world. However, as some of the English-speaking reviews note (e.g., Kermode, Taylor), the other plot that emphasizes the link between old age and childhood can be considered equally gratifying, and it is important that audiences of fairy-tale adaptations today have access to different ways of achieving narrative pleasures.

Conclusion

A cross-cultural comparison of the role played by the old in Grimm and Japanese tales reveals how age affects the plot pattern of the story and changes the way in which the reader attains narrative satisfaction at the end. Although old characters appear in both Western and Japanese tales, they perform different roles in these two narrative traditions. Whereas the elderly are cast in a supporting role to the coming-of-age plot of the Grimm tales, Japanese fairy tales cast the old as protagonists, who go through adventures themselves and attain eternal bliss when their kindness toward the magical child is finally rewarded. As my analysis of the Ghibli adaptation of "The Tale of the Bamboo Cutter" indicates, these two traditions have recently begun to interact with each other, revealing the different ways in which old age can be connected with childhood for the purpose of attaining a new equilibrium at the end of the narrative. As I suggest above, looking at such fusions and conflicts between different narrative traditions provides a new perspective on the way in which culture-specific representations linking old age and childhood in fairy tales have been affected by the current globalization of the genre mainly through Disney adaptations. The international circulation of cultural products works both ways, however, and it would be worth investigating whether such cross-cultural narrative merging is also affecting Western fairy-tale adaptations.

Notes

1. I use the term "canonical tales" to refer to the body of texts that have been more widely circulated than others by being included in fairy-tale collections or textbooks, or by being adapted to other media, such as picture books, novels, and films.

2. The English-language website *The Hylia* makes available 246 episodes from *Manga Nippon mukashibanashi*. See http://anime.thehylia.com/downloads/series/folktales-from-japan.

3. This number includes 210 tales in the Grimm collection's seventh edition and 32 tales omitted from it.

4. All quotations from works cited only in Japanese in the Works Cited list are given in my own translations.

5. Although the source is unknown, the classification "Five Great Fairy Tales" has been used widely by both the general public and researchers of fairy tales in Japan.

6. Today, Japan is estimated to have the world's highest proportion of the elderly. According to the Statistics Bureau, as of October 2014, 25.9 percent are aged 65 or above, compared to only 6.1 percent in 1960.

7. The percentage of the elderly living alone against the total population of the elderly rose from 15.5 percent in 1980 to 31.4 percent in 2010 (Cabinet Office).

8. Sung-Ae Lee's analysis of the abandonment of the elderly and children in contemporary South Korean films (this volume) throws light on how this old script produces different meanings depending on the specific social and cultural context.

9. One early example is the heroine of Takahata's 1974 adaptation of *Heidi's Years of Wandering and Learning* by Johanna Spyri for a TV animation series, in which it is not Heidi but the grandfather who undergoes moral development through his interactions with the innocent yet wise girl. Similarities between Takahata's *The Tale of the Princess Kaguya* and *Heidi* have been pointed out by many, including Takahata himself: these include the contrast between the countryside and the city, the characterization of the heroine who has a free and independent spirit, the presence of the repressive governess, and the close bond between the old man and the little girl. See Ingrid Tomkowiak's discussion of *Heidi* in this volume.

10. As of January 2015, *The Tale of the Princess Kaguya* has grossed 2.47 billion yen at the Japanese box office, while the production budget reached 5.15 billion yen, an unusually large amount for an animation film. It ranks fifteenth in the Ghibli films, whose top box-office earner, *Spirited Away* (2001), grossed 30.4 billion yen.

Works Cited

Cabinet Office. "Annual Report on the Aging Society: 2014 (Summary)." http://www8.cao.go.jp/kourei/english/annualreport/2014/2014pdf_e.html. Accessed on 6 December 2015.

Grimm, Wilhelm, and Jacob Grimm. *The Complete Fairy Tales.* Trans. Jack Zipes. London: Vintage, 2007.

Gullette, Margaret Morganroth. *Safe at Last in the Middle Years: The Invention of the Midlife Progress Novel.* Berkeley: University of California Press, 1988.

Kawai, Hayao. *The Japanese Psyche: Major Motifs in the Fairy Tales of Japan.* Trans. Hayao Kawai and Sachiko Reece. Woodstock: Spring, 1996.

Kermode, Mark. Review of *The Tale of the Princess Kaguya. Observer* (22 March 2015). http://www.theguardian.com/film/2015/mar/22/tale-of-princess-kaguya-review-kermode. Accessed on 1 May 2015.

Kubo, Kayo. *Nihon niokeru gaikoku mukashibanashi no juyō to hen'yō: Wasei Gurimu no sekai* (The reception and transformation of foreign folktales in Japan: The world of Japanised Grimm). Tokyo: Miyaishoten, 2009.

Lang, Andrew. *The Violet Fairy Book.* Longmans: London, 1901.

Ozawa, Toshio. "Minwa no naka no Nihonjin (II)" (The Japanese in the folktale [II]). *Nihonjin to minwa* (The Japanese and the folktale). Ed. Toshio Ozawa. Tokyo: Gyousei, 1976. 165-194.

Palmore, Erdman B. *The Honorable Elders Revisited: A Revised Cross-Cultural Analysis of Aging in Japan.* Durham: Duke University Press, 1985.

Schenda, Rudolf. "Nihon no Mukashibanashi no naka de Nihontekina mono wa nanika" (What is Japanese in the Japanese folktale). *Nihonjin to minwa* (The Japanese and the folktale). Ed. Toshio Ozawa. Tokyo: Gyousei, 1976. 106-116.

Schmiesing, Ann. *Disability, Deformity, and Disease in the Grimms' Fairy Tales.* Detroit: Wayne State University Press, 2014.

Seki, Keigo, ed. *Folktales of Japan.* Trans. Robert J. Adams. London: Routledge, 1963.

Someya, Yoshiko. "Japan." *Koreisha fukushi no hikaku bunka: Mareshia, Chugoku, Osutoraria, Nihon.* Ed. Jun Katata. Fukuoka: Kyushu University Press, 2000.

Statistics Bureau. "Population Estimates by Age (5-Year Age Group) and Sex." *Statistics Japan.* http://www.stat.go.jp/english/data/jinsui/2014np/index.htm. Accessed on 10 April 2015.

Takahata, Isao. "Intabyū: Yakudōsuru sukecchi o kyōrakusuru (Taking Pleasure in Vibrant Sketches)." *Yuriika* 45.17 (2013): 70–82.

The Tale of the Princess Kaguya. Dir. Isao Takahata. 2013.

Taylor, Ella. "Beauty and Loss in 'The Tale of Princess Kaguya.'" *NPR* (16 October 2014). http://www.npr.org/2014/10/16/356111666/beauty-and-loss-in-the-tale-of-princess-kaguya. Accessed on 1 May 2015.

Yamaori, Tetsuo. *Kami kara okina e* (From the god to the old man). Tokyo: Seidosha, 1984.

- 3 -

Vitalizing Childhood through Old Age in Hector Malot's *Sans famille*

An Intersectional Perspective

ELISABETH WESSELING

The social marker of "age" shapes identities in close interaction with affiliated variables of "gender," "class," "race," and "nationality." As intersectionality theory emphasizes, crucial social differences never operate in isolation from each other. Rather, they are mutually constitutive, with our social identities emerging at the points of intersection between these variables. While this theory was originally designed to address the intersections between gender and race within a feminist framework in order to come to terms with the differences between women (Crenshaw, "Demarginalizing," "Mapping," and "Whose Story"), it has by now also drawn other social variables into its orbit, including age (Hearn, Katz). These categories of identity define each other's meanings, shape each other's behavioral scripts, and enhance each other's social impact, determining the ways in which different social groups accumulate specific sets of advantages or disadvantages. Although some of these identity markers, most notably age, gender, and race, are often thought to be biologically determined, critical gender and age studies have driven the message home that they are in fact defined by culture rather than nature, as becomes manifest in their historical variability. Old age meant something completely different in pre-industrial societies than it does in industrial societies (and something different again in postindustrial societies), while its implications differ for men and women as well (Hearn). The desire to transcend the constraints that crucial differences impose on our social identities is likewise a persistent cultural phenomenon, which has strongly inspired the utopian aspects of narrative fiction. This chapter offers a historical and intersectional perspective on the interlinkage of childhood and old age through a detailed case study of Hector Malot's classic *Sans famille* (1878, No relations). This children's novel is set in late-nineteenth-century France, that is, in a social world that differs significantly from contemporary postindustrial, high-tech, urbanized Western societies. As such, it provides a research opportunity for generating detailed insight into the historicity of age, class, gender, and ethnicity.

Sans famille was an immediate success upon its publication in 1878. Only one year later, it went into its seventeenth printing. The fictional characters of the traveling musician Vitalis, who has reaped the wisdom and experience of a lifetime to pass it on to the foundling boy Rémi, have become widely known in different cultures through numerous translations and adaptations. The first English translation appeared in 1880, to be followed by translations into German, Dutch, Russian, Japanese, and Vietnamese (Willemsen 427). The book has never been out of print since. In addition, *Sans famille* was adapted to film and TV screens at least twelve times, the last coming out in 2000. New translations and editions of *Sans famille* have continued to appear around the last turn of the century,[1] even though the novel evokes a world that has ceased to exist, while it is written in the rather dated style of nineteenth-century literary Naturalism. The harsh poverty governing the first part of Rémi's life has been largely removed from now-affluent Western societies. The economic value commonly assigned to children in societies of scarcity, such as the one that *Sans famille* evokes, is now to be found, rather, in the developing regions of the world, where children are not yet considered to be "priceless" (Zelizer). In addition, the novel portrays elderly men in a way that is at odds with contemporary stereotypes of old age, such as physical weakness, mental feebleness, backwardness, dependence, and so on.[2] Vitalis displays none of these deficiencies. Weakness and vulnerability are associated solely with the young here, whereas the elderly characters excel in *savoir, savoir-faire*, and *savoir-vivre* and are held in high esteem as possessors of the wisdom and knowledge that come from a lifetime of learning and experience. Only elderly men are presented as suitable for instructing the young morally and intellectually in the school of life, as opposed to the parental generation, who are construed as a liability for the upcoming generations in *Sans famille*. Vitalis's strength, stamina, and intellectual and moral rigor are emphasized throughout the novel. His name already reveals that he is the personification of the very life force itself, which has an invigorating influence on the rather passive and melancholic Rémi. Clearly, this novel was published before a new "subclass" of retired men was created through the introduction of state pensions from the early twentieth century onward, which increasingly defined old age for men in terms of retirement versus employment. For sure, there is no pension or retirement for Vitalis, nor does he make the impression that he would need it.

The various characters in *Sans famille* are all fleshed out through specific positioning at the crossroads between the parameters of age, gender, class, and ethnicity. This chapter details how the intricate interplay between these markers is shown to determine their life course. At the same time, the novel articulates an intense longing to overcome these social constraints through art, more specifically through the supposedly universal language of music, which is celebrated as mankind's means par excellence to transcend all social barriers. After describing the narrative mode of *Sans famille*, I proceed to analyze how Vitalis's senescence supports his suitability and effectiveness as Rémi's principal teacher and guide in the school of life. I then elaborate how all social differences are supposedly erased by the unifying power of music in the utopian ending of the novel.

Naturalist Melodrama

The narrative structure of *Sans famille* displays the tempestuous succession of ups and downs that is typical of nineteenth-century melodrama, intended to stir the audience's feelings and soften their hearts so as to make them susceptible to a moral message (Brooks; Nemesvari 1–22). *Sans famille* might just as well have been called *Famille partout*, since Rémi's most outstanding virtue is his infallible adoptability. Rémi is deprived of kinsfolk seven times in the course of the story, which implies that he has been "adopted" by different parental figures six times in a row, if we also count his two reunions with his birth mother, the British aristocrat "madame" Milligan.[3] In addition to this succession of biological and substitute parents, he also gathers a considerable number of (adoptive) siblings along the way, such as his fellow street musician Mattia, and the six children of *père* (father) Acquin, who takes him into his own house after Vitalis has died on Acquin's doorstep. On top of all this, Rémi is also united with his younger biological brother, Arthur Milligan. Clearly, Rémi has a special talent for inducing familial attachment and devotion in others, and for answering them in kind.

The narrative voice of *Sans famille* is far from melodramatic, however. The novel plays the game of make-believe that the story is divulged to us in retrospect by Rémi himself, who sits down to write his memoirs after he has finally found his rightful place in society with a wife, son, mother, and brother, and a fortune and an estate, blessed with the necessary means to gather all his adoptive family members around him. Rémi's narrative voice is characterized by pensive, sober-minded maturity. His own survival into adulthood is the very warrant of the reassuring message that the numerous ups and downs in his life have finally stabilized in a steady, felicitous state. Even while depicting the most heart-wrenching circumstances, Rémi never drowns the (juvenile) reader in emotion, if only because it is made clear from the start that he has overcome the adversity at hand. Rémi's voice is also a learned one, which never tires of rendering highly detailed, fact-packed descriptions of the events and scenes under study.

This somewhat distanced, learned, and graphically descriptive narrative voice is quite typical of nineteenth-century Naturalism (Moore 45).[4] Malot used to be mentioned in one breath with literary giants whose place in the canon of French literature is still uncontested, such as Honoré de Balzac, Gustave Flaubert, and Émile Zola (Pottier 191–193). Malot was a committed, ambitious, and highly prolific author, skilled in achieving a "reality effect" through descriptive detail—the hallmark of Realist and Naturalist writing (Barthes 167–175). In *Sans famille* this quality becomes particularly manifest in Malot's gripping descriptions of turbulent atmospheric conditions, most notably the snowstorm that proves to be the undoing of Vitalis's *troupe*, eventually even killing the master himself (Malot 113–129). *Sans famille* turned out to be both a blessing and a curse for Malot's literary reputation. It earned him enduring fame, at the price of casting all his other literary works into oblivion.

As befits a Naturalist man of letters, Malot approached the business of novel writing as a (proto-)scientific endeavor (Ridley 170–200). *Sans famille* is packed with geographical, geological, botanic, physiological, and sociological data about late-nineteenth-century France. Malot obviously subscribed to the positivist tenet that human behavior and society are as much governed by laws as the natural world. More specifically, the traces of the authoritative literary critic Hippolyte Taine are quite noticeable in *Sans famille*.[5] According to Taine (1863), a staunch supporter of Naturalism in literature, human behavior—including aesthetic creation—is determined by the interplay between the three determining factors of "race, milieu et moment" (*Histoire* iii–xlix). "Race" here refers to one's entire physiological makeup or genetic heritage, which was widely associated with nationality in the nineteenth century. "Milieu" is the term Taine used for the environment in which one grows up—not just the social, but also the natural environment (climate, soil, nourishment, and so forth). "Moment" refers to the concrete historical circumstances in which people happen to find themselves at any given point in time (Terrier 27–31). Malot's adherence to Naturalist premises reveals itself in his portraits of the various characters in *Sans famille*, which place due emphasis on "race" in his graphic descriptions of French and English "milieux" (for example, the barren and poverty-stricken Chavanon where Rémi spends his first years, or the seedy side of London where the Driscolls ply their dubious trade), and in his fascination with the survival strategies of the lower social strata. In light of Taine's views on "race," the fact that Rémi is of British stock is an important clue to his character, just as the Italian origins of Vitalis and Mattia are to theirs. Malot's Tainean and overall Naturalist affinities need to be taken into account if we want to grasp the narrative functions of the connection between childhood and old age in *Sans famille*.

Intergenerational Conflict, Complementarity, and Affinity

Sans famille offers a complete inventory of the various commonplaces associated with the connection between childhood and old age, that is, conflict, complementarity, and affinity. Conflict is rife in the intergenerational relationships between adults and children in the lower social strata where the story of *Sans famille* is set. In fact, Rémi is targeted by the self-serving schemes of adults from the moment he is born. Cunning men put a price on his head to relieve their own misery and deprivation time and again, much to the detriment of the young child. As a baby he is snatched away from his aristocratic parents by the ruthless Driscolls, who hope to gain a handsome ransom for him. When they leave the baby boy briefly unattended, he is "found" by Barberin, who likewise regards him as a source of potential profit, as the fancy swaddling clothes of the baby betray his wealthy origins. When Barberin becomes disabled through an accident, he has no qualms in selling the boy to a traveling street musician, Vitalis, which makes it unlikely that Rémi will ever be reunited with his loving adoptive mother, Barberin's wife, again. When Vitalis is sent to prison, he makes the mistake of giving Rémi into the custody of the rather dubious guardian Garofoli, who is this novel's equivalent of Charles Dickens's Fagin (*Oliver Twist*). Garofoli is a corruptor of youth, running a gang of boy orphans and exploiting young children's begging and thieving only to enrich himself. Last but certainly not least, Rémi has an uncle who wants to have him out of the way so he can usurp the boy's inheritance. This uncle was instrumental in maneuvering the baby boy into the hands of the Driscolls. He repeats this trick when Rémi is about to be reunited with his biological mother toward the end of the novel. Clearly, adult men in reduced circumstances prey on Rémi throughout his childhood, always seeking to make profit out of him without the least regard for his well-being. There is a clear gender dimension to this schema: women do not figure as perpetrators in *Sans famille*; at worst they are only accomplices.

"Complementarity" characterizes the relationship between Vitalis and Rémi, who are very different from each other yet manage to establish a loyal and loving relationship that benefits both. Rémi embodies youthful innocence and ignorance, while Vitalis possesses the knowledge and wisdom that come with age. Yet a crucial aspect of their successful match is that their temperaments differ significantly. The complementary nature of their relationship becomes particularly clear when we compare it to Rémi's bonding with his adoptive mother, Barberin, and Mrs. Milligan, who turns out to be his real mother in the end. In spite of their poverty, mother Barberin and Rémi enjoyed almost paradisiacal harmony and peace. They were safely ensconced in their cottage, hidden away in the pit of a valley, leading a bucolic life of sober but perfect contentment that could have lasted forever, or so it seems, until father Barberin intruded upon the scene to sell off the boy. Rémi returns to this state of blissful contentment when he joins Mrs. Milligan and her son Arthur on their idyllic, flowery canal boat. The boat is pulled along at a slow and even pace, and all Rémi has to do is to go with the flow, while he is fed on cakes and pies. Here again, his extraordinary adoptability stands him in good stead, as Mrs. Milligan takes to the boy and is quite willing to accept him as her own son (which is what he actually turns out to be in the end).

Rémi and his two mothers appear to be of the same kind, as they merge in symbiotic union. Both maternal relationships cater to the passive streak in Rémi's nature. Like Zola, Malot drew upon the theory of the four humors to shape his characters.[6] Within this framework (Paster 1–24), it is quite obvious that Rémi has a phlegmatic temperament, verging on the melancholic (or "nerveuse," as Zola called it in *Thérèse Raquin*). Rémi's features are very fine and delicate, he is slim rather than robust, and his element is water. After all, his first reunion with his mother is set on the water (the canal boat), and he survives the flooding of a mine. His primary inclination is toward passivity (positively put: susceptibility or openness, hence his adoptability), repetition (positively put: loyalty, hence his talent for bonding with parent—and sibling—substitutes), submission (obedience) and giving in, up to the point of giving up. The state of perfect contentment or stasis thus suits him to a

T. Rémi does not seem to have a strong urge to make things happen; rather, things happen to him. In his whole disposition, he closely resembles his two mothers, who have similar temperaments. Rémi's utter passivity characterizes the domestic bliss with his mothers Barberin and Milligan, which is represented as perfect oral contentment. His mothers put food on the table, if not into his mouth, and there is a very real temptation never to grow out of this situation. Indeed, passivity bordering on resignation or defeatism seems to be the major pitfall or trap for Rémi's phlegmatic temperament.

As Rémi needs to develop into a man, his domestic bliss is not made to last. It is Vitalis, Rémi's highly esteemed mentor and guide, who actually tears him away from his mothers two times in a row. First, Vitalis rather callously conspires with Barberin in reducing the boy to the status of an indentured laborer. Vitalis does not even allow Rémi to take leave of mother Barberin, abducting him into the mountains by force. There, a life of hardship begins. This scene of violent rupture is repeated later on in the story, when Vitalis disrupts Rémi's equally blissful symbiosis with *madame* Milligan. Clearly, Vitalis is the main force to impose society's strictures on the young child, forcing him into manhood and a life of labor that befits his (supposedly low) social class. This time Vitalis takes Rémi away for what turns out to be the most horrendous episode in his life. Winter sets in and destroys nearly the whole group: the two carefully trained dogs Zerbino and Dolce are torn to pieces by a pack of wolves in a snowy night while the company is seeking shelter in a forester's hut. This already quite tragic event, which undercuts their livelihood, signals the onset of further disaster. The monkey Joli-Coeur is to follow suit soon after, dying of hypothermia, and finally the invincible Vitalis also perishes, as he vainly attempts to weather a cold winter's night out on the streets of Paris. This leaves Rémi virtually alone in the world, except for the dog Capi, the last surviving animal of Vitalis's troupe.

At first sight, Vitalis's intrusions upon Rémi's domestic idylls seem to put him in the same camp with the Driscolls and Garofolis. Nevertheless, the juvenile audience at which this book is addressed is to entertain the notion that Rémi carries away something useful from his repeated, cruel maternal deprivation. As Vitalis tells Mrs. Milligan in a rather high-flown manner, she might well have the means to educate Rémi's mind by providing him with a good upbringing, but he knows how to mold Rémi's character (Malot 111). Vitalis thus excuses Rémi's abductions by arguing that he can never grow up to be a man if he remains under female tutelage, all the more so because the phlegmatic temperament already seems to be rather effeminate in itself. Moreover, Malot clearly associates Rémi's phlegmatism with his British "race."[7] His sickly brother Arthur, who can only lie down and watch the world go by, even outdoes Rémi in terms of delicate vulnerability, passivity, and resignation. Whereas Arthur is prone to physical weakness, Rémi's usurper uncle James Milligan is a clear case of moral degeneration. And while his mother does not display any flaws, she does not manifest clear virtues either: life just happens to her, and she submits without much struggle. Like Rémi, she simply goes with the flow. Clearly, Rémi's genetic heritage is not flawless, and Vitalis is there to provide an important corrective to his character.

The gender politics of this rudimentary educational theory are quite glaring, gender conspiring with "race" in the Tainean sense of the word to cast doubt on Mrs. Milligan's suitability as educator. It takes a man, a father figure, and all that men are supposed to stand for (the wide world beyond the home, discipline, resilience in the face of adversity) to turn Rémi's natural inclinations to better use. But not just any man. Like Rémi, Vitalis embodies a specific temperament, which is associated with his nationality, in Vitalis's case, his Italian "race." Vitalis has a sanguine temperament, verging on the choleric. His soul has been forged in a warm and sunny climate. As a performing artist who obviously seeks company and attention, he is sociable, and quite capable of imposing his will on others through his choleric streak. Vitalis's element is air, not just the open air of the outdoors as opposed to domestic space, as becomes a wanderer, but also the air we breathe to recite verse, sing songs, and play musical instruments. With infinite patience, he teaches Rémi how to read and write, sing and act, bringing out the music in him (do-re-mi). Vitalis's musical talent turns out to be his most important defining feature, which epitomizes his sanguine nature.

However, Vitalis does not only teach lessons but also embodies them, and this is where senescence comes into the picture. Vitalis is obviously a man with a past, which remains shrouded in mystery until his true identity is revealed. Vitalis used to be the celebrated Italian opera singer Carlo Balzani, whose voice began to falter when he reached the very heights of fame. Ashamed of not living up to his audience's high expectations any longer, Balzani degraded himself to an anonymous expatriate who ekes out a living through a traveling circus act with trained dogs and a monkey. As the theatrical repertoire of trained animals is inevitably limited, Vitalis can never stay anywhere for long, and so he is forced to wander. These reduced circumstances, however, have not broken his spirit. Time and again, Rémi testifies to Vitalis's noble demeanor, his unblemished human dignity, his unshakable optimism, and his infinite patience with those who depend on his guidance. The old man's life story exemplifies (rather than informs) that no matter how low you sink, you need not lose your human dignity. Whatever Vitalis may have lost, there is one thing that he has retained: music. Music confers a universal dimension upon human interaction and communication in this novel, transcending age, class, gender, and ethnicity. Music, it seems, will always be there to lift one's spirits, whether it presents itself in the glamorous shape of a renowned opera singer or in the humble form of a poor street musician. In short, music is the medium of the very life force itself, which is personified by Vitalis.

Hence, Vitalis not only instructs Rémi in important skills (reading and writing, singing and acting, English and Italian) but also teaches the boy how to turn his temperament to good purposes by demonstrating that adversity can always be overcome. The lesson that Vitalis embodies provides an important antidote to Rémi's phlegmatic-melancholic temperament, which is naturally inclined toward passivity and surrender. Yet Rémi is also pensive, with a propensity for scholarship, which becomes manifest in his interest in father Acquin's horticultural books and in the fact that he is the only boy to pay attention to the learned discourses of "the professor," an experienced, autodidactic miner who has gathered considerable geological expertise during his lengthy career underground. Making the best of these melancholic traits,[8] Rémi eventually becomes a scholar or learned author.

The fact that Vitalis is succeeded by Mattia as Rémi's primary companion comes as no surprise. Vitalis and Mattia are interchangeable in that they both embody the animating principle of music, which seems to thrive optimally in men with a sanguine temperament that has been nourished by a sunny climate. Mattia shares Vitalis's extraordinary musical talent, his fiery temperament, and his optimism and stamina. They are obviously kindred souls, exemplifying the pattern of "affinity" in intergenerational relationships, meaning that age difference is negligible vis-à-vis their fundamentally identical take on life. Therefore, Mattia has the same vitalizing, invigorating effect on Rémi that Vitalis had before him. With Mattia, Rémi becomes even more successful as a street musician. It is quite obvious that Rémi would not have pulled through without Mattia, as he states quite explicitly on several occasions, while Mattia needs Rémi's loving fidelity to unfold his talents. In return, Rémi imparts his reading and writing skills to Mattia, who is the better musician but the poorer scholar of the two.

A Naturalist Despite Himself

Literary Naturalism and genetic determinism are almost synonyms. But not quite so in this novel, in which the author manifests himself as a Naturalist *malgré lui*. On the one hand, the author pays due tribute to the determining forces of "race, milieu et moment," forces that seem to seal his characters' fates, but not quite. *Sans famille* presents the reading audience with a mitigated, softened Naturalism, meaning that characters do not proceed toward their doom or victory according to the laws incumbent upon their genetic and class background; somehow some form of saving grace always operates in *Sans famille*, which disrupts linear progressions toward a preordained end, and in conclusion provides a rather un-Naturalist, blissfully happy, utopian ending that transcends all misery, deprivation, hardship, and adversity. Perhaps Malot felt that unredeemed Naturalism would be too harsh for a young reading audience, but whatever his motives were, it is clear that there is a counterforce in *Sans famille* that softens the hard lot of its characters and becomes increasingly noticeable as the story proceeds toward its ending.

First of all, departure and loss never appear to be as absolute as they seem to be at first sight, contrary to the dire fates of other famous Naturalist characters such as Zola's Nana, Flaubert's Madame Bovary, or Louis Couperus's Eline Vere. For example, the affinity between Vitalis and his successor Mattia articulates the reassuring message that the linear trajectory from life to death may be mitigated by various forms of retrieval and return. *Sans famille* relates many a departure that seems to be irreversible at first but is nevertheless repaired at a later stage. Rémi's forced withdrawal from Chavanon initially seems to be traumatically definite. The pathetic detail of mother Barberin's white cap becoming smaller and smaller as she is frantically looking for Rémi, who is climbing higher and higher out of their valley (41–42), seems to signal that they are lost to each other forever. Nevertheless, Rémi manages to return to her later on, providing her with another adoptive son (Mattia) and a cow, to boot. The gift has symbolic importance. Mother Barberin was forced to sell their cow Roussette when her husband turned into an invalid and thus became incapable of earning the family income. Rémi was sold likewise, almost simultaneously with Roussette, and for the same reason. Like the cow, Rémi started out in life as a creature of passive dependence. This dual loss is repaired by the return of Rémi and Mattia, which also indicates that Rémi has emancipated himself from the status of a helpless creature. Obviously, the boys are not dependent on maternal figures any longer for nourishment and care. Rather, they are turning into providers. In a similar fashion, Rémi leaves Paris as a baby, sold by his uncle, to disappear into an obscure corner of Chavanon, forever lost, or so it seems. However, thanks to Vitalis, he returns to Paris later on, where he learns about his British origins. Likewise, Rémi leaves England as a baby for France, where he is manipulated out of his inheritance by his uncle, but he manages to cross the channel twice later on, to reclaim his estate as rightful heir of Milligan Park in the end.

In this novel there is never a point of no return. This message is epitomized by the beatific reunion of all Rémi's loved ones in the concluding chapter, aptly titled "Ma famille." Only one person out of all the people who have crossed Rémi's path is absent—physically, that is. This is regrettable, but not unbearably so. Rémi has done everything he could to rehabilitate the great Italian opera singer posthumously, by burying him at Montparnasse, in the graveyard dedicated to artists of merit, with a proper tombstone that displays his real name. But according to Rémi, Vitalis/Balzani's spirit still presides over the reunion with his other loved ones, as well as over his writing, one could say, as Balzani's bust adorns Rémi's writing table. Thus, the fine art of belles lettres pays due tribute to what is suggested to be an even higher art: music.

Music is construed as superior to literature in that the latter always has to employ a particular language, whereas the language of music is presented as universal in *Sans famille*.[9] Here, music figures as the main force uniting people in crucial partnerships (Vitalis and Rémi, Rémi and Mattia, Rémi and Lise, Arthur and Cristina) that enable them to weather (almost) any storm, and to produce new life together. Therefore, the most typical musical expression in this novel is a love song. Under the spell of music, all social variables cease to matter. It is immaterial that Vitalis is old, and his soulmate Mattia young, or that Vitalis has gone from fame to ignominy, while Mattia is moving in the opposite direction, on his way to becoming a world-famous musician. Nor does it matter that Mattia is of lowly, and Rémi of aristocratic, origin, or that the first is of Italian and the second of British stock. The Italian love song that Vitalis teaches to Rémi is shown to have immediate appeal regardless of its language. Not only does it serve to ease both Vitalis's and Rémi's sorrows, but it is also used by the latter to soften the heart of Lise and to gain access to the mute girl, who learns to speak only after having listened to the language of music, and who will eventually marry Rémi and provide him with a son and heir. Appropriately, the last lines of the novel are therefore devoted to commemorating Vitalis/Balzani and to celebrating the power of music by singing this very song together as the whole company is gathered around the bronze bust of Rémi's mentor.

The irony of the happy ending to *Sans famille* is that Rémi has now returned to the very same state of blissful stasis that he was torn away from twice in a row for the sake of developing his character. As August Willemsen rightly remarks (430), domestic happiness is always represented by the timeless symbol of a garden in *Sans famille*: mother Barberin's cottage garden, the flowery canal boat of Mrs. Milligan (a floating garden, one could say), the nursery garden of the Acquin family, and finally, the most beautiful of them all: Milligan Park. At the end of *Sans famille*, the situation is once more so perfectly satisfactory, with plenty of both male and female kinsfolk around, that no one could possibly have any motive for change here. In retrospect, one might wonder why Rémi had to be taken away twice from the very situation that he eventually ends up in, and this time for good, it seems, a young man still. What first seemed to be a dangerous seduction, now turns out to be the final purpose of it all.

There are ways to resolve the paradox involved in the "happy ending." First, Rémi's character has reached a mature stage of development at which he can finally "afford" domestic bliss, with his circle of loved ones now widened to include male relatives and friends. One could speculate that these complex detours were necessary to make up for the absence of Remi's biological father, Mr. Milligan. In addition, Rémi now has the means to not only enjoy his own domestic bliss, but also to help those still in need, as becomes apparent in his declared intention to found and manage a charity for juvenile street musicians. Third, the final state of felicitous stasis can be interpreted as an iconic tribute to the power of art to immortalize (and thereby also to immobilize) all that we hold dear. Rather than living his adventures, Rémi is now content with recording them as an author, employing the power of art to safeguard the most important people and events in his life for posterity. Hence, his memoirs are on a par with the bronze statue of Balzani immortalizing Vitalis, or the iconic Neapolitan love song recurring throughout the novel and sounding its final note.

There is a price to be paid for everything. Rémi and Vitalis, who had to struggle so hard to survive, now seem to have moved beyond all vicissitudes into the transcendent realm of art, but at the price of losing life once more, albeit they have exchanged a death of ignominy for the lifeless stasis of perennial commemoration. In all this, Rémi hardly seems to be more alive than his deceased master, and in this sense their union still persists, first as a strategy of survival, now as means for joining each other in the immortal realm of art, which captures motion like flies caught in amber. The fourth and last solution to the paradoxical ending of *Sans famille* may be inferred from the fact that Remi himself now belongs to the parental generation, a generation that is portrayed quite negatively in *Sans famille*. Rémi's state of perfect bliss and contentment, one could say, is to keep him out of harm's way, and to turn him into a credible guardian of, rather than predator on, vulnerable youth, surely a reassuring message for the closing pages of the novel.

The Historical Variability of Crucial Differences

As I hope to have demonstrated, age is an important parameter for defining one's role and position in society in *Sans famille*, but only in close conjunction with the affiliated identity markers of class, gender, and nationality. The young boy Rémi has to be yanked out of the close companionship of women to grow up to be a man under the tutelage of an elderly, *déclassé* man of a different ethnic background, who has seen it all and knows how to face adversity, only to return to the felicitous symbiosis with women in the end, when he finally seems to have been sufficiently inoculated against its seductive lure of self-sufficient, perfect contentment. The novel renders in graphic detail how specific sets of social differences lead to the accumulation of advantages or disadvantages, but never in the linear, fatalistic way that is characteristic of so many Naturalist classics for adult reading audiences.

Literary Naturalism suggests that the vicissitudes of class, gender, and nationality are part and parcel of the genetic, rather than the cultural, heritage of its characters, and so does Malot. But it is in this very insistence on the biological, hence ahistorical, nature of social difference that Naturalism reveals the cultural determination of these social categories, given the fact that the meanings *Sans famille* assigns to age, class, gender, and ethnicity differ starkly from contemporary signifying practices. The association of femininity with passivity and resignation, let alone with the lure of the sirens, is not taken for granted any longer, nor do we find it self-evident that the Italian, French, or British are characterized by specific innate, collective temperaments. Malot's somewhat un-Naturalistic transcendental investment in music has become equally dated. With the emergence of popular mass culture in the course of the twentieth century, music has acquired the function of marking the differences between specific subcultures (punk, Goth, emo, techno, and so forth). And the ideal of the universal family of men, which is embraced in the concluding chapter of *Sans famille*, has been shattered by the two World Wars. Naturalism's sociology *avant la lettre* ultimately reveals its historicity in its ahistorical determinism.

Notes

1. In France, a new edition was released in 2000 by Librairie Générale Française. The last translation in English appeared in 2007 under the title *Alone in the World* (2007). The book was translated into Dutch by August Willemsen in 1999, reappearing in a hardcover luxury edition, which has been reprinted. Various other types of adaptations, such as comic strip versions, audio books, and adaptations for the theatre continue to be produced to date.

2. This means that the novel is not affected by what Margaret Morganroth Gullette (1997), one of the founding mothers of age studies, has criticized as "the narrative of decline."

3. *Sans famille* is thus a perfect illustration of the foundling fantasy as described by Sigmund Freud in his essay "Die Familienroman der Neurotiker" (1909). According to Freud (227–231), this fantasy is a widespread feature of the Oedipal complex, signaling the onset of the child's emancipation from its parents.

4. The combination of a melodramatic narrative structure and a realistic, (proto-)scientific voice is not uncommon at all in nineteenth-century Realism and Naturalism, for example, in the novels of Thomas Hardy (*Tess of the d'Urbervilles*) or Émile Zola (the Rougon-Macquart cycle).

5. Taine admired Malot's writing and actively encouraged him, together with Zola and Guy de Maupassant, to enter in the republic of letters (see Zola's *Les romanciers naturalistes*).

6. Although positivists such as Taine, Zola, or Malot were unlikely to express explicit adherence to such a speculative paradigm as humoral theory, they nevertheless share the basic premises of this paradigm, namely, the idea that our behavior is determined not so much by inner spirit or individual character as by physiological constitution, that is, by specific combinations of and balances between physical properties. Hence, the theory of the four temperaments is quite noticeable in, for instance, Zola's *Thérèse Raquin* (1867) and *Sans famille*.

7. In this respect, Malot definitely departs from his mentor Taine, who attributed much more robust features to the British temperament in *Notes sur l'Angleterre* (1872).

8. Melancholics, because of their immense inwardness, have an inclination toward bookish learning, as becomes apparent in the most famous of them all, Shakespeare's Hamlet, who typically makes an entrance upon the scene while engrossed in a book (for instance, in act II, scene II). For the close association between melancholy and learning, see Trevor (9).

9. Malot's concept of music as a universally transcendent language differs strikingly from late modern views on music, which belabor music's importance in marking subcultures, that is, the border between "ingroup" and "outgroup" (Shuker 161–187).

Works Cited

Barthes, Roland. 1968. L'effet de réel. *Le bruissement de la langue*. Paris: Seuil, 1984. 167–175.

Brooks, Peter. *The Melodramatic Imagination: Balzac, Henry James, and the Mode of Excess*. New Haven: Yale University Press, 1976.

Crenshaw, Kimberlé. "Demarginalizing the Intersection of Gender and Race: A Black Feminist Critique of Antidiscrimination Doctrine, Feminist Theory, and Antiracist Politics." *University of Chicago Legal Forum* 14 (1989): 538–554.

Crenshaw, Kimberlé. "Mapping the Margins: Intersectionality, Identity Politics, and Violence against Women of Color." *Stanford Law Review* 43.6 (1991): 1241–1299.

Crenshaw, Kimberlé. "Whose Story Is It, Anyway? Feminist and Antiracist Appropriations of Anita Hill." *Race-ing Justice, En-gendering Power*. Ed. Toni Morrison. New York: Pantheon, 1992. 402–440.

Freud, Sigmund. *Gesammelte Werke*. Vol. 7. Frankfurt am Main: Fischer Verlag, 1976.

Gullette, Margaret Morganroth. *Declining to Decline: Culture Combat and the Politics of the Midlife*. Charlottesville: University of Virginia Press, 1997.

Hearn, Jeff. "Imaging the Aging of Men." *Images of Aging: Cultural Representations of Later Life*. Eds. Mike Featherstone and Andrew Wernick. London: Routledge, 1994. 97–115.

Katz, Stephen. "What Is Age Studies?" *Age Culture Humanities: An Interdisciplinary Journal* 1 (2014). http://ageculturehumanities.org/WP/what-is-age-studies/. Accessed on 25 January 2017.

Malot, Hector. 1878. *Sans famille*. Paris: Librairie Générale Française, 2000.

Marcoin, Francis, ed. *Hector Malot et le métier de l'écrivain*. Paris: Magellan, 2008.

Moore, Grace. *The Victorian Novel in Context*. London: Bloomsbury, 2012.

Nemesvari, Richard. *Thomas Hardy, Sensationalism, and the Melodramatic Mode*. New York: Palgrave Macmillan, 2011.

Paster, Gail Kern. *Humoring the Body: Emotions and the Shakespearean Stage*. Chicago: Chicago University Press, 2004.

Pottier, Jean-Michel. "Hector Malot: Écrivain classé/déclassé. Le cas de *Victimes d'amour*." *Hector Malot et le métier de l'écrivain*. Ed. Francis Marcoin. Paris: Magellan, 2008. 191–207.

Ridley, Hugh. *Darwin Becomes Art: Aesthetic Vision in the Wake of Darwin: 1870–1920*. Amsterdam: Rodopi, 2014.

Shakespeare, William. 1599–1602. *Hamlet: Prince of Denmark*. Cambridge: Cambridge University Press, 2003.

Shuker, Roy. *Understanding Popular Music Culture*. London: Routledge, 2013.

Taine, Hippolyte. *Histoire de la littérature anglaise*. Vol. 1. Paris: Hachette, 1863.

Taine, Hippolyte. *Notes sur l'Angleterre*. Paris: Hachette, 1872.

Terrier, Jean. *Visions of the Social: Society as a Political Project in France, 1750–1950*. Leiden: Brill, 2011.

Trevor, Douglas. *The Poetics of Melancholy in Early Modern England*. Cambridge: Cambridge University Press, 2004.

Willemsen, August. "Nawoord." *Alleen op de wereld*. Hector Malot. Groningen: Wolters-Noordhoff, 2004. 422–431.

Zelizer, Viviana A., 1985. *Pricing the Priceless Child: The Changing Social Value of Children*. Princeton: Princeton University Press, 1994.

Zola, Émile. *Les romanciers naturalistes*. Paris: Charpentier, 1881.

Zola, Émile. *Thérèse Raquin*. Paris: Flammarion, 1887.

- 4 -

The Right to Self-Determination

Ageism in Two Dutch Children's Books on the Voluntary Death of Elderly People

HELMA VAN LIEROP-DEBRAUWER

Learning about the meaning of age and ageing is an important part of children's socialization process. Developmental psychologists have argued that "age is a fundamental dimension along which children organize their perception of people in their social world." It is "one of the first and most important social attributes to which children develop a sensitivity" (Montepare and Zebrowitz 77). How they become agewise and how they learn to perform age depends on their culture's age ideology, as Margaret Gullette claims in *Aged by Culture*. Because Western societies today have a "cultural bias in favor of youth" (Nelson, "Ageism: Strange Case" 38), it does not come as a surprise that children already develop old-age prejudices at a very young age (Montepare and Zebrowitz 82). Children as young as three years have a more negative impression of older adults than of younger adults. Although their perception of the elderly becomes more differentiated as children get older, negative prejudices tend to prevail also in adolescence, Mary Kite and Blair Johnson (1988) found. The main sources of children's and young adults' knowledge about old people (apart from their own experience) are (grand)parents, teachers, and the media, which all tend to focus on youth rather than old age (Montepare and Zebrowitz 104–109).

Research on children's literature as a medium specifically intended for children yields a rather ambiguous picture of the portrayal of old people. In a study of popular picture books in the 1970s, Edward Ansello (1978) concludes that negative characteristics, such as physical unattractiveness and passiveness, are emphasized. An analysis of ninety-five award-winning American picture books published between 1972 and 1995 revealed that senescence is relatively invisible in these books: only eleven of the ninety-five books featured older adult characters (Dellman-Jenkins and Yang). However, the image of old people in these award-winning picture books was far more positive than in the popular books investigated by Ansello: in the former the elderly were attributed mainly positive characteristics, such as being healthy, friendly, happy, caring, and not at all lonely. Patricia Crawford (2000) comes to a similar conclusion after the analysis of sixteen "quality" children's books. Vanessa Joosen found both positive and negative characteristics in the description of the elderly. In her introduction to an analysis of the portrayal of old people in the work of three British children's authors, she observes that while old people tend to be represented as evil in popular fairy tales, we also find positive images of them in numerous other children's books. There, understanding and friendly grandparents tell their grandchildren stories and guide them through life, often siding with children on issues that their parents feel differently about. In these books the companionship between children and old people is romanticized (Joosen, "Boeken" 52).

Although various children's books provide "starting points for personal and curricular explorations of the aging process, age-related biases, and intergenerational relationships" (Crawford 169), they seldom have ageing (in the sense of getting and being old) as their central theme. Most focus on young children facing minor and major problems that are part of growing up, one of which may be the illness and loss of a beloved grandparent. However, in 2013 and 2014, two realistic Dutch children's novels were published in which old people and their performance of age are central to the plot: *De regels van drie* (The rules of three) by Marjolijn Hof (2013) for readers aged ten and up, and the young-adult novel *Lang zal ze leven* (Long life to her) by Koos Meinderts (2014). Both books, the former more explicitly than the latter, discuss the right to self-determination, in this case the right of older people to die when they feel ready, either because they see their life as completed or because they suffer from old age or want to prevent future misery. It is a topic that is still highly controversial if not taboo in children's literature outside the Netherlands, a country known for its relatively liberal position on euthanasia. As early as 1957, An Rutgers-van der Loeff published a children's novel about an old man preferring a voluntary death over living in a nursing home (*Ze verdrinken ons dorp*; They are drowning our village). Personal communication with children's literature experts from various other countries reveals that realistic books dealing with (in)voluntary euthanasia of older characters are exceptional outside of the Netherlands. The best-known is *Postcards from No Man's Land* (1999) by the British author Aidan Chambers, which features the euthanasia of a terminally ill old woman. However, the novel is set in the Netherlands and the woman is Dutch, which once more confirms that euthanasia is considered to be a typically Dutch issue, at least in children's literature. To my knowledge, the only other non-Dutch realistic children's book that touches upon the euthanasia of older people is *Going Backward* (1986) by the American author Norma Klein. The protagonist is sixteen-year-old Charles Goldberg, whose grandmother is suffering from Alzheimer's disease. The night before she is to be moved to a nursing home, Charles's father gives her an overdose of Valium, which causes her death. Chambers's and Klein's books are certainly related to the Dutch novels that I will discuss in this chapter, because they reflect upon the quality of life and the voluntary death of old people as an option. Yet neither contains older characters choosing to die because they want to keep the dignity and freedom they have always enjoyed or because they are simply done with life.[1]

Because of their shared topic, the books by Hof and Meinderts present two interesting case studies to examine how children's literature in the Netherlands interacts with social views of old age. To what extent do these books confirm or criticize ageist stereotypes? How do the elderly characters perform their age; in other words, do they or do they not "take on roles that expand cultural perceptions about what aging can be, using the transformative power of theater to disrupt stereotypes about aging" (Basting 8)? Because of the recurrent *puer senex* trope in Western society and the fact that the topic of euthanasia in senescence is discussed in novels written for children, I will supplement my exploration of old age and ageism by an analysis of the image(s) of childhood as presented in the books by Hof and Meinderts, to see what unites and separates these two life stages. The analysis will be framed by sociological research on ageing and ageism in contemporary Western cultures, Dutch culture being one of them, and more in particular, about the issue of the voluntary death of old people.

Ageism

"Age comes with ailments" (leeftijd komt met gebreken); "Everybody wants to grow old, but nobody wants to be old" (iedereen wil oud worden, niemand wil oud zijn); and "You can't teach an old dog new tricks" (je kan een oude hond geen nieuwe kunstjes leren). These are well-known Dutch proverbs, all three of them referring to old age in a negative way. By implying that older people form a homogeneous group sharing the same characteristics, these proverbs exemplify the verbal stereotyping of the elderly. Although proverbs are often considered to be part of the folklore of a country, they are far from harmless. Proverbs are omnipresent in the mass media and can play an important role in social and political life (Mieder 4). They can be used as significant tools in promoting or supporting certain ideologies. Seen from this point of view, the three proverbs confirm a view of older people that is widely accepted in contemporary Holland as well as in other Western societies and that is commonly referred to as ageism.

The term *ageism* was coined in 1969 by Robert Butler, who described it as age discrimination, stereotyping individuals or a group of people on the basis of their age. Although ageism can affect members of any age cohort, the term is mainly applied to refer to prejudices against old people, which is also the sense in which it will be used here. *Ageism* then refers to generally negative "evaluative judgments toward a person or persons simply due to their advanced age" (Kite and Wagner 131). According to Todd Nelson ("Prejudice" 208), the elderly "tend to be marginalized, institutionalized, and stripped of responsibility, power, and, ultimately, their dignity." His observation echoes Gullette's lament that in Western society, "[a]ging equals decline" (*Culture* 7). Old people are assumed to be less healthy; to think, speak, and move more slowly than younger people; to become forgetful, dependent, and thus unable to exercise self-determination. Nelson argues that this negative view of the elderly is a fairly recent development, thereby underlining that the way ageing is viewed is not predominantly a matter of nature or biology (and thus more or less identical over time and across cultures), but that instead it is historically and culturally determined. In prehistoric and agrarian societies, older people were highly respected and, because of their age and experience, valued as teachers who were "the custodians of the traditions and history of their people" (208). Two historical developments are held responsible for the change in the way the elderly are viewed: the printing press, which reduced their role as cultural gatekeepers, and the industrial revolution, with its concomitant changes in family structure and its influence on the job market, where experience became less valued than mobility and the ability to work with new technologies (Nelson, "Ageism: Prejudice" 208). More recently, the emergence of youth culture, the concomitant ideal of youth that cuts across the life course (Blatterer 8; Gilleard and Higgs 65), and the digital revolution (Brabazon 23–24) are considered to be important influences on the negative attitudes toward old age. As a consequence, "[o]lder persons today are treated as second-class citizens with nothing to offer society and the negative attitudes about aging that give rise to ageism tend to manifest themselves in subtle ways in the daily life of the average older person" (Nelson, "Prejudice" 209). Although age is one of the three dimensions for categorizing people, most people in Western culture never reflect on ageism in the way they do on the other two categories of sex and race, the main reason being the institutionalization of ageing in society (Nelson, "Strange Case" 40). As a result, even elderly people themselves tend to internalize many of the negative stereotypes (North and Fiske 983).

"Rational" Suicide

At its worst, ageism can quench in the elderly the desire to live. In a response to the self-inflicted death of seventy-seven-year-old feminist and anti-ageist Carolyn Heilbrun, Gullette (*Agewise* 43) reveals "the power of ageism in the United States to push older people over the edge into despair." Heilbrun, married with adult children, financially secure, and a popular writer, chose to kill herself because internalized ageism and the widely accepted ideology of decline pulled her into an age-related depression that made her think that it was better to exit life before becoming a burden to society. Gullette argues that her colleague's so-called rational suicide to cut short old age has less to do with the *right* to die, as advocates of voluntary death tend to think, than with the *duty* to die because of society's "hostile rhetoric about the unnecessary and expendable costs of 'aging America'" (49).

American seniors often commit suicide because physician-assisted suicide (PAS) is not allowed in the United States, except in Oregon and Washington, and euthanasia is legally considered a crime (Gullette, *Agewise* 56). In the Netherlands, known as one of the most progressive countries with respect to the legalization of euthanasia and PAS, the law has built-in safeguards to control the practice. Euthanasia is permitted only when the requester is experiencing unbearable suffering, physically or psychologically, with no prospect of improvement. A number of requirements explicitly laid down in the law must be met: explicit written consent from the applicant that the request is voluntary and well considered, and the help of a physician who has to submit a written report of the process. However, some people argue that in the Netherlands the practice is much more widespread than the law would permit, and that in thirty years the country "has moved from euthanasia of people who are terminally ill [. . .] to euthanasia simply if a person is over the age of 70 and 'tired of living'" (Pereira e43). The ongoing debate in Dutch society on this liberal attitude toward voluntary death may explain why it is a central issue in the two recent Dutch children's novels by Hof and Meinderts. As a consequence of this discussion about willful death and the relatively widespread practice of euthanasia in the Netherlands, it stands to reason that some Dutch children will be confronted with it and that others will hear about it in the media or at school. Children's books such as Hof's and Meinderts's can help children reflect on the topic.

"A Man Prefers to Die the Way He Lived"[2]

In *De regels van drie,* the twins Twan and Linde, who are approximately twelve years old, travel to Iceland to visit their great-grandfather "Grampy Kas."[3] The twins' mother and grandmother want to take Grampy Kas to a nursing home in the Netherlands, because his neighbors feel that the old man—he is over ninety years old—is no longer able to look after himself. Grampy Kas wants to escape to the mountains to die there instead and needs the help of his great-grandchildren to accomplish his plan. The story then revolves around the question of whether Twan and Linde should obey their mother and grandmother or help their great-grandfather instead. Who knows what is best for whom? Are the two women right in taking Grampy Kas with them to Holland? Or should the children listen to their great-grandfather, a man accustomed to living the unfettered life of a free man in Iceland for most of his life, who tells them that he would rather die than move to a nursing home in Holland? Once the twins have decided that Grampy Kas has the right to decide about his own life and death, they set out to assist him. To help prepare their great-grandfather for his escape into the mountains, they use Twan's *Big Survival Handbook* and the so-called rules of three in life-threatening situations to make him ready for his last journey. The irony in Twan and Linde giving their great-grandfather survival tips (Joosen, "Bergen") reveals that although the twins do understand and respect his decision, they still have mixed feelings about it.

De regels van drie addresses Nelson's observation that the elderly are treated as second-class citizens who are denied self-determination. Grampy Kas's neighbors are convinced that he is no longer capable of living on his own. Rather than leaving it up to the old man himself, they decide that—in his own interest—he should no longer be allowed to drive his car. They simply take his car keys away. They keep a close watch on him, stripping him of his responsibility and dignity: they check if he still washes properly and if he is still physically capable of doing so. They also alert his daughter and granddaughter that Grampy Kas does not cook any meals, take his pills, or clean the house. For his daughter and granddaughter, Grampy's messy house confirms their belief that he needs daily supervision. They see no other option than to take him with them to a nursing home in the Netherlands, although they know that their (grand)father does not want to leave. However, they do not communicate this to him directly but only talk about him in a patronizing way, as if he were a child: "We know he prefers to stay, but sometimes things simply do not go the way you would like," and "For once Daddy will have to adjust," Twan's grandmother says (Hof 95).[4] She rejects Twan's alternative solution—his grandmother staying with his great-grandfather in Iceland—by arguing that she has a life of her own in the Netherlands. It is implied that the life that Grampy Kas leads in Iceland is valued less than the grandmother's. The fact that she does not consider the possibility of taking him into her own house suggests that she considers the care for her father to be too much of a burden.

Hof exploits the supposed freshness of a child's gaze in revealing the adults' ageist stereotypes. This does not mean that Twan himself is exempt from ageist assumptions, though. His first extensive description of his great-grandfather, when they visit the swimming pool together, reveals discomfort with his Grampy's appearance. The scene confirms the observation by age sociologists, including Joann Montepare and Leslie Zebrowitz (83), that children dislike the outer signs of old age:

> [His back] was bent and white with brown spots. Like moles, but much bigger. And I saw his shriveled bum and his legs with thick veins. Soon he would turn around and then I would see the worst. A shriveled willy. [. . .] In the hot tub he looked even older. White aged skin with brown spots, a thin wrinkled neck and a crumpled face with two enormous ears. (Hof 33)[5]

Twan is dismayed that he has to share a bedroom with his great-grandfather and repelled by his yellow nails and watery eyes. Gradually, however, the boy's negative view of his Grampy changes. Twan, and soon afterward his sister Linde too, begins to trust Grampy Kas and appreciate his sense of humor. They enjoy his stories about his life as a fisherman and come to understand why Grampy wants to stay in Iceland and determine where and how he dies:

> maybe, just maybe, I would want the same as Grampy Kas. Die the way I'd choose to. I could not imagine how I'd feel if I were ninety

years old, but maybe that's what I would want to do too. To go into the mountains. Yes. If I was going to die anyway, that's what I would want. Into the mountains. I understood Grampy Kas, and I understood gran and mom. But Grampy Kas I understood best. (Hof 76–77)[6]

Finally, when their mother and grandmother discover that Grampy has left, Twan and Linde defend him: "Grampy Kas has the right to decide for himself where he is going" and "Grampy Kas is the master of his own life" (116).[7] With their plea they manage to make their grandmother understand that her father does not want to be found. They decide to let him be, although none of them knows what to do. The story concludes with an open ending and a comment by Twan: "I think that in this case there is no such thing as the best thing to do" (117).[8] The changing attitude of the children toward their great-grandfather reflects the idea expressed by some age sociologists that intergenerational contact can successfully counteract ageism (North and Fiske). In particular, the intensity of the contact, rather than the frequency (Knox, Gekoski, and Johnson) and the exposure to atypical older adults (Duval et al.) tend to reduce age biases among young people. Indeed, in *De regels van drie*, the positive change in the children's attitude toward the old man is brought about by their intense contact and because Grampy's behavior clashes with their expectations.

Through the conversations between the children and the old man, the novel gives the reader insight into what may motivate the elderly's decision to part with life. Illness is not the main issue. Grampy Kas does grant that he is physically deteriorating yet treats his doctor's announcement that he has only a few more months to live with distinct irony: "Telling someone well over ninety that he's got about a month or so left—how very intelligent. Yes, it takes years of study to come to that conclusion" (64).[9] He does not fear death, because for him it is the natural end to life. Although his body's decline is not denied, the novel highlights his mental vigor. In that respect he is still very much the man he used to be: vivid, witty, stubborn, freedom loving, and convinced of his right to self-governance: "I decide about when I'm going somewhere. [. . .] And where I'm going, that too is for me to decide. That is how I've always done things. Ever since I was a little boy" (42).[10] By relating his present state of mind to his behavior as a child, Grampy Kas emphasizes that for him life is a continuum rather than divided into separate stages. By dying the way he chooses, he wants to stay true to the way he lived.

Both Grampy's Icelandic neighbors and his daughter and granddaughter equate ageing and decline with the loss of independence, responsibility, and dignity as "natural" consequences. However, their ageism is counteracted by the positive attitude of the twins toward Grampy Kas and by the figure of the great-grandfather himself. The latter in particular shows that people of advanced years should not be treated as inarticulate infants and that instead their privacy, dignity, and ability to govern themselves should be respected. His performance of old age contradicts the view held by the younger adults around him that ageing by definition implies a devaluation of the quality of life, highlighting instead the variety of norms that may constitute this quality. To the two women, it is a clean house, a healthy body, and a home-cooked meal; to him, it is the freedom to do what he pleases. In contrast to Gullette's argument that Catheryn Heilbrun's choice to die is a symptom of an ageist society, Grampy's decision to choose the conditions of his death proves his agency and can be interpreted as counteracting ageism.

The question of agency may be exactly the reason why Twan finds it easier to sympathize with Grampy Kas than his mother and grandmother do. Grampy Kas is patronized like a child. The two women function as gatekeepers for both Twan and Grampy Kas—in a figurative sense by keeping secrets from them, and in a literal sense by shutting Twan from their bedroom, forcing him to share a room with his great-grandfather. Grampy Kas, in contrast, functions as an enabler for Twan and Linde, sharing with them adult knowledge. For example, he tells them stories about the women he loved, in order to underline that a "free boy always will be a free boy" (71).[11] By treating the children as equal partners in dialogue, Grampy Kas gives them opportunities to learn about (adult) life.

Having been bossed around himself, Twan understands the old man's need to assert his rights and rebel against the two meddling women. Moreover, both the children and the old man are presented as facing an important transition. For Grampy Kas, this is the transition from life to death, while the children are in the process of leaving one stage of life (childhood) and entering another (adolescence). They all sense that it is important to do so on their own terms. The novel features a number of initiation rites to mark these transitions. Linde's initiation is marked by her first menstruation. Twan comes of age through his sympathizing with Grampy's anti-authoritarian attitude. The Icelandic setting is significant in this context of initiation. In *De regels van drie*, this isolated and rural country functions as a liminal space in which both the twins and their great-grandfather are given a voice as they transit to a new situation in a ritual manner. Grampy's choice to go into the mountains is inspired by his belief about ancient ritual customs among Eskimos and Native Americans: "Did you know that? Eskimos and Indians did it like that. They went into the wilderness and the end of their lives" (71).[12] It is interesting to note here that according to Gullette, there is no such tradition among Eskimos and that "the Eskimo on the ice floe" is a myth. To her, the proliferation of this myth in today's American society underlines the fact that because of the ideal of youth, Americans think of suicide as a possibility to escape old age (Gullette, *Agewise* 21–23). For Grampy, who is obviously familiar with this myth, the wilderness symbolizes his idea of death being as natural as life. Through the Icelandic setting with its impressive natural environment and Grampy's wish to die as he lived, *De regels van drie* emphasizes ageing and dying as a natural instead of a culturally determined process.

Long Life to Her?

Koos Meinderts's *Lang zal ze leven* (2014) tells the story of eighty-three-year-old Ms. Ida de Graaf and sixteen-year-old Eva Seghers, who meet literally "by accident"—at least that is what it initially appears to be. On her way to school, Eva sees the old lady standing on a railroad track while a train is approaching. She saves the lady at the risk of losing her own life. The story alternates between Eva's first-person and Ida's third-person perspective. Because of this changing perspective, it is clear from the beginning that the old lady in fact wanted to die, although she was not fully aware of this wish at the moment the girl "saved" her. Eva's shocked reaction when Ida confesses this raises Ida's awareness that the way she tried to commit suicide was selfish, because she would have harmed other people. The chapters told from Ida's perspective are partly flashbacks, giving us insight into the life she has led, and partly reflections on why she does not want to live anymore. The chapters told from Eva's perspective narrate how she copes with the knowledge of having saved someone against her will and deal with her daily life as an adolescent. *Lang zal ze leven* ends with Ida's second, successful suicide attempt by taking a combination of pills and alcohol, and Eva's acceptance of her death.

Given the subject, the title of the book is ironic, referring to a Dutch birthday song expressing the wish for a long life. The subtitle immediately ties in with the issue of so-called rational suicide as a means to escape a life no longer experienced as worth living: "When life is no longer a party."[13] This quote applies to Ms. De Graaf, who is tired of life and who, in her own words, does not want to become an "old-aged toddler." When the doctor she consults to check on her broken arm tells her that her insomnia could be a sign of depression, she thinks to herself:

> I am old, I've had my fill of life, and I do not want to serve it out, with the risk of ending as an old-aged toddler with a bib around my neck, dribbling over a plate of lukewarm lumpy porridge. Having been a toddler once is enough and lumpy porridge I couldn't eat even if I wanted to, now, nor when I was a kid. So, doctor, spare me the misery and prescribe me a last-will-pill. (Meinderts 114)[14]

Lang zal ze leven is fiction, but in many ways the book mirrors Carolyn Heilbrun's life story as told by Gullette in *Agewise*. Although Ida de Graaf never married or had children, the flashbacks reveal that she lived a good life with ups and downs, having enjoyed a wonderful love experience and an intense lifelong friendship with another woman who died from breast cancer a few years earlier. But it is old age that bothers her. The quote above is one of the many examples of how the internalization of age prejudices is responsible for Ida's loss of lust for life. She is still in good health but hates being a member of the old-age cohort because she fears all the discomforts associated with ageing.

The flashbacks reveal that Ida had already internalized the myths of old age at a very young age. For example, thirteen-year-old Ida discusses with her friend Guusje what they will be like when they are eighty: "Two warped friends with caved-in murmuring little mouths, little old witches who are no longer capable of anything" (21).[15] They strike a deal that when they reach that age they will go to Crete to jump off Mount Ida hand in hand. Thus, already at an early age, Ida wished to exit life to avoid old age. At eighty-three she hates living together with other old people in a serviced apartment, although she made the decision to move there herself. She is annoyed by the dull conversations with the other residents, in particular the women of her age who are all alike: "grey, squatting doves" (72).[16] When she goes to an art exhibition of a painter she used to adore and discovers that she is no longer touched by an important painting, she realizes that she has changed. She diagnoses herself as suffering from "old-age autism" (24): beauty still exists, but it does not touch her anymore. In contrast with Grampy Kas's view on life as a continuum, Ida's conclusion that she is not the same anymore suggests that, for her, life consists of separate stages in which people have different states of mind. For Ida, deep old age in this respect is very much like early childhood. Ida wants to stay away from geriatricians and their so-called solutions. The wish to escape from nursery homes, walkers, and mobility scooters is expressed several times through metaphors such as "as far as she was concerned the game was over, the referee could blow the whistle" (50),[17] not wanting to become "an old, crippled blackbird" (78),[18] and being "a small bunch of slack flowers of which the leaves are falling one by one" (93).[19] As in *De regels van drie*, ageing in *Lang zal ze leven* is represented by the use of organic metaphors, but whereas in the former, ageing and dying as natural processes have positive connotations, in the latter most images of nature underline Ida's internalization of the idea of ageing as decline.

Ida de Graaf marginalizes herself here as someone whose position in society has become completely useless and irrelevant. The text gives no explicit reasons for this attitude toward life. It merely suggests that it is because of Ida's personality that she wants to commit rational suicide. However, anti-ageists such as Gullette explain this age-related despair as a result of the internalization of society's negative evaluations of older people and their position in the margins of society. In a culture hostile to seniors, one which promotes the age-as-decline ideology, many older people come to the conclusion that death is preferable to life. Because of the harshness of ageism in American society (and in other Western societies as well), Gullette argues, suicide seems to become "a rational response to normal aging" (*Agewise* 57).

What role does Eva play in the age ideology of *Lang zal ze leven*? As a character she is far less fleshed out than Ida. She is interested to know why Ida wants to die, but her thoughts about Ida's answer that she is just tired of life remain unclear. She goes on with her life, enjoying a holiday job and a vacation in the company of a good friend. When she tries to visit Ida again, the old woman tells her it is not a good time. Eva suspects that something is up, keeps thinking about it, tries to telephone her, but does not do anything besides that, which seems to suggest that she respects Ida's wish to die. The next day she gets a phone call that Ida is dead. When her mother expresses sadness about the news, Eva's only comment is that Ida was old. For her mother, and Eva agrees, this is not a sufficient reason: "'Still,' my mother says, and she was right. She was old, but still" (138).[20] It is a rather implicit comment on being old as a reason to commit suicide. How Eva feels about old age beyond that remains unclear, except for one ageist remark she makes when she gets up one morning. Looking in the mirror and seeing her sleep-wrinkled face and her hair sticking out every which way, she comes to the negative conclusion that she looks like "an old bag." It is a rather loose comment on old age, which does not compare to Ida's aforementioned ageism as a teenager.

Because Eva's story is told in the first person and because of her young age, she presents a subject position that young readers can identify with, although they get less insight into her emotions and thoughts than they do into Ida's inner life. With respect to age and ageing, taking Eva's perspective means that readers can learn from *Lang zal ze leven* that young people should be conscious of what being old means to people, but first and foremost that every individual should get a chance to live his or her own life. Because of Ida's internalization of age prejudices, ageism, rather than being criticized, is accepted as a given in society. The relationship between childhood and old age in *Lang zal ze leven* is present only in Ida's negative comparison of old people with toddlers. Although they get to know each other better in the course of time, Ida and Eva never become really close. In contrast to the mutual understanding between Grampy Kas and his great-grandchildren in Hof's novel, enabled by his freedom-loving mentality that remains constant throughout life, Ida's gradual resentment of life inhibits an intense contact between her and the future-oriented Eva.

Conclusion

Aging and ageism are big issues in Western societies today: "In the modern world, older people face reduced social and economic opportunities, damage to self-esteem, and exacerbated physical health problems, to name just a few consequences of ageist treatment" (North and Fiske 982). With the predicted increase of life expectancy and the concomitant rise in numbers of people over sixty-five, age sociologists emphasize the importance of counteracting the negative consequences of ageism and of taking better care of old people's well-being. *De regels van drie* by Marjolijn Hof and *Lang zal ze leven* by Koos Meinderts both try to raise young readers' interest in the social debate on ageing by zooming in on old people's right to self-determination, more in particular their right to decide about their own deaths. In doing so, both novels emphasize children's right to know about the adult world. They express the idea that children are competent enough to give meaning to complex issues, questioning the "widespread tendency to think of adults and children as fundamentally different types of humans" (Lee 5). Rather than confirming the traditional division between adult "human beings" and child "human becomings" (Lee 5), the two books evoke the image of the child and the elderly person as that of individuals simultaneously being and becoming.

However, the stance that the two novels take on ageing and preferable attitudes toward old people is quite different. Both assert the right of older people to die when, where, and how they want. But they differ in their perspective on the meaning of old age, which is underlined by the way childhood and old age are paired. In *De regels van drie*, ageing is represented as a continuum: every stage of life brings many changes, and growing older inevitably and naturally leads to the end of life. The view of life as a continuum implies that people should be able to continue their lives in the way they have always done. Therefore, the novel criticizes the patronizing attitude of some adults toward old people and emphasizes the benefits of intergenerational contact for each age cohort, thus endorsing sociological findings (by, among others, Knox et al.) that intense interaction between young and old people counterbalances ageism. On the one hand, young people can learn a lot about life through old people's stories and by observing their lifestyles. On the other hand, when young people leave their prejudices behind, they can be supportive to the elderly in an unpatronizing way. *De regels van drie* underlines that both old and young people and the adults of the generations in between can act as competent agents.

Lang zal ze leven is far more ageist than *De regels van drie*. The story thematizes the age segregation typical of present-day Western societies and the age prejudices that go with it. Youth, adulthood, and old age are presented as separate life stages, each with its own characteristics and relative indifference toward the other age cohorts. Old age is presented as definitely the least preferable life phase, quite set off from the previous ones, as the internalization of age prejudices by Ida de Graaf shows. Rather than being seen and accepted as the natural end of life, death is felt to be preferable. Her own diagnosis that she suffers from "old-age autism" reflects Gullette's observation that accepting the ideology of decline can pull people in an age-related depression (*Agewise* 49). Ida's refusal to see old age and death as natural processes is reflected in the way she commits suicide (by a combination of alcohol and pills), which stands in sharp contrast with Grampy Kas's natural death in the mountains. The rift between the life stages is reinforced by the absence of any real intergenerational contact. A comparison of the two books reveals that *De regels van drie* certainly provides (young) readers with a thought-provoking exploration of different perspectives on what ageing means, thus making the novel an interesting tool in becoming agewise. *Lang zal ze leven* is more problematic in this respect, because it confirms rather than challenges prejudices against old age.

Notes

1. However, willful or sacrificial deaths of old people are not completely absent from children's literature. A famous example is Albus Dumbledore's death in *Harry Potter and*

the Half-Blood Prince (2005). Dumbledore is killed by Snape, but it is suggested that his death was the result of an agreement between both.

2. All translations from Hof and Meinderts are my own. This is a quote from Hof (72). "Een man gaat graag dood zoals hij geleefd heeft."

3. In Dutch he is called "opi Kas." For the translation I followed the sample translation provided by the Dutch Foundation for Literature, in which "opi Kas" was translated as Grampy Kas.

4. "We weten dat hij liever hier wil blijven, maar soms gaan de dingen nou eenmaal anders dan je zou wensen." / "Papsie zal zich voor één keer moeten aanpassen."

5. "[Zijn rug] was krom en wit en er zaten bruine vlekken op. Moedervlekken, maar dan veel groter. En ik zag zijn schrompelige billen en benen met dikke aderen. Straks zou hij zich omdraaien en dan zou ik het allerergste zien. Een schrompelige piemel. [...] In het bubbelbad zag hij er nog ouder uit. Wit vel met bruine vlekken, een dunne rimpelnek en een gekreukeld hoofd met twee enorme oren."

6. "Maar misschien, heel misschien, zou ik hetzelfde als opi Kas willen. Doodgaan op mijn eigen manier. Ik kon me niet voorstellen hoe ik me zou voelen als ik negentig was, maar misschien zou ik dat willen. De bergen in. Ja. Als ik toch dood zou gaan, dan zou ik dat willen. De bergen in. Ik snapte opi Kas, en ik snapte oma en mama. Maar opi Kas snapte ik het meest."

7. "Opi Kas mag zelf beslissen waar hij naartoe gaat" / "Opi Kas is de baas over zijn eigen leven."

8. "Ik denk dat het beste niet bestaat."

9. "Tegen iemand van dik over de negentig zeggen dat het ongeveer een maand of wat gaat duren—dat is knap hoor. Nou. Daar moet je jaren voor studeren."

10. "'Ik beslis zelf wanneer ik ergens heen ga,' zei opi Kas. 'En wáár ik heen ga, dat beslis ik ook zelf. Zo ben ik altijd geweest. Van jongs af aan.'"

11. "Een vrije jongen blijft altijd een vrije jongen."

12. "Wisten jullie dat? Eskimo's en indianen deden het net zo. Die gingen de wildernis in aan het eind van hun leven."

13. "Als het leven niet langer een feest is."

14. "Ik ben oud en der dagen zat, ik heb geen zin om mijn leven te moeten uitzitten, met het risico te eindigen als een bejaarde kleuter met een slabbetje om, kwijlend boven een bord lauwe lammetjespap. Eén keer kleuter geweest te zijn, is wel genoeg en lammetjespap krijg ik niet door mijn strot, vroeger al niet. Dus, dokter, bespaart u me ellende en schrijf me een laatste-wil-pil voor."

15. "Twee kromgetrokken vriendinnen met ingevallen mompelmondjes, ouwe heksjes die niks meer kunnen."

16. "Grijze, in elkaar gedoken duiven."

17. "Wat haar betrof was de wedstrijd gelopen, de scheidsrecht mocht affluiten."

18. "Een oude vleugellamme merel."

19. "Een bosje slaphangende bloemen waarvan de blaadjes een voor een beginnen uit te vallen."

20. "'Maar toch,' zegt mijn moeder, en daar had ze gelijk in. Ze was al oud, maar toch."

Works Cited

Akveld, Joukje. "Interview Marjolijn Hof: Woutertje Pieterse Prijs voor *De regels van drie.*" *Parool* (8 March 2014). http://www.joukjeakveld.nl/boeken/item/interview-marjolijn-hof. Accesssed on 19 June 2015.

Ansello, Edward F. "Ageism: The Subtle Stereotype." *Childhood Education* 54 (1978): 118–122.

Basting, Anne Davis. *The Stages of Age: Performing Age in Contemporary American Culture.* Ann Arbor: University of Michigan Press, 1998.

Blatterer, Harry. *Coming of Age in Times of Uncertainty.* New York: Berghahn, 2009.

Brabazon, Tara. "Wiring God's Waiting Rooms: The Greying of the World Wide Web." *The Revolution Will Not Be Downloaded: Dissent in the Digital Age.* Ed. Tara Brabazon. Oxford: Chandos. 21–72.

Crawford, Patricia A. "Crossing Boundaries: Addressing Ageism through Children's Books." *Horizons* 40.3 (2000): 161–174.

Dellmann-Jenkins, Mary, and Lisa Yang. "The Portrayal of Older People in Award-Winning Literature for Children." *Journal of Research in Childhood Education* 12.1 (1997): 96–100.

Duval, Laura L., Janet B. Ruscher, Kathryn Welsh, and Sarah P. Catanese. "Bolstering and Undercutting Use of the Elderly Stereotype through Communication of Exemplars: The Role of Speaker Age and Exemplar Stereotypicality." *Basic and Applied Social Psychology* 22 (2000): 137–146.

Gilleard, Chris, and Paul Higgs. *Ageing, Corporeality and Embodiment.* London: Anthem Press, 2013.

Gullette, Margaret Morganroth. *Aged by Culture.* Chicago: University of Chicago Press, 2004.

Gullette, Margaret Morganroth. *Agewise: Fighting the New Ageism in America.* Chicago: University of Chicago Press, 2011.

Hof, Marjolijn. *De regels van drie.* Amsterdam: Querido, 2013.

Joosen, Vanessa. "De bergen in." Review of *De regels van drie. De Standaard Letteren* (8 March 2013). http://www.standaard.be/cnt/dmf20130307_00495650. Accessed on 14 April 2016.

Joosen, Vanessa. "Boeken over oude en jonge kinderen: De romantische beeldvorming van kinderen en oude mensen in de boeken van drie Britse schrijfsters rond de jaren vijftig." *Literatuur zonder leeftijd* 22.7 (2008): 52–64.

Kite, Mary E., and Blair T. Johnson. "Attitudes toward Older and Younger Adults: A Meta-analysis." *Psychology and Aging* 3.3 (1988): 233–244.

Kite, Mary E., and Lisa Smith Wagner. "Attitudes toward Older Adults." *Ageism: Stereotyping and Prejudice against Older People.* Ed. Todd D. Nelson. Cambridge: MIT Press, 2002. 129–161.

Knox, V. Jane, William L. Gekoski, and Edward E. Johnson. "Contact with and Perceptions of the Elderly." *Gerontologist* 26 (1986): 309–313.

Lee, Nick. *Childhood and Society: Growing Up in an Age of Uncertainty.* Buckingham: Open University Press, 2001.

Meinderts, Koos. *Lang zal ze leven.* Utrecht: De Fontein, 2014.

Mieder, Wolfgang. *The Politics of Proverbs: From Traditional Wisdom to Proverbial Stereotypes.* Madison: University of Wisconsin Press, 1997.

Montepare, Joann M., and Leslie A. Zebrowitz. "A Social-Developmental View of Ageism." *Ageism: Stereotyping and Prejudice against Older People*. Ed. Todd E. Nelson. Cambridge: MIT Press, 2002. 77–128.

Nelson, Todd D. "Ageism: Prejudice against Our Feared Future Self." *Journal of Social Issues* 61.2 (2005): 207–221.

Nelson, Todd D. "Ageism: The Strange Case of Prejudice against the Older You." *Disability and Aging Discrimination: Perspectives in Law and Psychology*. Eds. Richard L. Wiener and Steven L. Willborn. New York: Springer, 2011. 37–47.

North, Michael S., and Susan T. Fiske. "An Inconvenienced Youth? Ageism and Its Potential Intergenerational Roots." *Psychological Bulletin* 138.5 (2012): 982–997.

Pereira, José. "Legalizing Euthanasia or Assisted Suicide: The Illusion of Safeguards and Controls." *Current Oncology* 18.2 (2011): e38-e45. http://dx.doi.org/10.3747/co.v18i2.883. Accessed on 24 February 2015.

- 5 -

Extremely Close Generations

Childhood and Old Age in Jonathan Safran Foer's Novel

VANESSA JOOSEN

Children's literature has a long tradition of connecting the young and the old, both in portraying relationships between children and elderly characters, and in drawing thematic and symbolic parallels between them (Joosen, "As If" and "Second Childhood"). In this volume, Helma van Lierop-Debrauwer, Ingrid Tomkowiak, and Elisabeth Wesseling unearth and explore the connection between childhood and senescence both in children's classics and in more contemporary fiction for young readers. Adult literature has no match for the large corpus of children's stories about young characters engaging with their (great)grandparents, elderly neighbors and relatives, or other sympathetic old characters. While senescence is a topic that is gaining ground in adult literature—think of such bestselling titles as Jonathan Franzen's *The Corrections*, Philip Roth's *Everyman*, or some of Alice Munroe's short stories—child characters seldom play a big part in these narratives. There are a few classics that feature close relationships between children and elderly characters in the margins of the story: Marcel Proust's *A la recherche du temps perdu* (In Search of Lost Time; see Hauck), for example, or Isabelle Allende's *La casa de los espíritus* (The House of Spirits). Most recently, Ali Smith's *Autumn* (2016) describes the friendship between a young woman and an elderly man that started when she was a child. Yet few novels for adults explore the relationship between childhood and old age as extensively as Jonathan Safran Foer's bestselling, post–9/11 novel *Extremely Loud and Incredibly Close* (2005). Foer's story is narrated by three characters: nine-year-old Oskar Schell and his two grandparents. In this chapter I explore how the combination of children's and senior voices, as well as the adult target audience of Foer's novel, affects the implementation of the connection between childhood and old age. I relate my close reading of the novel's character construction to its narratological features (including Wolfgang Iser's concept of the implied reader) and age-related ideology.

Extremely Loud and Incredibly Close tells the story of nine-year-old Oskar Schell, one to two years after 9/11, when he is coming to terms with the death of his father in the collapse of the Twin Towers. Oskar, now living alone with his mother, has found a key labeled "Black" in his father's handwriting. In an attempt to find the lock that matches this key, Oskar navigates New York, visiting various people called Black that he has found in the yellow pages. His account of this search is marked by his verbosity, intelligence, and broad knowledge, as well as by various anxieties. In the movie adaptation of *Extremely Loud and Incredibly Close* (2012, directed by Stephen Daldry), Oskar mentions having been tested for Asperger syndrome, but the novel never labels him as such. In the book's reception, the figure of Oskar has been called "an unreasonable invention" (Barbash cited in Brauner 189) for being an excessively "precocious" and "overly knowledgeable child"—a child too mature to be realistic for the nine years of age ascribed to him (see, among others, Uytterschout 186; Mullins 298, 310; Brauner 189). As Foer himself has indicated, "expectations of realism were misplaced" (cited in Brauner 189) with regard to the maturity of his child narrator. Like all child characters, Oskar is a fictional construct, invented by an adult, for a certain purpose. His "childness," to use a term coined by Peter Hollindale, with associated features of weakness and innocence, evokes sympathy in the adults that Oskar visits in search of the lock. Most of the adult characters that Oskar meets immediately enter into a protective mode. I endorse Matthew Mullins's interpretation of the novel as promoting community in New York after the traumatic events of 9/11 and would argue that Oskar's childness is a crucial factor in building that community: the child is, after all, a symbol of the future, and for several characters in this novel, a reason to move on with life.[1] Oskar himself shows an awareness of the power of age to elicit certain responses. In fact, he uses his own childness to his benefit. Asked about his age on one of his visits to a person called Black, he lies, claiming he is "seven, because I wanted him to feel more sorry for me, so he would help me" (90). The same effect seems to be encouraged in the implied reader: Oskar's childness, combined with his loss, serves to evoke sympathy for the novel's young protagonist—even though he does not always comply with the idealized image of childhood innocence, as I explain below.

Oskar's account of his memories of his father and his search for the lock alternates with two adult first-person narrators. The first is his grandfather,

Thomas Schell Sr., who writes letters to his son (Oskar's father) describing the key moments in his life. Oskar's grandfather survived the bombings of Dresden, during which he lost his pregnant fiancé. He first writes about his attempts to build up a new life in New York shortly after the war. There he meets again his fiancé's sister, who will later be Oskar's grandmother. When she in turn becomes pregnant with Thomas's child, he cannot face the potential loss of another baby, and he abandons his family. He is reunited with his wife only several decades later, after his son—Oskar's father—has died in 9/11. The second adult narrator is Oskar's grandmother, whose name the reader never learns. Her account is addressed to Oskar. She shares with her grandson details about her youth and family in Dresden, the bombing, her marriage to Thomas, her life as a single parent and grandparent, her pain after her son's death, and the subsequent reunion with her husband. The story is thus composed of three strands, told by narrators of three different generations and life stages (childhood—adulthood—old age).[2] The most striking recurrent theme is the three characters' experiences of trauma and their subsequent difficulties to live and communicate with their loved ones.

Connecting Childhood and Old Age in Oskar's Narrative

In Oskar's account, the close connection between characters in childhood and old age is first established. The reader learns that three aged characters play a central role in his life: his grandmother; his 103-year-old neighbor Mr. Black, whom he meets in search of the lock that matches his father's key; and his grandfather. Since his grandmother keeps his grandfather's presence secret, Oskar and his mother call him "the renter" until his true identity is revealed. As Tomkowiak (this volume) illustrates for Johanna Spyri's *Heidi*, and as Van Lierop-Debrauwer (this volume) shows for Marjolijn Hof's *De regels van drie*, various children's books suggest that it is easier for children to connect with the elderly than with the generation of their parents.[3] That recurrent trope also appears in Foer's novel, as the list that Oskar makes of the people he most loves makes explicit: his deceased father comes first, but of his living relatives, he ranks his grandmother above his mother. Oskar explains their closeness by referring to their shared social status as professionally inactive members of society: "Grandma didn't work, obviously" (14). She has cared for Oskar since he was a baby and hosts him every afternoon after school: "We spent so much time together. I don't think there's anyone that I spent more time with, at least not since Dad died" (105). Her lack of professional responsibilities means that Oskar's grandmother has ample time to care for him, in contrast to his mother, who works six or seven days a week.

The grandmother's physical availability is matched with a constant emotional availability. I discuss below how her narrative proves Oskar's impression of her life to be flawed. Nevertheless, his grandmother invariably caters to his needs for attention, joining him on a nightly visit to Central Park, buying him a stamp collection as soon as he expresses an interest in stamps, and attending every single school performance of *Hamlet* that Oskar features in. At night they are connected by two-way radios, and Oskar observes: "She was always waiting for me on the other end. I don't know how she knew when I'd be there. Maybe she just waited around all day" (102). His comment makes explicit what Sylvia Henneberg calls a form of "reverse ageism," with the elderly being staged as "wise mentors who have no needs of their own" (121). Foer's novel explicitly addresses the ageist stereotype of the wise mentor a second time through Oskar's relationship with his elderly neighbor, Mr. Black. After Oskar has visited the old man in search of the lock, they become friends. For a few months, the old man joins the boy on his quest and helps him conquer some of his fears, such as riding on the subway. When Mr. Black eventually decides to step down, Oskar is deeply frustrated. His anger reveals a sense of entitlement to the elderly and is only relieved when the friendship with Mr. Black is replaced with the renter's (his grandfather). Oskar's narrative thus appears as a series of successive friendships with the elderly, on which he relies to fulfil his emotional needs.

In contrast to his ever-available grandmother and—for a while—his elderly neighbor, Oskar's mother is reproached by him for being physically absent. His frustration dates back to 9/11, when he was sent away from school and arrived home before his mother, while his father was trapped in one of the Twin Towers and tried to reach his family. Oskar had to listen to his father's agonizing messages on their answering machine in solitude, and he rebukes his mother—in a manner that comes across as childish and irrational—for being at work during the 9/11 attacks. A year after his father's death, Oskar is frustrated that his mother is not constantly available. For example, she cannot attend every performance of his school's *Hamlet* because she has to work. He says, "The whole time I was thinking, *What trial is more important than the greatest play in history?*" (144, emphasis in original). Moreover, just as *Hamlet* deals with a son's reproaches to a mother who remarries too soon after his father's death, Oskar is angry that his mother is emotionally involved in other relationships, especially with her new friend and potential partner Ron. While Oskar testifies to his love for his mother, their relationship is loaded with contradictory reproaches, which gravitate around Oskar's grief about his father's death.

Oskar's family attachments display a seesaw effect that is also recurrent in children's literature: the child's intimacy with an elderly person is matched with the debasement of the generation in between. As Anna Altmann (1994) points out for feminist fairy tales, a seesaw effect is not unusual in literature that tries to promote the agency of weak or previously downgraded groups: what was up comes down, and vice versa. In some children's books that empower the young and old in their alliance, the middle generation, and mothers and fathers in particular, are presented as unimaginative, and too preoccupied with work or with their own needs to attend to their children or know what really matters in life. When children and elderly characters become allies, members of the middle generation often appear as antagonists—in this volume, we see this effect applying to, among others, Fräulein Rottenmeier in *Heidi* and the mother in Hof's *De regels van drie*. The implied adult audience in *Extremely Loud and Incredibly Close* complicates that seesaw effect, however. Oskar's mother gets neither a name nor a direct voice, but the adult reader is invited to fill in the gaps in the boy's account and imagine how she feels. After all, Oskar is positioned as a highly subjective, emotional, and unreliable narrator, who does not value the various attempts that his mother undertakes to decrease the emotional distance between them. He also contradicts himself. With regard to his father's messages on their answering machine, Oskar says: "I could never let Mom hear the messages, because protecting her is one of my most important *raisons d'être*" (68). Yet, when Oskar thinks about her relationship with Ron, he insists that she must remain sad over his father's death.

Although we find a seesaw effect in *Extremely Loud and Incredibly Close* that may look similar to some children's books, its effect and function in the narrative are thus quite different. In children's literature, preoccupied or incompetent parents often serve the development of the plot: once the parents are out of the way, the children's adventures can begin. *Heidi* makes that particularly clear: the young heroine's adventures with her grandfather are much more exciting than those in the city, where she is under the strict surveillance of the middle generation. Oskar's narrative hints at this recurrent pattern when he goes on his search for his lock and finds his mother surprisingly at ease to let him go and explore. What he interprets as lack of interest, however, is in fact her conscious decision. She has found out about his plan to find the lock and makes sure to call the people he meets in advance to check that he is okay. The revelation of his mother's involvement in his journey through New York, which occurs towards the end of the novel, has a threefold function: it serves to make his solitary adventures plausible,[4] exposes—once again—the limitations of Oskar's perspective (and potentially that of the reader, if the reader took Oskar's views to be true), and illustrates the mother's love and concern for her son, to the extent that she finds a way of fostering his well-being without his being aware of her control. Oskar's mother is thus shown to recognize the fact that her son wants to keep her at a distance, and she finds a way of granting him the time, space, and independence that he needs without compromising his physical safety and emotional well-being. Oskar's explicit reproaches to his mother are thus not endorsed by the narrative, which invites the implied reader to fill in other gaps in his story and imagine her point of view. This requires an awareness of the professional responsibilities and emotional and potentially sexual needs of Oskar's mother. In addition, a second element counteracts the seesaw effect, since the special relationship between Oskar and the elderly can be said to compensate for the loss of a bond that was even more intense: that between Oskar and his father. The latter is described as an adult who was both professionally active and a dedicated, imaginative, and loving father, who liked storytelling and spending time with his son. Although Oskar can be said to idealize his father after his death, their strong relationship is never disavowed by the rest of the narrative.

Reconsidering Oskar's Perspective on Old Age

Although the intergenerational relationships in *Extremely Loud and Incredibly Close* are marked with ambivalence, it is obvious that Oskar can share his feelings more easily with his elderly relatives and friends than with his mother. Conversely, Oskar is constructed as a boy who sympathizes with the elderly. In his list of things that make him sad, for example, Oskar includes "old people who sit around all day because no one remembers to spend time with them and they're embarrassed to ask people to spend time with them" (42). The latter is a dubious form of sympathy, however, since it reinforces the ageist "decline narrative" criticized by Margaret Gullette (1997), where growing old is conceived as a steady ride downhill, as well as the stereotype that senescence is inevitably lonely and pitiful.[5]

Oskar's ability to connect with the elderly seems at least in part grounded in his perception of their weakness, in particular their loneliness, which he attempts to relieve together with his own. In age studies, the connection between childhood and old age is deplored when it is motivated by perceived weakness rather than strength, as, for example, in Jenny Hockey and Allison James's study of institutionalized care (135). Foer's novel at first endorses and then challenges this ageist connection. A revealing instance is the mention of "the renter." At the beginning of the novel, Oskar's mother treats the "renter" as if he were Grandma's imaginary friend. This is a common trope in children's literature, where an imaginary friend or pet is regularly cast as the product of a solitary or disturbed child's fancy.[6] In Foer's novel the trope of the imaginary friend is mapped onto Oskar's grandmother:

> The renter had been living with Grandma since Dad died, and even though I was at her apartment basically every day, I still hadn't met him. He was constantly running errands, or taking a nap, or in the shower, even when I didn't hear any water. Mom told me, "It probably gets pretty lonely to be Grandma, don't you think?" I told her, "It probably gets pretty lonely to be anyone." "But she doesn't have a mom, or friends like Daniel and Jake, or even a Buckminster [a pet]." "That's true." "Maybe she needs an imaginary friend." "But I'm real," I said. "Yes, and she loves spending time with you. But you have a school to go to, and friends to hang out with, and *Hamlet* rehearsals [. . .] you can't be around all the time. And maybe she wants a friend her own age." "How do you know her imaginary friend is old?" "I guess I don't." (Foer 69–70)

As the novel develops, however, the assumption that Grandma has no life of her own and needs an imaginary friend to alleviate her loneliness is revealed to be a false one. The renter *is* real: it is Thomas Schell Sr., Oskar's grandfather, who has learned about his son's death and returned to his wife. Oskar's and his mother's speculations about Grandma's imaginary friend are then exposed as ageist misconceptions—and this is also true for the implied reader in case he or she has followed their point of view uncritically. Likewise, the notes that Oskar believes Grandma puts up for him (for instance, "Don't go away"; Foer 70) are in fact directed at her husband, and the boy's misunderstanding arises from the ageist trope of the wise mentor and a lack of understanding of the complexities of her life that lie beyond his scope.

Time and again, Oskar's limited perspective is used to address ageist prejudices and prove them wrong. Oskar's first meeting with the 103-year-old Mr. Black is also colored by age-related prejudice. When he invites his neighbor to join his search and does not get an immediate reply, he muses, "[M]aybe he'd fallen asleep, which I know that old people, like Grandma, sometimes do, because they can't help it" (164). Oskar may have derived his association of old age and narcolepsy from popular culture—in *The Simpsons*, for example, Grampa regularly falls asleep in the middle of a conversation.[7] Oskar does not consider the option that a man who has not left his flat for twenty-four years will not take the decision to step out in a mere few seconds. It is by no means the only ageist stereotype that Oskar reproduces in his narrative, even though he explicitly mentions that he wants to refrain from ageism and all other –isms. That claim in itself seems to parody political correctness, which Oskar flouts in the same sentence. His intention to avoid being "discriminatory to handicapped people or mental retards" (87) is, after all, immediately undermined by the disrespectful term "retard."

While Oskar's misconceptions about old age sometimes carry a tragic load, at other times they are mobilized to produce comic effect. For example, upon his first meeting with his elderly neighbor, Oskar also asks Mr. Black whether he is gay. When the old man replies, "I suppose so," Oskar is puzzled: "'Really?' I asked, but I didn't take back my hand, because I'm not homophobic" (194). One may guess that Mr. Black is not aware that the predominant meaning of "gay" has shifted from happy to homosexual in the quarter of a century that he stayed in his flat.[8] He is thus likely to have misinterpreted Oskar's question, who in turn misapprehends his answer.

On the whole, Oskar's stance toward old age is marked by ambivalence. His narrative comes across as containing authentic sympathy with senescence on the one hand, and being filled with humor and sentiment at the expense of the elderly on the other. Oskar does not hesitate to use his grandmother's weaknesses for comic effect. Early on in the book, he resorts to mild mockery to assert his superiority over her ignorance: "For my ninth birthday last year, Grandma gave me a subscription to *National Geographic*, which she calls 'the *National Geographic*'" (3). Their relationship is also marked by shame. For instance, she embarrasses him with her disruptive behavior in the audience during *Hamlet*: "Inside, I was wishing she was tucked away in a portable pocket, or she'd also had an invisibility suit" (144). Her supportive act of attending every staging of the play thus ironically becomes a source of repeated embarrassment for Oskar. However, his discomfort seems to be mostly related to other people's opinions, because a portable pocket or invisibility suit implies that he still wants her to be close, and he fantasizes about the two of them going somewhere far away together. Then again, as I have explained above, his behavior toward his grandmother is marked with a sense of entitlement and a lack of understanding or even general interest, and sometimes it even borders on plain cruelty. Shortly after his father's death, for example, Oskar deliberately fools Grandma into thinking he has disappeared in the park, watching her panic from a distance: "She was crying and touching everything, but I wouldn't let her know where I was, because I was sure that the cracking up at the end would make it all OK" (101). Oskar's relationship to Grandma is complex and characterized not only by affection and need but also by ageism, shame, pity, and even cruelty. The implied reader is first invited to extend Oskar's perspective and to fill in the adult characters' motives and emotions, while later in the novel the adult characters' narratives serve to supplement his account of events with their own.

Connecting Childhood and Old Age for Adult Readers

In children's books the connection between childhood and old age is marked by features that are specific to this kind of literature. First of all, the fact that the young are (part of) the implied readership of children's literature entails a number of conventions and may even set certain restrictions to what is expressed and in what form. The stories are often told by a young first-person narrator or by a third-person narrator with a child focalizer, whose knowledge, understanding, and interests may be confined (Nikolajeva 115), as they are constructed according to the adult author's image of a child of a certain age. The author assesses not only what his child character but also what his young reader may be interested in and able to cope with. This assessment may explain the recurrence of the stereotype of the wise old man/woman in children's books, as well as in Oskar's narrative—children are then constructed as being rather uninformed about or uninterested in the lives of the elderly beyond their immediate relationship with them.

A further comparison with Foer's novel is revealing about the impact of the inclusion or exclusion of child readers in the address.[9] As explained above, *Extremely Loud and Incredibly Close* offers a combination of a young and two adult first-person narrators, and Oskar is constructed as an unreliable narrator. In the chapter "The Only Animal," Oskar admits that he does not know much about his grandmother. At that point the reader has already had access to her memoirs, which disclose various details about her past and present. As a result, the reader is positioned at an ironic distance from Oskar, with a surplus of knowledge that reveals Oskar's ignorance.

Interestingly, the two adult narrators make the addressee of their writing explicit, and in both cases, the narratives are addressed to children: Thomas

Schell Sr. writes letters to his son, Thomas Jr., still a child at the time of the early writing, while Oskar's grandmother repeatedly mentions Oskar as the addressee of her narrative. The young age of the overt addressees, however, does not lead to any restrictions on the content that is expressed, or on the complexity of the form in which it is expressed. For example, Oskar's Grandma includes painful details about the sexual relationship with her husband:

> We made love in nothing places and turned the lights off. I felt like crying. We could not look at each other. It always had to be from behind. Like that first time. And I knew he wasn't thinking of me. He squeezed my sides so hard, and pushed so hard. Like he was trying to push through me to somewhere else. (Foer 177)

Grandma motivates the candid nature of her confession by the close relationship with her grandson: "I can tell you these things because I am not ashamed of them, because I learned from them. And I trust you to understand me. You are the only one I trust, Oskar" (84). However, the intimate details of their intercourse—both physical and emotional—seem far removed from their usual conversations and from Oskar's limited familiarity with sex: "I don't know very much about the birds and the bees. Everything I do know I had to teach myself on the Internet, because I don't have anyone to ask" (192). The last remark underlines the taboo on sex that he experiences with his close relatives, and this makes his grandmother's revelation all the more surprising. Oskar's repertoire to talk about sex—with terms like "monster cocks," "cunts," and "dildos" (192)—is clearly based on Internet pornography and rather distinct from the intimate feelings that his grandmother spells out for him. The end of Foer's novel reveals that though Oskar may be her addressee, he will never actually read her letter. She writes it, after all, on a typewriter with no ribbon. Earlier in the novel, she had used this same typewriter to produce an autobiography consisting only of piles of blank paper.

Rather than being an actual letter to Oskar, then, his grandmother's writing seems to function first and foremost as a form of therapy for herself. Her love for her grandson motivates the writing, and its function in the narrative is both to illustrate their connection and to inform the adult reader about her point of view, without any restrictions on its content. In light of the connection between the young and the elderly, moreover, it serves a third function: Foer gives an intertextual dimension to the root metaphor that links the two generations ("children are like old people"). Oskar and his grandmother not only describe the same events, as many polyphonic narratives do, but also use similar images to describe their states of mind. For example, Oskar has hidden the answering machine that recorded his father's final messages from the World Trade Center. He feels oppressed by this secret, describing it as "a hole in the middle of me that everything happy fell into" (71). His grandmother is traumatized by the loss of her family in the Dresden bombing. She writes about her husband: "His attention filled the hole in the middle of me" (83). These emotional cavities point at a gap in the succession of generations after Thomas Junior's death: the line of succession between the generations is broken, leaving a hole that both Oskar and his grandmother attempt to fill.

Not only do grandmother and grandson use similar metaphors, they also share comparable experiences. The picture that she paints of her former child self bears striking resemblances to Oskar's youth: just as Oskar goes about like a detective gathering clues to find the lock that matches his father's key, his grandmother describes how she used to go through her father's letters, making comparisons and trying to find out what happened to an uncle of hers who had disappeared (78). Moreover, Oskar's grandmother describes how she became fascinated by her own grandmother's life when the latter wrote her a long letter about her childhood (78–79). This intergenerational correspondence is repeated by Oskar's grandmother in her writing to him. Also, both Oskar and his grandmother were the last people to hear or see their fathers alive, with each describing the burning and collapse of the buildings in which their fathers perished. Both buildings were surrounded by flying papers and contained burning paper inside. Here too, their narratives converge. Grandma wonders, "If I hadn't collected them [her letters], would our house have burned less brightly?" (83). Oskar recalls: "I read that it was the paper that kept the towers burning. [. . .] Maybe if we lived in a paperless society, which lots of scientists say we'll probably live in one day soon, Dad would still be alive. Maybe I shouldn't start a new volume" (325). Finally, both Grandma's last letter (309–313) and Oskar's final chapter (325–326) end with a thought experiment in which they reverse a course of events. While Grandma dreams about the Fall and the creation of Earth being undone, Oskar rewinds the tape of 9/11, bringing both his father and the iconic, so-called falling man back to life. In the intertextual links that Foer establishes between Oskar's and Grandma's narratives, he underscores on the one hand how much their personal lives are connected, and on the other hand that loss and trauma are not exclusive to one generation or stage in life. As Mullins argues, Foer's novel shows that "[t]rauma can be a unifying experience, one that encourages solidarity across various boundaries of identity" (Mullins 299), including age. Grandma's experience of loss and despair as a young girl may further explain why it is easier for her to connect with Oskar than for his mother, of whom we learn only that she has experienced loss as an adult.

An Unromantic Connection

As Ingrid Tomkowiak's discussion of *Heidi* in this book makes particularly clear, the connection between childhood and old age in classic children's literature often relies on romantic discourse. In *Heidi* the young and the old are shown to thrive in a pastoral setting, cherishing animals and enjoying simple lifestyles. Lucy Boston's *Children of Green Knowe* relies on a similar romantic discourse, casting a young boy and an elderly lady in a pastoral setting, engaging in adventures with characters from a past that is imbued with a nostalgic aura (see Joosen, "As If"). In Foer's novel the setup is quite different from these children's books. The setting is urban, and the adult characters' need to revisit the past is not motivated by nostalgia or a sense of adventure, as it is in Boston's novel. Rather, they need to come to terms with loss and work through traumatic experiences. Read in the light of their use in children's literature, some aspects of *Extremely Loud and Incredibly Close* get an almost perverse twist. Early on in the novel, we learn for example—from Oskar's grandmother—that his grandfather "loved animals more than he loved people" (6) and later that "[h]is apartment was like a zoo" (82), filled with all sorts of animals. Not only does the grandfather's affection for animals connect him to elderly characters in children's books who feel more at home with their pets and children than with other adults (for example, Vitalis in Hector Malot's *Sans famille* or the grandfather in *Heidi*),[10] it also links him with Oskar's attachment to his cat, Buckminster, who comes fourth on the list of creatures he loves most (after his closest relatives, but before his friends; Foer 73). The origin of Thomas Schell's care for animals, however, has little to do with a romantic closeness to nature or the affection for a pet to alleviate loneliness. It is rather motivated by a traumatic experience. Halfway into the book Thomas Sr. describes the bombing of Dresden, in which he "lost everything"—his fiancée and unborn child. He explains that after the first raid of bombs, he ran past the zoo, where "the cages had been ripped open" and "dazed animals cried in pain and confusion" (213). He then describes himself shooting a range of animals, both carnivores who could pose a danger to humans, and animals that he wants to release from their misery, such as a bear cub climbing its dead mother. The fact that Thomas Schell Sr. fills his house in New York with animals is not motivated by a romantic connection with nature but by his painful memories and a possible attempt to make up. This is another layer of the story that Oskar remains oblivious to, as he never gets to read his grandfather's memoirs.

Conclusion

Extremely Loud and Incredibly Close is a rare literary narrative for adults that places the relationship between a child and his grandparents at its center. If we compare it with children's texts that employ the same trope, such as those that are discussed elsewhere in this volume, it becomes apparent that Foer's novel adds different dimensions to the link between childhood and old age, which can be explained by its implied adult readership. Because of the juxtaposition of child and adult voices, the range of topics that are addressed is broadened, drawing attention at least as much to differences in interest, experience and forms of expressions as to the shared features of childhood and old age. Moreover, even though the adult strands position a child as their overt addressee, these young characters never get to read the texts that were addressed to them, nor is there an implied child reader for the novel as a whole. As a consequence, the novel addresses aspects of old age that children's books engaged with old age do not, such as detailed memories of sexual intercourse or traumatic experiences.

In connecting youth and senescence, Foer's novel repeatedly highlights the weaknesses of these two stages in life: the subjection to ageism for the old, for example, and the limited perspective, sense of disempowerment and emotional immaturity of the child protagonist. Nevertheless, the relationship between members of various generations, and especially the connection between the young and the old, is constructed as an empowering one in spite of all the ageism, differences and misunderstandings that are addressed. The importance that the novel attaches to community—especially in the light of conflict, loss and trauma—implies respect for all generations, not only children and the elderly, but also the hardworking generation in between, which is also likely to comprise a substantial part of its readership. Although Foer connects the stories of young and old via intertextual links and descriptions of shared experiences, a close reading of the novel and comparison between the three narrators' accounts reveals numerous divergences, contradictions and gaps. The abundant inconsistencies between certain characters' experiences and other figures' understanding of their lives underline the need for intergenerational communication. Only then can the community that Foer envisages be based on a genuine interest in other people's life phases and experiences, rather than rooted in ageist preconceptions and nostalgic sentimentalism.

Notes

1. Although Foer refutes standards of realism to judge his novel, a child character makes the plot lines more plausible than an adult character would. Oskar's childlike "openness" is crucial in creating the community that the novel endorses. Second, the use of the child narrator creates significant gaps in the story, which in turn allow for narrative tension and the reader's active engagement with the text. Finally, Oskar's precociousness, combined with his childlike idioms ("Jose!"), lack of decorum, and patchy knowledge in certain areas, provides for various humorous and dramatic effects.

2. Oskar's grandfather evolves from being a young father in the first letters to an elderly man in the final letters—this does not produce, however, any significant change of voice.

3. See Joosen ("As If" and "Second Childhoods) for further examples.

4. Nevertheless, the lack of plausibility of Oskar's search was criticized by John Updike (Brauner 189).

5. The narrative partly contradicts his prejudice, showing that Oskar's neighbor, 103-year-old Mr. Black, chose to isolate himself in his flat for a quarter of a century and made a living that suited his needs. Nevertheless, when he discovers first Oskar's company, and on their journey meets a woman who is suggested to become a love interest, he turns out to be much happier than when he lived alone.

6. See, for example, a survey in the *Guardian* with children's books about an imaginary friend: http://www.theguardian.com/childrens-books-site/2014/oct/23/top-10-imaginary-friends-in-fiction-af-harrold.

7. See also Mariano Narodowski and Verónica Gottau's chapter in this volume.

8. Mister Black is said to have been married to a woman, and at the end of the story, it is suggested that he has fallen in love with another woman. No mention of any homosexual love interest is ever made with regard to this character.

9. One children's book that breaks many taboos is Ted van Lieshout's *Driedelig paard*, a humorous book that mentions incontinence, among others. Nevertheless, even Van Lieshout steers away from sexuality in senescence. The same is true for Bette Westera's *Aan de kant, ik ben je oma niet* (Move to the side, I'm not your grandma), which covers a wide range of topics related to old age, but not sex.

10. See Elisabeth Wesseling's contribution to this volume.

Works Cited

Altmann, Anna E. "Parody and Poesis in Feminist Fairy Tales." *Canadian Children's Literature* 73 (1994): 22–31.
Brauner, David. *Philip Roth*. New York: Manchester University Press, 2007.
Foer, Jonathan Safran. 2005. *Extremely Loud and Incredibly Close*. New York: Penguin, 2006.
Gullette, Margaret Morganroth. *Declining to Decline: Culture Combat and the Politics of the Midlife*. Charlottesville: University of Virginia Press, 1997.
Hauck, Nicholas. "Proust's Grandmother." *Modern Horizons* (2013). http://modernhorizonsjournal.ca/wp-content/uploads//Issues/201306/201306_Hauck.pdf. Accessed on 17 January 2017.
Henneberg, Sylvia B. "Of Creative Crones and Poetry: Developing Age Studies through Literature." *NWSA Journal* 18.1 (2006): 106–25.
Hockey, Jenny, and Allison James. "Back to Our Futures: Imaging Second Childhood." *Images of Aging: Cultural Reflections of Later Life*. Eds. Mike Featherstone and Andrew Wernick. London: Routledge, 1995. 135–48.
Hof, Marjolijn. *De regels van drie*. Amsterdam: Querido, 2013.
Hollindale, Peter. *Signs of Childness in Children's Books*. Stroud: Thimble Press, 2001.
Iser, Wolfgang. 1970. *Die Appellstruktur der Texte: Unbestimmtheit als Wirkungsbedingung literarischer Proza*. Konstanz: Universitätsverlag, 1972.
Joosen, Vanessa. "'As If She Were a Little Girl': Young and Old Children in the Works of Lucy M. Boston, Eleanor Farjeon, and Philippa Pearce." *Interjuli: Internationale Kinder-und Jugendliteraturforschung* 1 (2013): 21–34.
Joosen, Vanessa. "Second Childhoods and Intergenerational Dialogues: How Children's Literature Studies and Age Studies Can Supplement Each Other." *Children's Literature Association Quarterly* (2015): 126–140.
Mullins, Matthew. "Boroughs and Neighbors: Traumatic Solidarity in Jonathan Safran Foer's *Extremely Loud & Incredibly Close*." *Papers on Language and Literature* 45.3 (2009): 298–324.
Nikolajeva, Maria. *The Rhetoric of Character in Children's Literature*. Lanham: Scarecrow Press, 2002.
Spyri, Johanna. *Heidi: A Little Swiss Girl's City and Mountain Life*. Trans. Helen B. Dole. Boston: Ginn, 1899.
Uytterschout, Sien. "An Extremely Loud Tin Drum: A Comparative Study of Jonathan Safran Foer's *Extremely Loud and Incredibly Close* and Günter Grass' *The Tin Drum*." *Comparative Literature Studies* 47.2 (2000): 185–199.

- 6 -

The "Strawberry Generation"

Two Views on Intergenerational Relations in Post–Cold War Taiwan

EMILY MURPHY

In 2011 the film adaptation of Jimmy Liao's *The Starry Starry Night* (2009) was released, making this captivating story about the relationship between a little girl and boy finally available to an international audience. At the root of both the book and the film is the special relationship between a girl and her grandfather. In both versions, the death of the old man becomes the catalyst for the adventures of the two children who are the main characters. The story of love and loss has an international appeal, yet the views exposed by Liao and director Tom Shu-Yu Lin reveal the story's relation to national social issues in Taiwan, especially the shifting relation between the younger and older generations as a result of the radical economic and political developments on the island. These changes can be placed into relief through a comparison of *Starry Starry Night* to an older, yet equally popular, Taiwanese children's book: Chang Ta-Chun's *Wild Child* (1996).[1] While Chang has not gained as much international recognition overseas, with the exception of mainland China, his work has been translated into multiple languages. The English translation of *Wild Child* provides a dark and cynical view of Taiwanese society and suggests that adversity can never be overcome, even with the help of an elderly person who is more equipped than the young to navigate the social landscape. The two fictional works, then, serve as a useful point of comparison to explore current views about intergenerational relations in Taiwan, and similarly add to our understanding of age relations in an international context.

As this collection suggests, the relationship between childhood and old age is an important yet often overlooked subject in academic research. Age studies, for example, focuses primarily on the later stages of life, or what we might refer to as "old age."[2] Stephen Katz's definition of age studies is telling in this regard. While Katz defines age studies as the interdisciplinary study of age, he links this field to gerontology and admits that in the social sciences the goal of age studies is "redefining later life and old age." Similarly, children's literature scholars tend to focus almost exclusively on childhood and young adulthood, neglecting to consider the relationship between the young and the old, even as examples of intergenerational relations in children's fiction and other media abound. As Vanessa Joosen remarks in her essay "Second Childhoods and Intergenerational Dialogues" (2015), "except for their respective fields' overlapping in childhood studies, age scholars and children's literature specialists rarely draw on each other's work. Yet both start from the same constructivist approach to age and have many insights to offer to each other" (127). Joosen's point is that scholars in both fields begin from the assumption that age, in *all* stages of life, is socially constructed (126). Indeed, as I will demonstrate through my comparative analysis of Chang Ta-Chun's *Wild Child* and the film adaptation of Jimmy Liao's *Starry Starry Night*, Taiwanese juvenile fiction and media reflect these changing social constructions in their representations of the young and the old. While the examples I provide draw upon popular tropes of aging in Western literature, they also subvert these tropes in order to address the specific social issues in Taiwan, such as the recent phenomenon of "economically worthless children" due to rapid modernization (Zelizer 3).

Intergenerational Relations in Post–Cold War Taiwan

The meaning of both childhood and old age in Taiwan is difficult to understand without some basic knowledge of the recent social and political developments on the island.[3] As Shelley Rigger indicates, Taiwan is made up of four distinct generations: the Colonial Generation, the Authoritarian Generation, the Transitional Generation, and the Democratic Generation ("Looking" 67–70). They are distinguished by their experiences of some of the most pivotal historical and political events in Taiwan. The members from the older generation recall the period of Japanese colonization, which lasted from 1895 to 1945, whereas those in their middle years will strongly remember the period of martial law (1949–1987), a time when many were persecuted for their political beliefs. These two historical periods were also marked by rampant poverty, with most still living rural lifestyles with limited access to modern luxuries. With the intervention of the United States in the 1950s, Taiwan began to change rapidly as new buildings and a modern infrastructure, including the high-speed rail, were built as a way of strengthening the island's economy and its political clout in East Asia. As a result, the number of middle-class workers rose, and expectations for both children and the elderly shifted along with these changes. Children, who may have worked on a farm or in the night markets that populated the city streets, were expected to exceed their parents in wealth, so that their academic success was valued more than their ability to contribute to their family's business. In this respect, the changing social construction of childhood in Taiwan is similar to the developments in twentieth-century American childhood, which Viviana Zelizer famously describes as a turn from the "economically worthless child" to an "emotionally priceless" one (3). The difference, however, is that the experience of colonialism and especially martial law left a lasting impact on the older generation in Taiwan and has shaped age relations in ways that differ radically from the American experience.

One contemporary example is the controversy over the younger generation's supposed inability to handle difficult situations, which gained attention with the outbreak of the Wild Strawberry movement in 2008 and again with the Sunflower student movement in 2014. In both instances, student protestors rejected the label "Strawberry Generation," which was first coined by Christina Ongg in the 1990s with the publication of her book *Office Stories* (1993).[4] The term, which describes Taiwanese youth as lazy, naive, and even selfish, is based on the belief that the younger generation "bruises easily" (like a strawberry), because they have enjoyed a period of unprecedented wealth and were spoiled and sheltered as a result. In recent years the term has made its way to mainland China as well, largely due to the rising middle-class population. In their news report for *Asia One* (16 May 2012),[5] Geraldine Mark and Lim Yufan suggest that the number of youth that can be classified as "strawberries" is growing in Asia. While the names differ (they are called "freeters" in Japan and "Gen Y" in Singapore), the associations remain the same: youth are uniformly described as spoiled, lazy, and naive. In Taiwan the term "Strawberry Generation" is loaded with negative connotations and is particularly detested by the young, who have attempted to infuse the term with positive connotations by insisting that they are "wild" strawberries (hence the name of the 2008 student movement). The addition of "wild" to the moniker "Strawberry Generation" indicates that Taiwanese youth are not sheltered (that is, raised in a greenhouse-like environment similar to strawberries) but instead are hardened and prepared for adult life in a way that parallels the tougher wild strawberries growing outdoors.

The debate over the term "Strawberry Generation" sheds light on intergenerational relations in post–Cold War Taiwan. Much of the controversy stems from irreconcilable differences between the younger and older generations, especially when it comes to views about work ethics, politics, and other major areas of social life. The views of the younger generation are reflected in popular culture and social media, whereas mainstream media outlets voice the opinions of the middle generation. Tsai Ming-liang, a popular "Second New Wave" film director, has argued that "Taiwan's young people have been brought up in an extremely materialistic environment, by parents whose only concern has been to acquire a new car or a new house. The children's material needs are all satisfied, and they are asked in return only to succeed at school" (cited in Michelon 63). Youth are often accused of being spoiled and unable to handle pressure, with the moniker "Strawberry Generation" acting as a kind of shorthand that expresses the disapproval of elders. In their popular song "Mickey Mouse," the Taiwanese band Mayday challenges this perception of youth: "Who are you calling the Strawberry Generation? You are the durian generation. You are a body of stinging stubbornness, then you hurt me, and you ask me not to cry."⁶ Speaking up for fellow youth, Mayday challenges the middle generation by denying that they are in fact "strawberries," followed by a comeback to the label often given to youth. By calling the middle generation "durians" (a popular fruit in Taiwan and mainland China well known for its prickly exterior and pungent smell), the band suggests that the younger generation is innocent in comparison to their elders. They likewise add a note of resentment through the use of "才," which often occurs in arguments between two people and serves to intensify the tone in the line "You are the durian generation."

While the elderly seem to be absent from this conversation between the younger and middle generations, the emphasis on respecting one's elders in Chinese culture dictates that they, too, have a part to play in shaping the next generation. In speaking of Taiwan's "youth problem," Nakamura Akira, a former professor at Taiwan National University, claims that it is the responsibility of the elderly to "pave the way for the next generation" and that "if we do not nurture a passionate youth, there will be no one to carry on the legacy of the current generation" (Nakamura and Long 132). Nakamura subscribes to the typical Confucian value of *xiao* (孝), or filial piety, positioning the elderly as wise leaders who must usher in the next generation. As Mayako Murai indicates in her contribution to this volume, children and old people have traditionally had a close relation in Chinese culture, largely due to the predominance of the *puer senex* trope: the wise man who is "at once an old man and a little child" in Taoist philosophy. However, Murai cautions against overzealously applying this image of the "old man on the mountain" to East Asian literary works featuring the elderly, a warning that might equally apply to Taiwanese literature. While the childlike old man can be found in popular contemporary works of fiction, such as Grace Lin's Newbery Honor book *Where the Mountain Meets the Moon* (2009), narratives produced in Taiwan trouble this stereotype as a way of reflecting the current shifting age relations in Taiwan. As we shall see, the authors of *Starry Starry Night* and *Wild Child* take dramatically different positions on the role of the elderly and their ability to aid Taiwanese youth as they seek to navigate through a rapidly changing society. In *Wild Child*, Chang presents the elderly as foolish and naive, while Liao prefers to present the elderly as wise and compassionate, even childlike in their ability to see the wonder in the world. These differing characteristics point toward similarly opposed views about children and their role within Taiwanese society.

Wise Man or Childish Fool? Dismantling Ageist Stereotypes

Long before Jimmy Liao published his first picture book and gained international recognition for his illustrations, Chang Ta-Chun rose to national stardom with the publication of his *Big Head Spring* series. The first volume, which roughly translates as *The Weekly Journal of Young Big Head Spring* (1992), was so popular in Taiwan that Chang's editors insisted he write two sequels. The final installment in the series, *Wild Child*, is the darkest of the three books and arguably the most rigorous social critique of Taiwanese society in the 1990s. The book's "wild child" is a literary precedent to the rebel child that is now popular among young Taiwanese seeking to buck the negative label "Strawberry Generation." As Andrea Mei-Ying Wu explains, these "social rebels" began appearing in the literature of the 1990s and are characterized by their desire to "revolt against or radically negotiate with/in the (post) modern society of Taiwan after the lifting of martial law" (30). Wu is referring to the end of the Chinese Nationalist Party's authoritarian rule, which lasted from 1949 to 1987. In this dark period in Taiwanese history, many were imprisoned or executed for expressing beliefs that conflicted with the government's agenda. The lifting of martial law in 1987 ushered in a new era of political freedom and led to a series of changes in Taiwan. Not only was the island rapidly modernizing, but the people were also adjusting to the new freedoms provided by the relaxation of governmental rules. In

1990, for example, thousands of students gathered in Liberty Square in Taipei to urge the government to allow direct elections. This student-led protest, known as the "Wild Lily Movement," was one of the more visible revolts of Taiwanese youth, who wanted to create a truly democratic state. Today, the leaders of the Wild Lily Movement serve as a source of inspiration for the younger generation, which is facing a new set of challenges as the declining economy continues to make it difficult for young people to find employment in their home country.

In *Wild Child*, Chang evokes the radical changes that led to the development of youth-led social movements by depicting the troubled relationship between the younger and older generations. His main character, Ho Shichun, must deal with the oppression of adults who ignore or belittle his everyday problems. The tension between Shichun and the adult authority figures in his life is captured in one particular scene where his grandfather pummels him with a stuffed bun. The boy is distraught because the soupy mess from the stuffed bun has destroyed a letter from a former classmate who recently committed suicide in order to escape the pressures of the educational system. In response to his grandfather's careless action, Shichun screams, "Why don't you just drop dead!" (181). His rage may be sparked by his grandfather's careless action but points at a sense of injustice: why is his grandfather still alive while his schoolmate is gone? Frustrated, Shichun claims that the elderly will "just keep ticking on for an eternity" (181). Shichun's response indicates that he blames his grandfather for a crime much more profound than his prank with the stuffed bun. Indeed, earlier in the narrative Shichun relates how his grandfather did a poor job raising his father, which resulted in the family's misfortune and Shichun's ultimate turn to street life (158). The grandfather therefore becomes a scapegoat for the troubles that Shichun faces in his youth.

Shichun appears to be so quick to blame his grandfather because he accepts common stereotypes about the elderly that are especially predominant in Western culture. In her overview of ageism and its destructive tendencies, Margaret Morganroth Gullette explains that ageist stereotypes, such as the feeble and senile old man or woman, are tightly embedded in several popular tropes of decline in US culture. Gullette focuses on one myth in particular, the Eskimo on the ice floe, which derives from the American belief that this indigenous group chose to commit senicide rather than care for its elderly. In her analysis of this myth, Gullette argues that this story depicts three competing views of old age: "One group dreads aging-into-old-age. The second dislikes 'the aged.' The third, cognitively and psychologically dissimilar from the others, is characterized by its fear and criticisms of ageism" (30). Gullette makes several arguments for increased rights for the elderly, but the thrust of her argument deals with the views of the second group, who often wrongly perceive that the elderly are weak, feeble, and downright useless and therefore deserve to be placed on a metaphorical ice floe so that they will no longer burden the younger generation.

The ageist stereotypes that are the second group's most powerful tools clearly shape Shichun's views of his grandparents, who are both described as feeble and out of touch with reality. Shichun first describes his grandmother, whose most noticeable feature is her slow gait and her insistence on maintaining a regular schedule. Shichun can always predict when his grandmother will arrive home with a bag of stuffed buns. Shichun's grandfather is livelier, but he still fails to successfully integrate into the modern lifestyle of the younger members of the family and often feels isolated as a result. Indeed, it is the grandfather's boredom, in Shichun's opinion, that prompts the old man to act out. This need for attention also stimulates the grandfather to tell stories about his life as a young adult, in the hopes of being useful by playing the role of the "wise man" that is so predominant in Chinese literature. Yet the old man fails miserably, only boring his young grandson, who claims that his grandfather's stories from the past are "bearable to hear [. . .] once, but after you hear it more than twice it gets really irritating" (181). In fact, Shichun is so uninterested that he admits to falling asleep, only to be forcibly wakened by his grandfather, who will then continue with his story.

Shichun's reaction to his grandfather may also be attributed to the immense amount of pressure to respect elders, which derives from the Confucian value of filial piety. As Weimin Mo and Wenju Shen explain, *The Classic of Filial Piety* and *The Twenty-Four Examples of Filial Piety* are both considered classics of Chinese children's literature (15). Published in the fourth century BC, *The Classic of Filial Piety* is modeled on a conversation between Confucius and one of his disciples, Tseng-tzu, and includes edicts such as the five acts of filial piety, which encourages children to respect their parents both in life and death:

> A filial son serves his parents in the following ways: he offers them the utmost respect when at home; he serves them so as to give them the greatest joy; if they are ill, he feels the greatest anxiety; he is completely devastated at their funerals; when he sacrifices to them (as ancestors), he is completely reverent. If he can do these five things, we can say that he is able to serve his parents. (cited in Rainey 24)

The Twenty-Four Examples of Filial Piety, in contrast, is more narrative in form and might be compared to James Janeway's *A Token for Children* (1671–1672). Rather than instilling within children a sense of reverence for a higher power, however, the book asks them to respect their elders and obey them without question. Mo and Shen explain that "to the disappointment of Confucius, love and respect became a one-way street, and the 'rectification of names' became a tool to discourage the younger generation's desire to protest or rebel and to keep children in a subservient position" (19). The veneration of elders at the expense of the younger generation has led to filial piety being "one of the Confucian ideas that has been most severely criticized for imposing on the individual humiliating, subservient obligations and suppressing the desire for freedom and democracy" (Mo and Shen 22).

Although the incident with the stuffed bun plays a minor role in Shichun's narrative about his journey on the streets, it demonstrates the deeply troubled relationship between the younger and older generations in Taiwan. These age relations, as Shichun's relationship with his grandfather indicates, are characterized by tension and conflict and fall far short of the harmonious grandfather-grandchild relationship that often appears in works of children's literature. Joosen writes that literary representations of old age and childhood have developed from the tense relations portrayed in works of Victorian literature, such as Charles Dickens's *The Old Curiosity Shop* (1841), and are now more often characterized as being "in the child's best interest, fostering his or her agency, emotional strength, and imagination" (128). Such a relationship, which is based on mutual love and trust, is certainly a far cry from the parasitic relationship of the elderly that appears in Dickens's works of fiction. Little Nell, for example, is practically killed, and is certainly aged far beyond her tender years, due to her grandfather's irrational decisions and constant abuse of the young girl's trust. The endless bickering between Shichun and his grandfather, and the violent culmination of their animosity for each other, suggests that, at least in part, such nineteenth-century tropes of old age are revived in Chang's work of juvenile fiction. However, the bitterness that Sichuan feels may be better attributed to the imbalanced power structure created by the Confucian value of filial piety, which gives children few rights, since they must put the needs of their parents and elders before their own.

The departure from a positive portrayal of intergenerational relations reflects the increasing burden that the younger generation must carry in Taiwan. With growing unemployment and increasingly complex social issues arising out of the rapid modernization of the 1990s, many Taiwanese youth feel incapable of growing up. Their course to reach maturity is hindered by various obstacles that stall and even prevent the movement into adulthood. Tanguy Le Pesant attributes some of this difficulty to parental pressure to perform well in school, which "enclose[s] them [young people] in a 'school bubble' from which they emerge only after the university entrance examinations" and prevents them from engaging with the "real world" (73). Yet Le Pesant also recognizes that college students are more engaged with politics than their elders assume, and that those finishing their degrees are plagued by concerns about unemployment (73, 75). Indeed, although Taiwan once rose to fame as one of the four "tigers" of Asia due to the rapid development of its economy, today the situation is much bleaker.[7] In the campaign leading up to the 2012 election, unemployment of recent graduates aged twenty to twenty-four was said to be as high as 12.97 percent, and those who did have jobs were severely underpaid and overworked (Le Pesant 75). This trend has continued, and as of 2016 Taiwan has the highest unemployment rate among its neighbors, including South Korea, Hong Kong, Japan, and Singapore (Liu), with one survey citing under- or unemployment among 2015 graduates as high as 35 percent (Vanderklippe). As Taiwanese scholar Ning Yin-bin suggests, "[w]hen unemployment rate is high, glass ceilings are low, and even master's degrees get you nowhere in the job market, what is the motive for vocational privatism?" (cited in Ho 545).

This is not to say that the younger generation is incapable of handling the social pressures surrounding a bleak economy, as the moniker Strawberry Generation suggests, but rather that the current social and economic conditions in Taiwan prevent the attainment of traditional markers of adulthood, such as financial independence. In his discussion of the youth movement of *kuso*, a form of parody that celebrates flaws, Nishant Shah contextualizes the frustration felt by the younger generation by citing the complaints of several bloggers whose concerns are representative of Taiwanese youth. One young blogger, Henry, bemoans the charges of the middle generation, arguing that "the problems of the Strawberry Generation are largely economic in nature and may lead to serious problems for Taiwan's economy" (23). The current economic conditions of Taiwan, especially for recent graduates, demonstrate that concerns like those of Henry are justified. In her philosophical study of coming of age, *Why Grow Up?* (2014), Susan Neiman insists that many young people fail to see the point in growing up when so little incentive is given to them to do so. She addresses the increasingly popular feeling that it is in fact preferable to extend childhood, in some cases indefinitely. While Neiman is speaking about American youth, her claim that we are living in an "infantile age" can also apply to Taiwanese youth, who strive to reach adulthood and yet fail to do so because of forces beyond their control. The frustrations that emerge from this modern crisis of aging help to explain some of the difficulties surrounding intergenerational bonding. Shichun, who so desperately wants to grow up, cannot imagine why a clown like his grandfather should hold the honors of the wise old man. With his childish pranks, the grandfather appears less like an adult and more like a child. This inability to fulfill his role of wise mentor is all the more frustrating for Shichun, since he is desperately trying to leave childhood and enter the adult realm that his grandfather is a part of simply due to his age.

While Shichun's feelings of powerlessness are significant, it is important to recognize that the elderly feel equally disempowered. Chang begins to develop this point through his depictions of Shichun's grandfather, but he goes on to more fully support it through another relationship between a young character and an elderly person. Annie, one of the young adults in the street gang that Shichun will eventually join, describes her close relationship with an elderly woman. Annie was kidnapped as a teenager by a gang leader, who forced her to care for his elderly mother in his place. Although the events that bring the women together are rather violent, culminating in the death of Annie's entire family, the two grow very close. The elderly woman, who suffers from an autoimmune disease called lupus erythematosus, has sores all over her body. "Her cheeks," Annie explains, "looked as if she had a pair of eggs fused onto her cheekbones, and almost all of her hair had fallen out" (189). The deformation of the old woman's body only increases with time, and yet Annie cares tenderly for her, buying her groceries and ensuring that she takes her daily medications. When the old woman is about to pass, she asks Annie to bury her body in secret, explaining: "Alive I have already completely lost face. When I die how can I dare let anyone know? Please, I beg you to take care of this for me" (193). The aged woman's request reveals her shame about her condition and her dependence on young Annie, who she knows has lost everything in order to care for her. Aware of her son's desire for Annie, she attempts to protect the girl in one particularly riveting scene. The old woman storms down to her miserable son, strips naked, and cries, "If you've got what it takes, why don't you take me on?" (192). This scene demonstrates the old woman's desire to protect Annie, who has already been violated once by the gang leader. The swapping of bodies is indicative of the fragile state of both women. The mother's frail body, covered with sores, mirrors the internal wounds caused by the gang leader's evil deeds. Likewise, it highlights the old woman's strong desire to make amends for the past, especially her failure to protect Annie from her son's first sexual advance. While this scene ends in victory, the old woman still knows that she cannot retrieve the things that her son has stolen from Annie (her family, her childhood innocence), and that all she can do is ask Annie for one more favor in the hopes of finally having her shame buried along with her body.

Annie's relationship to her abductor's mother, while still unbalanced in terms of power, is marked by care and even genuine affection. Although Annie remarks that the woman's body was "hideous" (190), she still stays with her until she dies; and even though she has the freedom to leave at this point, she even carries out the old woman's death wish. The tenderness of this relationship, however, does not mask the fact that the old woman is incapable of protecting the young girl. The two, living at the top of a high-rise building, are fittingly described as being in a "cage" (189), and this entrapment is symbolic of the feelings of powerlessness that affect both the younger and older generations. The old woman is trapped due to her feeble body, which is never strong enough to protect the girl that she comes to care for in her final days. Similarly, Annie is powerless to stop the middle generation (in this case the gang leader) from encroaching on her childhood, first through the elimination of her family and then through the loss of her virginity. The comparison of the plight of these two people, both at very different stages of life, illustrates how the rapid modernization of Taiwan has affected intergenerational bonding. The happy grandparent–grandchild relationship that Joosen describes in her study of contemporary Western children's books is simply not possible in this novel.

While these are extreme examples, they amplify the real conditions in post–Cold War Taiwan as a way of making a social critique of rapid modernization and its effect on city dwellers. In addition to a rapidly declining birthrate, which has led the government to offer a "baby bonus" to those who have more than one child, along with other incentives (Branigan), Taiwan also faces a rising aging population. In her study of elder-care practices, Chen Yen-Jen argues that the "demographic issue in Taiwan has become vital for the island's economic and social development" (123). In a society that continues to uphold the Confucian principle of filial piety, the changing demographics present a problem, since traditionally children held the responsibility to care for their parents in their old age. This creates an "'up-side-down triangle'; as elderly dependency population increases and depended labor population decreases, maintenance burdens will grow" (Chen 125). Such burdens have already begun to reveal themselves as an overworked middle generation searches for a substitute to fulfill their duties of filial piety.

"Culturally and morally restrained," Chen argues, "children can't cope with harsh social criticisms for abandoning filial piety; nevertheless, they do hope to relieve themselves from elderly care duties" (129). In *Wild Child*, Annie and the old woman's plight parallels the shifting family dynamic, where Annie acts as the substitute for the gang leader who is not willing to commit the time needed to care for his mother now that she is severely ill, but who still wishes to ensure that she is provided for, so that he is still technically caring for his mother's needs. Such situations demonstrate that, given the choice, children are much more willing to provide money than time when it comes to elder care (Chen 129).

Reviving the Image of the Wise Old Man and Recovering Childhood

In contrast to Chang's critical view of intergenerational relations in Taiwan, Jimmy Liao, with the help of director Tom Shu-Yu Lin, has brought to life a touching story of a young girl's relationship with her grandfather that is more in keeping with contemporary portrayals of grandparent–grandchild relationships in children's literature. Based on the original picture book written by Liao (Figure 6.1), the film *Starry Starry Night* provides a more detailed account of the relationship between the female protagonist (known as Mei in the film version) and her grandfather and suggests that the elderly can and do still have much to offer the younger generation. The film opening underscores this continued need for an older generation, as thirteen-year-old Mei sits in Taipei Main Station. Distraught by her parents' ongoing fighting, Mei fails to complete her journey to her grandfather's house and returns home instead. From there, Mei immediately calls her grandfather. The two playfully chat, and Mei tells her grandfather that she wants him to make her a blue elephant. As the story unravels, we learn that the elephant is one of many handmade toys that her grandfather has crafted for her. These colorful animals are not meant to reflect the real world but are instead more reflective of the imaginative world associated with childhood. "Being grown up," as Neiman relates, "is widely considered to be a matter of renouncing your hopes and dreams, accepting the limits of the reality you are given, and resigning yourself to a life that will be less adventurous, worthwhile and significant than you supposed when you began it" (1). In *Starry Starry Night*, however, it is the grandfather, rather than young Mei, who has access to this world of hope and wonder, which he continues to share with his granddaughter as a way of fostering her childlike innocence.

Figure 6.1. Book cover for *Starry Starry Night* by Jimmy Liao. © Jimmy Liao. Licensed by Jimmy S.P.A. Co., Ltd.

When an illness unexpectedly takes her grandfather away, Mei must find a way to carve out her own safe space. At first she tries to overcome her feelings of anger and sadness in the city, but she eventually succumbs to her desire to return to her grandfather's remote home. Mei's search for "Grandpa's house" provides a sharp contrast with city life, where Mei is typically indoors doing homework or other school projects. In contrast, on their journey to Grandpa's house, Mei and her friend Jei walk along a road that is surrounded by a dense tropical forest and then hop onto a farmer's watermelon truck, munching on the juicy fruits. These bright scenes underscore how childhood in the city fails to live up to the happy-go-lucky lifestyle that is often associated with the younger generations in Taiwan. The children, who do not feel sheltered and protected at home, can experience the more romanticized version of childhood only when they leave their parents behind. Lifted of the weight of the middle generation's mistakes, the children can enter a world that is preserved for them by the older generation, here represented by Grandpa. These older characters, like the watermelon farmer, have maintained the old agrarian ways of life, as well as traditional crafts (for example, Grandpa's wooden toys). Grandpa's dwelling further reinforces this divide, as it is a brightly colored wooden house, rather than a grey high-rise building. The house is also filled with paintings, as at Mei's home, but in this case they are works of art created by Mei in her younger years rather than professional artists' productions.

Through its depiction of "Grandpa's house," the film reinforces a recurring trope that Joosen identifies as the "seesaw effect," where the disempowered groups (namely, the young and the old) gain power at the expense of another generation (131). By celebrating Mei's childhood innocence, and demonstrating Grandpa's wise choice to protect and preserve this childhood, the film underscores the flaws of the middle generation, who are unhappy and bitter due to their hectic city lives. As the previous scene from Mei and Jei's journey demonstrates, "Grandpa's house" represents a safe haven from both the city and its destructive forces, which have left the middle generation tired and overworked. These outside pressures are blamed for the demise of the modern Taiwanese family, which is cracking under the strain of contemporary city life. In this respect, Liao's touching tale of young love between Mei and Jei dovetails with Chang's more cynical story of juvenile delinquency. While the children in *Starry Starry Night* may have homes to which they can return at night, the film version makes it clear, in a way that is not apparent in the original picture book, that these children do not have happy families. In fact, the houses are so infested with negative energy that Mei and Jei must leave Taipei City behind and journey to the country, where Grandpa's house still remains. The building is all that Mei has left of her grandfather after his death. Her journey is motivated by a desire to find a place clear enough to see the stars, so that she might show her friend the wonders that lie beyond the city's borders. This need to see the stars is not simply testament to the growing air pollution in Taipei; it is also symbolic of the way in which the city literally "clouds" the lives of those who live in it. The dark cloud, like the thick smog that often waves over the city's low-rise buildings, chokes the life out of what is good.

The beauty of the starry night is continually contrasted with the smog-filled environment of modern Taipei. In the city Mei struggles to create a world that is as fantastic as her grandfather's house. This is made apparent in earlier scenes where the girl seeks to create an imaginary world as a way of escaping from the pressures of her daily life. The blue elephant, whose missing leg symbolizes Mei's feelings of incompleteness, limps alongside her in one scene as she ventures out into the night to visit her Grandpa right before his death. The elephant gives her the strength to complete the journey and serves as a source of comfort for Mei. It is soon joined by other animal figures, who help to express Mei's internal feelings throughout the film. As her affection for her friend Jei grows, for example, the animals begin to increase in number, hopping and prancing playfully behind the children as the two cross the famous Tamsui Bridge, a popular romantic spot for young lovers. This peaceful moment in Mei's emotional journey is disrupted when a bully tears down the children's art project, but Mei will eventually find solace after she visits her grandfather's house and comes to terms with his death.

Mei's development is represented in ways that bring together Eastern and Western perspectives. Whether it is a hat, a scarf, a shirt, or a shawl, Mei is always clad in some kind of red attire (Figure 6.2). In Chinese culture red is considered a symbol of power and luck. It is for this reason that red is often seen during the Lunar New Year Festival. However, red also has associations with sexual development and the loss of innocence. In his famous reading of "Little Red Riding Hood," for example, Bruno Bettelheim explains that the titular heroine's red hood is representative of her sexual desire and that her experience with the wolf marks her ultimate transition to adolescence (173). Similarly, young Mei is on the threshold of childhood and adolescence, as she finishes middle school and falls in love for the first time. Mei struggles with this transition, as is evident in one scene where she changes clothes in Jei's presence. While Mei insists that Jei "doesn't look," she later learns that the boy was watching her shadow as she undressed. At first, Mei is horrified by this revelation, but then she playfully cries "pervert," suggesting that she is also flattered by the fact that Jei wanted to watch her. Other intimate scenes occur that generally end with the two characters touching innocently, whether it is holding hands or gently resting a head on the other's shoulder. The red of Mei's clothing is therefore a constant reminder of her budding sexuality and her need to find a successful transition into adolescence, and ultimately adulthood.

We can see Mei's resolution of her internal battle when she comes face-to-face with her grandfather. While this is an imaginary encounter that is enabled by Mei's illness, a high fever that she develops after getting soaked in the rain on her way to her grandfather's house, it helps Mei resolve many of her feelings of anger, hurt, and frustration. Angered by her parents' decision

Figure 6.2. Still from *Starry Starry Night,* directed by Tom Shu-Yu Lin.

to divorce, hurt by the loss of her grandfather, and frustrated that her friend Jei must leave her just as she has managed to express her feelings, Mei's entire world literally falls apart during a dream sequence that she experiences after falling ill in the forest. After each important person in her life has come undone like the pieces of a puzzle, she finds herself in the warm living room of her grandfather and sees the old man at his workbench. At first, Mei appears to be distraught, even though she is reunited with her beloved grandfather. It is only when he touches her shoulders lightly and softly speaks her name that Mei relaxes and embraces him, letting out her emotions in a flood of tears. The film then cuts to scenes of the forest in the morning and finally to a sickly Mei. This time Mei is shown on a hospital bed, pale from her illness. As she wakes, we see tears softly rolling down her cheek, showing that her dream elicited a visceral response from her.

As the search for Grandpa's house and Mei's lively imagination (fueled by her grandfather's creations) demonstrate, the elderly play a pivotal role in *Starry Starry Night*. Released in 2011, the film appeared during a time when Taiwanese youth were more actively asserting their independence. In light of these changes, author Liao and director Tom Shu-Yu Lin express a stirring message about the need to preserve childhood, even when it appears that this version of childhood is merely a figment of the imagination. This message is clearly articulated in the closing scene of the film, when Mei returns to school after her illness. No longer in the company of Jei, Mei reflects on the significance of her journey with her first love:

At 13, we're very fragile. But at 13, we're also very tough. So, before we have to face this cruel world, please be gentle with us. We don't ask for much: a glance, a kind word, a rainstorm, a gust of wind, or just a nod of the head goodbye. It's these little kindnesses that make us feel special.

Mei's closing speech reinforces some of the modern views of Taiwanese youth, especially the fact that young people are fragile and "easily bruise." Yet, at the same time, it presents childhood, especially the threshold age of thirteen, as a time of contradiction. Children like Mei are both "fragile" and "tough," in need of both protection and greater independence. After Mei has returned home, she discovers a letter from Jei with the missing piece from the "brightest star" in her Van Gogh *Starry Starry Night* puzzle. As tears roll down her face, Mei concludes, "Everything passes. But before letting go. Hold on, as tight as you can." These final lines urge young people to cling to childhood rather than rushing forward into adulthood.

The message in the closing scene of *Starry Starry Night* differs dramatically from the one that appears in Chang's *Wild Child*. In the novel Chang makes clear that there is no place for childhood innocence in modern Taiwan, as the destructive forces of modernization have made it impossible for youth to have carefree experiences in their early years. This view is supported by scholarship in Taiwan studies, such as Ban Wang's assertion that the globalization of Taipei has emotional, cultural, and ideological disadvantages that are bound up in the term *modernity*. Although modernity elicits "visions of the future [that] may promise progress, emancipation, freedom, and universal prosperity," Wang concludes that it "is [often] little more than a euphemism to conceal the global standardization and unequal relations that pave the way for the penetration of capital into underdeveloped countries" (370). In contrast, film director Tom Shu-Yu Lin brings to life Liao's story of childhood innocence and suggests that there is in fact a space where this innocence can still exist, even if one must fight to obtain it. The fragility of this state of innocence makes it all the more special and reinforces the idea that it is something worth holding onto. These two diametrically opposed views are exemplary of the way that the meaning of childhood has shifted over time in response to social and political changes on the island.

The two views of intergenerational relations that appear in *Wild Child* and the film version of *Starry Starry Night* depart from contemporary children's books that suggest that the relationship with a grandparent, or grandparent-like figure, is in fact good for the child (Joosen 128). In both the novel and the film, the bonds between the young characters and their grandfathers are troubled by the challenges of modernization, which appear to have the greatest effect on the middle generation. The focus on the ability (or lack thereof) of the elderly to aid children in the process of growing up suggests that children may need a "wise" mentor to help them along the way. In this respect the two texts provide a window into an ongoing debate about age, particularly the (in)ability and (un)desirability for youth to "grow up" and become adults. Neiman's *Why Grow Up?* is just one of a series of recent publications about the crisis of youth. Yet these studies fail to consider the role that the older generation, and particularly the elderly, might play in the process of growing up. They also fail to consider the international scope of this "crisis." As my analysis of Taiwanese texts shows, the struggle of growing up reflects a more global concern about the declining economy and the inability of youth to secure a more "adult" self. Scholars in both children's literature and age studies might benefit from considering the crisis of youth from such an intergenerational, transnational perspective.

Notes

1. Throughout this essay, I refer to the English edition of *Wild Child*, which was published under the title *Wild Kids: Two Novels about Growing Up* (2000). This edition also includes a translation of *My Kid Sister*, which is the second book in the series featuring Big Head Spring. The quality of this translation was placed into question with the publication of Amanda Tsai's 談張大春《野孩子》的英譯 (Michael Berry's translation of Chang Ta-Chun's *Wild Child*). I respond to Tsai's concerns in my article "Postnational Possibilities in Two YA Novels about Taiwan: The American Trace" (2015) and include original comments from author Chang Ta-Chun.

2. For the purposes of this chapter, I will define "old age" as people aged sixty and above. The "middle generation" will be those aged thirty to fifty-nine, whereas "children" is used for those under eighteen. This, admittedly, leaves a gap for those who fall into the awkward category of "young adulthood," a term that is highly contested. However, much has been written about the extension of childhood (see, for example, Jeffrey Arnett's essay "Emerging Adulthood"), which may easily include young men and women in their twenties.

3. For a general overview of Taiwan's history, see Denny Roy's *Taiwan: A Political History* (2003) and Nancy Bernkopf Tucker's *Taiwan, Hong Kong, and the United States, 1945–1992* (1994).

4. In "Strawberry Jam: National Identity, Cross-Strait Relations and Taiwan's Youth" (2011), Shelley Rigger discusses some of the national and social issues in Taiwan and how the "Strawberry Generation" might contribute to resolving them.

5. Before being published online by *Asia One*, Mark and Yufan's report appeared in *The New Paper* in Singapore.

6. Original text: "谁是草莓族 / 你才是榴梿族 / 一身伤人顽固伤害我 / 还要我不哭"

7. In order to address these problems, former president Ma Ying-jeou ran on a campaign slogan of "6-3-3" (6 percent annual growth, GDP of 30,000 USD per capita, and a reduction in unemployment to below 3 percent) in 2008, but his failure to uphold this promise left young voters feeling disenfranchised (Le Pesant 74).

Works Cited

Arnett, Jeffrey. "Emerging Adulthood: From the Late Teens through the Twenties." *American Psychologist* 55.5 (2000): 469–480.

Bettelheim, Bruno. 1976. *The Uses of Enchantment: The Meaning and Importance of Fairy Tales*. New York: Random House, 2010.

Branigan, Tania. "Taiwan Offers Baby Bonus to Fix Plummeting Birth Rate." *Guardian* (23 January 2012). https://www.theguardian.com/world/2012/jan/23/taiwan-low-birth-rate. Accessed on 2 January 2017.

Chang, Ta-Chun. *Wild Kids: Two Novels about Growing Up*. Trans. Michael Berry. New York: Columbia University Press, 2000.

Chen, Yen-Jen. "More Choices for Families? Changing Elderly Care Models in Taiwan." *International Journal of Sociology of the Family* 33.1 (2007): 123–143.

Gullette, Margaret Morganroth. *Agewise: Fighting the New Ageism in America*. Chicago: University of Chicago Press, 2011.

Ho, Josephine Chuen-juei. "Queer Existence under Global Governance: A Taiwan Exemplar." *positions: east asia cultures critique* 18.2 (2010): 537–554.

Janeway, James. 1671–1672. *A Token for Children, Being an Exact Account of the Conversion, Holy and Exemplary Lives and Joyful Deaths of Several Young Children*. Miami: HardPress, 2016.

Joosen, Vanessa. "Second Childhoods and Intergenerational Dialogues: How Children's Literature and Age Studies Can Supplement Each Other." *Children's Literature Association Quarterly* 40.2 (2015): 126–140.

Katz, Steven. "What Is Age Studies?" *Age Culture Humanities: An Interdisciplinary Journal* 1 (2014). http://ageculturehumanities.org/WP/what-is-age-studies. Accessed on 20 August 2015.

Le Pesant, Tanguy. "A New Generation of Taiwanese at the Ballot Box: Young Voters and the Presidential Election of January 2012." Trans. Michael Black. *China Perspectives* 90.2 (2012): 71–79.

Liao, Jimmy. *The Starry Starry Night*. Taipei: Locus, 2009.

Liu, John. "Unemployment Rises with Entry of New Graduates into Market." *China Post* (23 July 2016). http://www.chinapost.com.tw/taiwan/business/2016/07/23/473116/Unemployment-rises.htm. Accessed on 2 January 2017.

Mark, Geraldine, and Lim Yufan. "A Soft Generation Y?: Is a Strawberry Generation Emerging in Singapore?" *AsiaOne* (16 May 2012). http://www.asiaone.com/print/News/Latest%2BNews/Singapore/Story/A1Story20120515-345887.html. Accessed on 15 April 2015.

Mayday. "Mickey Mouse." *Born to Love*. Rock Records, 2007. MP3.

Michelon, Laurent. "Youth Culture and Urban Life in Taiwanese Cinema during the 1990s: In the Grip of the City's Evil Ways." *China Perspectives* 18 (1998): 61–67.

Mo, Weimin, and Wenju Shen. "The Twenty-Four Paragons of Filial Piety: Their Didactic Role and Impact on Children's Lives." *Children's Literature Association Quarterly* 24.1 (1999): 15–23.

Murphy, Emily. "Postnational Possibilities in Two YA Novels about Taiwan: The American Trace." *Jeunesse: Young People, Texts, Cultures* 7.2 (2015): 16–39.

Nakamura, Akira, and Yingzong Long. "A Conversation on Taiwanese Culture." *The Columbia Sourcebook of Literary Taiwan*. Ed. Sung-Sheng Yvonne Chang, Michelle Yeh, and Ming-ju Fan. New York: Columbia University Press, 2014. 129–133.

Neiman, Susan. *Why Grow Up? Subversive Thoughts for an Infantile Age*. New York: Farrar, Straus, and Giroux, 2014.

Rainey, Lee Dian. *Confucius and Confucianism: The Essentials*. Oxford: Wiley-Blackwell, 2010.

Rigger, Shelley. "Looking toward the Future in the Taiwan Strait: Generational Politics in Taiwan." *SAIS Review of International Affairs* 31.2 (2011): 65–77.

Rigger, Shelley. "Strawberry Jam: National Identity, Cross-Strait Relations and Taiwan's Youth." *The Changing Dynamics of the Relations among China, Taiwan, and the United States*. Ed. Cal Clark. Newcastle upon Tyne: Cambridge Scholars, 2011. 78–95.

Roy, Denny. *Taiwan: A Political History*. Ithaca: Cornell University Press, 2003.

Starry Starry Night. Dir. Tom Shu-Yu Lin. Perf. Jiao Xu and Hui Ming Lin. Deltamac, 2011.

Shah, Nishant. "Now Streaming on Your Nearest Screen: Contextualizing New Digital Cinema through *Kuso*." *Journal of Chinese Cinemas* 3.1 (2009): 15–31.

Tsai, Amanda. 談張大春《野孩子》的英譯 (Michael Berry's translation of Chang Ta-Chun's *Wild Child*). *Journal of Taiwan Literary Studies* 32 (2011): 44–51.

Tucker, Nancy Bernkopf. *Taiwan, Hong Kong, and the United States, 1945–1992*. New York: Twayne, 1994.

Vanderklippe, Nathan. "Taiwan's Economic Woes Top of Mind for Unemployed Grads before Election." *Globe and Mail* (14 January 2016). http://www.theglobeandmail.com/news/world/taiwans-economic-woes-top-of-mind-for-frustrated-youth-ahead-of-election/article28196086/. Accessed on 2 January 2017.

Wang, Ban. "Reenchanting the Image in Global Culture: Reification and Nostalgia in Zhu Tianwen's Fiction." *Writing Taiwan: A New Literary History*. Ed. David Der-Wei Wang and Carlos Rojas. Durham, NC: Duke University Press, 2007. 370–388.

Wu, Andrea Mei-Ying. "From the 'Good Child' to 'Wild Kids': Childhood Discourse and Cultural Imagination in Taiwanese Juvenile Fiction." *Tinker Bell: Journal of the Japan Society for Children's Literature in English* 58 (2013): 30.

Zelizer, Viviana. 1985. *Pricing the Priceless Child: The Changing Social Value of Children*. Princeton: Princeton University Press, 1994.

- 7 -

Intergenerational Bonding in Recent Films from South Korea

SUNG-AE LEE

A common ground that children and the aged share is that the structures of a social ecology can position them as society's others, lacking coherent subjectivities and agency, so that they are always deficient in some ways, and incomplete. Wholeness, in contrast, presupposes the development of the individual as a social being with an accepted function within social ecology. In recent South Korean films that portray grandparent/grandchild relationships, the interaction of these socially distant generations pivots on the assumption that members of neither generation constitute whole social beings. They are thus cast as the most vulnerable members of society, deprived of agency because of their age: while children's actions are often constructed in these films as clumsy and misplaced, their emotions disproportionate to everyday situations, and their understanding of the world grounded in misapprehensions, the aged may be deemed to have lost the competence to deal with a world that has moved beyond their comprehension, and cannot adequately support themselves in a society that has no further use for them except to exploit them as caretakers for unwanted children. The idea of dual abandonment—that is, abandonment of both children and the aged—was thematized in the first decade of the twenty-first century in the three important films that are the corpus of this study: *The Way Home* (*Jibeuro*, 2002; directed by Lee Jeong-Hyang), *Cherry Tomato* (2007; directed by Jeong Yeong-Bae), and *Treeless Mountain* (2008; directed by Korean American Kim So Yong). I will first contextualize these films within social scientists' observations about the abandoned members of South Korean society and then develop an analytic methodology that draws upon conceptual metaphors, script theory, and the metonymic characteristics of realist cinema.

A perceived loss of competence of the elderly corresponds to trends observed by sociologists. In two of the films discussed here—*The Way Home* and *Cherry Tomato*—a grandparent is presented as illiterate. As a 2008 study reports (see Kim Jung-Wan et al. 911), approximately 20 percent of the population over the age of seventy in Korea is illiterate. In agricultural areas, the illiteracy rate is 26.4 percent of adults aged sixty-five and older.[1] Research into the relation between literacy and cognitive ability suggests that reading ability has significant effects on a range of cognitive tasks, including measures of orientation, visual and verbal memory, visuospatial ability, attention, language, calculation, and praxis (see Deloche et al.; Manly et al.; Reis, Guerreiro, and Peterson). Associations between illiteracy and cognitive decline have also been reported.

The elderly and the young may face common problems through a need to survive somehow in a disrupted ecology. Statistical evidence indicates that the living conditions of the elderly in South Korea are the worst of any country in the developed world, and these conditions will continue to produce emotional and behavioral problems unless there are significant changes in cultural values, economic systems, and public policies. As a Confucian-based society, Korea traditionally respected senior family members, but the age-old concept of filial piety has collapsed and not been replaced by a social safety net to sustain the elderly. Thus, the current generation of old people who were born between 1930 and 1950 and who bore the burden of Korea's economic transformation in the second half of the twentieth century has not been treated justly by their children or by the government (Jeong). Without any effective preparation for old age, elderly Koreans easily fall into destitution, so that the poverty rate of 45 percent is the highest among the thirty-four member countries of the Organisation for Economic Co-operation and Development (OECD) and 14 percent above the second-highest (Ireland, at 31 percent).

A second consequence of South Korea's disrupted social ecology is the high level of neglect and abuse experienced by the elderly. Precise figures are not available, but it is estimated that between 20 and 35 percent are abused by their children, relatives, or others. Figures from the Department of Health and Welfare show that reported cases of abuse increased by 50 percent between 2005 and 2010 (from 2,038 to 3,068 cases). This is just the tip of the iceberg, however, as not all victims share their experiences. The number of people seeking counseling because of abuse increased by a factor of 3.5 (from 13,865 to 47,988) during the same period. Abuse of the elderly occurs in a variety of forms, but particularly as physical abuse, verbal abuse, abandonment of support, and total abandonment. Mentally and physically driven into extreme situations, Koreans aged seventy-five and above have a rate of suicide more than eight times the average for OECD countries (160.4 out of 100,000), and with 81.8 out of 100,000 suicides, people aged between sixty-five and seventy-four also have the highest suicide rate among OECD countries. An officer from the Bureau of Statistics has commented that the key factor that makes South Korea's suicide rate the highest in the world (24.7 out of 100,000) is suicide of the elderly (Jeong).

The Jige (A-frame) Script

A metaphor for Korean attitudes to the elderly can be found in an ancient folktale, "The Son Who Abandoned His Old Father in the Mountains." I will refer to the instrumental script that underpins it as the *jige*-script. The sense of *script* I am using here has been employed widely in cognitive theories: individuals normally hold in memory specific, detailed knowledge of standard actions or situations, such as undertaking a journey; similarly, as a narrative form, a script enables us to make predictions about a recognizable sequence of events on the basis of some key components or schemas. Adaptations of folktales are often based more on scripts than on specific recorded versions, and those scripts may draw core schemas from several related or similar folktales (see Lee, "Fairy-Tale Scripts" and "Lures"). "The Son Who Abandoned His Old Father in the Mountains," already recorded in the thirteenth century in the *Tripitaka Koreana*, alleges a practice of senicide, whereby elderly family members were transported to the top of a mountain, where they were left to die of starvation or exposure, rather than living on to consume scarce resources.[2] Structurally, the tale blends three conceptual metaphors seemingly inconsistent with each other: down–up, domesticity–wilderness, and carrying. Traveling up a mountain usually signifies spiritual height, but traveling from home (civilization) to wilderness signifies danger, and carrying normally functions as a metaphor for support and nurturance, not destruction. Because conceptual metaphors move from a concrete domain (such as the physical act of carrying) to a less concrete (and hence less accessible) domain, as George Lakoff and Mark Johnson (1980) have shown, the figurative significance may be more fluid.[3] Thus, one can carry (support, nurture, bear) a hope, a dream, a curse, or a family, but there is a shift in connotation with "carry a research team" (prop up, do most of the work). In the folktale, three generations ascend the mountain together:

when the abandoning son's own child alludes to the day when he will have to bring his father to the mountain in turn, the son reconsiders his plan and carries the old man back home. With this reversal, "up" now signifies not the spiritual enlightenment of the old, but the social enlightenment of the middle generation, and carrying switches to the nurturing significance proper to family relations.

An instrumental element within the tale is the actual carrying device, known as a *jige* (literally, back carrier). The *jige*, a lightweight, A-shaped structure used to carry a load, and generally referred to as an "A-frame" in English, allegedly functioned in past eras as the instrument of senicide. The *jige* has four functions that structure the narrative as a script available for later reference: it is used to transport the elderly parent; as an emblem of abandonment, it is to be left on the mountain; as the younger generations set off to return home, the child picks up the *jige* and remarks that he will need it himself when the time comes to abandon his father in turn; and the man, thus prompted to repent his folly, then uses the *jige* to carry his aged father home again. James H. Grayson (327) observes that the theme of the tale is "the virtue of filial piety," and that it validates "a core value of Korean culture, concern for one's parents." The moral point of the tale is that "if the older generation does not practice filial piety, how can they expect the younger generation to carry out their filial responsibilities?"

It is not surprising, in light of the statistics quoted earlier, that metaphorical references to the *jige* continue in contemporary usage, if sometimes allusively. The motif of abandonment of the old for the sake of self-interest has been most famously treated in Kim Ki-Young's historical film *Goryeojang* (Burying the old alive, 1963),[4] in which upon reaching the age of seventy, a parent is routinely abandoned. Thus, in the first few minutes of the film, a son comes with a *jige* and carries his mother away, and the extended close of the film includes a long episode in which the protagonist, Guryong, carries his mother to the mountaintop to a place littered with the skeletons of those who have gone before (Figure 7.1).

The episode invokes the *jige*-script but enacts only three of its four components: the abandonment of the parent, the intention to abandon the *jige*, and the request by the accompanying child to be given the *jige*. Although Guryong is reluctant to part from his mother, plot circumstances prevent him from bringing her back: he believes that her death will bring rain to break the drought that has caused widespread famine, and rain does begin to fall as she is devoured by the Divine Spirit in the form of a large eagle. The variation on the folktale is foregrounded by the child's citation of its

Figure 7.1. Scenes from *Goryeojang* (1963). Guryong carries his mother to the mountaintop.

common form: "Uncle, the *jige* . . . get the *jige*. I know the way now, so I can take you up here when you are old." Guryong offers no reply and, after a short pause, turns back for the *jige* and explains to his mother why he has returned. The eagle arrives soon after he leaves her. His apparent acquiescence in his own future death thus further reinforces the connection of the *jige* with the abandonment of the elderly.

The *jige*-script is invoked in both *Cherry Tomato* (2007) and *The Way Home* (2002). It is reprised by mirror isomorphism in the opening scene of *Cherry Tomato*, in which a young porter wearing an A-frame is juxtaposed with seventy-year-old Park Goo. The conjunction functions as a premonition that Park Goo will be abjected by society before the film ends. *Goryeojang* anticipated a crisis situation in relation to the elderly members of the population that has now existed for several years in South Korea. Today's A-frame is globalization, urbanization, the disappearance of Confucian family values, and a society motivated by self-interest, although few of the elderly will say, with Guryong's mother, "I shan't eat. It is a sin for an old, useless woman like me to squander the gift of heaven while the young ones starve."

The Abandonment of Children

At the other end of South Korea's social ecology lies the abandonment of children, which takes two forms: leaving behind newborn babies, on the one hand, and older children on the other. Most babies born to unmarried mothers will spend their lives in orphanages, as there are taboos in Korea's residual, self-regarding Confucian values against single motherhood and the adoption of unrelated children. Parents often ostracize a daughter who has a child out of wedlock, and newborn babies are apt to be abandoned anonymously rather than accepted into the family. The cohort most likely to be raised by grandparents thus consists of older children who are abandoned because they have lost their parents or whose parents have failed in business and/or are divorced. The children are cast aside and left with their grandparents. A characteristic pattern of temporary relocation followed by complete abandonment, which grounds the fuller script enunciated in the focus films, was identified by Kim Dong-Cheol (2005):

> "Lee Sung-Min," aged nine, lives with his seventy-year-old grandfather and sixty-seven-year-old grandmother in a rural village in Cheongha-Myun. He was taken to his grandparents when he was three. His mother had left home because of the family's poverty and his father was unable to raise him alone. Money was occasionally sent to the grandparents over the next three years, but then there was no further contact from his father. The primary school "Sung-Min" attends has only seventy-nine students, twelve of whom have been abandoned by parents. Each year the number of students in the school decreases, but the number of children being raised by grandparents increases. (my translation)

Variations of this pattern of abandonment to dependency upon grandparents are employed in the three films under discussion, and each film raises the question of whether the grandparents' unconditional love for the children can compensate for social exclusion and material lack. The *jige*-script is invoked early in *The Way Home* when Cheol, a child from a neighboring house, brings a gift of apples to the film's elderly protagonist. Cheol, for no physical purpose at this point, is wearing an empty *jige*, and it seems that the *symbolic* purpose lies in the contrast between the apples, which sustain life, and the A-frame, which may signify the ultimate abjection and death of the elderly. Whereas Cheol expresses a warm affinity with the old woman, the child protagonist, Sang-Woo, is an urbanized, ageist (and mostly dislikable) child who may dream of a figurative *jige*. The scene thereby underlines Sang-Woo's emotional isolation, as he fails to engage effectively with either his grandmother or Cheol but instead expresses hostility to both. From here, the main arc of the film depicts the slow growth of Sang-Woo's love for his mute, patient grandmother. In their representations of developing affect at one generational remove, the films may romantically affirm traditional values that are lost from Korea's social ecology (*The Way Home*) but also express a sense of profound helplessness in the face of society's self-interest and moral anarchy (*Cherry Tomato*). Incorporating some predictable variations, the three films draw on an underpinning *abandonment script*.

The First Abandonment Script: The Abandoned Elderly

At some point after reaching adulthood, children abandon their parents. An optional component of the script is that the abandonment occurs after the children have acquired most of their parents' resources. As pointed out earlier, South Korea has one of the highest rates of poverty amongst the elderly of the OECD countries. As the economy has expanded, the cost of urban living has exceeded the resources of many elderly Korean citizens, and, together with programs of "development" that eradicate cheap housing, they are easily rendered homeless. Further, as young people tend to have moved to the cities, many rural villages are inhabited almost entirely by old people with little income. There is no adequate welfare structure, and the South Korean state continues to assume that the responsibility for supporting the old rests with their children. Middle-aged people still divest themselves of their assets by overspending on the education of their children, and by selling their property to set their children up in poorly conceived businesses or to buy homes for their sons and to stage lavish weddings for their daughters.[5] They thus have few resources for their old age once they are abandoned by those same children. Choices available to low-income elderly citizens within South Korea's market economy are constrained by four factors adduced in the focus films: the engagement in caring for grandchildren (and sometimes a dysfunctional partner); compulsory altruism (children are imposed upon grandparents they have never met without prior consultation); limited economic resources and remoteness of location; and ageist (and educational) barriers limiting or preventing paid work.

The Second Abandonment Script: The Abandoned Child

This script begins with a version of the scenario sketched by Kim (2005): a man or woman abandons spouse and children, and the remaining parent subsequently abandons the children as well, leaving them with grandparents they may never have met before. The script may then unfold in one of three ways:

Option 1:   The children lead materially impoverished lives but may be relatively safe and happy (*Treeless Mountain*).
Option 2:   The mother gets her life in order and retrieves the child (*The Way Home*).
Option 3:   The child dies (*Cherry Tomato*).

The fate of abandoned children may be dire if they are compelled to share the lives of their grandparents. In *Cherry Tomato*, six-year-old Da-Sung is being raised by her seventy-year-old, illiterate grandfather, as her mother has disappeared in unexplained circumstances, and her father has been jailed. Jin and Bin, in *Treeless Mountain*, are abandoned by their mother when she goes after her runaway husband. When she decides not to return for the girls, she advises the aunt she left them with to further leave them to the care of their elderly grandparents. In *The Way Home*, Sang-Woo is left for about two months with his mute, illiterate, and osteoporosis-afflicted seventy-five-year-old grandmother while his divorced mother strives to establish a career.

A child may thus be left in an unfavorable environment with an impoverished grandparent who has long lacked the economic, social, and intellectual resources to keep up with society's technological advances. This problem of the technological gap between generations is comically represented in *Cherry Tomato* and *The Way Home* in the form of toilet adventures. At what proves to be a turning point in *Cherry Tomato*, Park Goo and Da-Sung creep into the temporarily empty mansion of a developer who has violently evicted the residents of a slum area and demolished their houses. Urgently needing to relieve herself, Da-Sung is bewildered by her first encounter with a Western-style lavatory, as she has only ever seen a squat toilet. The incident presages the inability of the pair to understand much of what they find in the house, although they could not have known that the expensive meat that Da-Sung eats has been prepared for the owner's beloved dog and poisoned by a resentful house servant. In the crucial scene (Figure 7.2), a vector connects Da-Sung's backpack (which ironically reads "Hope") to a duck in the

Figure 7.2. Screenshot from *Cherry Tomato*. Park Goo and Da-Sung squat in the developer's luxurious home, but the meat has been poisoned.

top background, symbolizing prosperity and progeny. A second vector, the extended arms as Park Goo passes the (poisoned) meat, duplicated by its reflection on the polished surface of the table, embeds a further irony.

Da-Sung's subsequent death is an enigma grasped only by viewers outside the film, since only the servant knows the meat was poisoned, and only the viewers know that Da-Sung has been in the house. The enigma serves to highlight both Park Goo's practical incompetence and the careless contempt shown by the medical profession for the urban poor, as a young doctor dismisses Da-Sung's illness as typical childhood malingering. Further, though, the doctor's attitude emphasizes a social disregard for the very young and the very old if they are economically underprivileged.

In *The Way Home*, Sang-Woo's equally urgent need to use the bathroom also causes him to panic, now because his grandmother's under-resourced house has only a dark and primitive outhouse. He is given a handsome pot to use (the grandmother uses a metal bucket), probably the most valuable object in the house. He later smashes the pot during a tantrum when his Game Boy batteries need to be replaced. The sequence accentuates the technological gap between the very young and the very old, as Sang-Woo resists the imperative to adjust his expectations. He never becomes one with the pastoral ambience, in contrast with Jin and Bin in *Treeless Mountain*, as I discuss below.

It is possible to tease another, deeper meaning out of these encounters between bodily fluids and containers, in that they reflect a metaphor underlying the three films. The basic conceptual metaphor that children are like old people, and vice versa, is developed in terms of the ground of the analogy, children and elderly people are incomplete vessels, and, further still, children and elderly people are leaky vessels. Jenny Hockey and Allison James note that "the apparent 'limitations' of childhood are mapped on to a parallel series of 'inadequacies' believed to characterize old age," and that the elderly are denied their adult status and capacities (135). Because a conceptual metaphor unfolds from a concrete concept to one that is less concrete, old and young are equally judged according to a social expectation of fullness (fullness is an optimal state). The child has the prospect of completion, although this prospect becomes evident only in *The Way Home*, after Sang-Woo develops empathy and affection for his grandmother. Jin likewise progresses in *Treeless Mountain*, but she and Bin remain metonymic of a society within which only limited positive change, at best, seems possible, because any development is always constrained by larger economic conditions. Finally, in *Cherry Tomato* the child dies because of society's entrenched inequalities, lack of safety net for the poor, and the resentments this structure spawns. The aged person can only become increasingly "leaky," but—in *The Way Home* and *Treeless Mountain*—the young may come to realize that the old are not necessarily as useless as stereotypes would suggest.

Children as Incomplete Vessels

The children in each of the films are marked as incomplete in various ways. Da-Sung (*Cherry Tomato*) has very poor eyesight and is continually falling over, which suggests that she lacks balance and perception. She is emotionally volatile and prone to stubborn tantrums. She has, however, acquired limited reading skills, so at times she can understand things her illiterate grandfather cannot. Her incompleteness is expressed metonymically by the yellow backpack she always wears to assert that she attends kindergarten, which she does not, as Park Goo cannot afford the fees. The backpack, which (ironically) bears the insignia "Hope Kindergarten," is empty, apart from the cigarette butts that Da-Sung has scavenged from the streets as a present for Park Goo.

Early in *Treeless Mountain*, the older sister, Jin, is constructed as clumsy and not in control of her bodily fluids: she is first depicted colliding with a pedestrian and dropping what she is carrying; soon after, she wets the bed and cries while her mother cleans her up (she leaks at both ends, as might be expected of a leaky vessel). In the representation of both incidents, the child either occupies only a segment of the screen or is depicted by fragments

Figure 7.3. Screenshot from *The Way Home*. Sang-Woo appears as an "incomplete vessel," as he does not see his heavily burdened grandmother.

(as when her mother washes her). These filmic tactics visually affirm the conceptual metaphor of incompleteness.

Representations of Sang-Woo's incompleteness (*The Way Home*) focus less on the physical, and more on the social and emotional. He is indulged, materialistic, selfish, and petulant; he hits his mother when she refuses to bribe him to stay with his grandmother, and kicks her repeatedly when he does not wish to follow her; he kicks Cheol's dog at their first meeting and is also verbally abusive toward his grandmother. Sang-Woo is oblivious to the relentless work performed by his grandmother to survive. In one scene (Figure 7.3), Sang-Woo is playing with his toys and does not notice his grandmother, who is toiling hard to carry water up the mountain. The contrast between the two is visually emphasized by the shallow depth of field (Sang-Woo is shot out of focus) and by the use of urban and rustic motifs—Sang-Woo's Transformers toy and the grandmother's buckets to carry water. Because he cannot contain his negative emotions, which burst out violently from his usual state of self-absorption, Sang-Woo presents as emotionally "leaky," incapable of the kind of intersubjective relationships that society develops to contain aggression.

These examples from the three films exemplify how in narrative fiction verbal and visual metaphors, metonymies, and images may lay bare underlying cultural processes and constructions, and pose questions about the impact on individuals of economic inequality and ageist social practice. In all three films, the metonymic use of objects, landscapes, and actions is a major source of expressive power, to the extent that each abandonment functions as an overarching metonymy of social dysfunction, with a multitude of more specific metonymies. Realist narratives tend to favor metonymy over symbol or metaphor, because metonymy combines the often heart-rending particularity of things with the potential significance of something else, to which the metonymic antecedent is only a small part. The easily accepted validity of the antecedent (for example, the excessive cost of an object) then validates the implication about the consequent (the inequitable workings of a national economy), and viewers move from one perception to the other with minimal cognitive processing. Metonymy is so pervasive in these films that it functions structurally to interlink scripts and conceptual metaphors/metonymies. As Maricel Oró-Piqueras observes, "Fiction interconnects outer and inner both at an individual and social level by interrelating not only the self and body of the ageing individual, but also the individual with his or her society" (48).

In one scene in *Cherry Tomato*, Da-Sung scavenges for recyclables in the wasteland where her home once stood, watched by the thugs hired to evict the residents and guard the demolished site. The image is a powerful visual metonymy for the plight of homeless and disadvantaged children in a heartless economy. In a later scene, at a gathering of the rich, the president of the development company receives compliments for his "patriotic work" in demolishing the slum. He is one of the privileged elderly, introduced as a contrast to Park Goo and all the elderly citizens abandoned by society: he possesses immense wealth, an expensive house, a chauffeur-driven car, and a young trophy wife. In contrast, Park Goo is shown rummaging in the refrigerator after creeping into the president's house, and picking up a carton of yogurt that costs as much as he can earn in a day. Simple metonymies like the carton of yogurt—metonymic of a national economy that precludes participation by the poor and prevents social mobility—accumulate toward the film's great metonymy, the incomprehensible poisoning of Da-Sung in the house of the company president.

Such contrasts are also evident in filmic strategies whereby perspective fluctuates between viewer alignment with the point of view of one or more characters and the camera perspective of those characters, the latter being characteristically evoked by long shots and zooms. In *The Way Home*, for example, "interest" point of view, a perspective from which viewers make ethical judgments, is established by the camera, as point of view fluctuates between Sang-Woo's way of seeing (by camera alignment with his visual perspective) and the visual representation of his physical manifestation of selfishness and unreasonableness. The shifting between different camera perspectives also prompts viewers to understand that Sang-Woo's intolerance toward his grandmother is metonymic of a more general attitude. For example, his demand for money to buy batteries for his Game Boy is metonymic of the expectation that the elderly will give up whatever resources they have to their children/grandchildren, and indeed Grandmother does so by walking home from the distant village in order to save the bus fare and pay for the batteries. Having returned home alone, Sang-Woo grows anxious and returns to the bus stop to wait. The camera then alternates between a focus on Sang-Woo's physical signs of anxiety and his view of the road and each bus that arrives, until Grandma emerges through a cloud of dust thrown up by a passing bus. Her sacrifice is accentuated by her proximity to the bus she did not take and, ironically, by Sang-Woo's complaint that she was away a long time. His self-focus prevents concern for others or reflection on the consequence of his demands.

The conceptual metaphor of the incomplete vessel can function as an unexamined justification for the expulsion or abjection of those who fail to meet what are assumed to be social norms. They are relegated to the margins as outsiders—to the urban slums or remote rural villages—from where their *incompleteness* and *difference* do not pose a threat to normative middle-class society. Da-Sung's imperfect vision (*Cherry Tomato*) and the muteness and illiteracy of Sang-Woo's grandmother (*The Way Home*) are metonyms for the imperfection and incompleteness of abjection, although Sang-Woo's unfolding love for his grandmother, like Jin's developed affection for her grandmother in *Treeless Mountain*, overturns the stereotypical perception of the elderly as abject. It seems that such a transformation is most likely to occur through the routines and traditional practices of everyday rural life, far from the self-regarding materialism of the city.

Youth, Old Age, and the Pastoral Mode

In traditions of pastoral literature, youth and old age share a situation "on the periphery of socially defined reality" (Marx 22) that is removed from urban centers. They are thus liminal to the world of active adults. Such a conjunction is found in *Treeless Mountain* and *The Way Home*, in which Jin and Bin find a home in a remote rural area with their grandparents, and Sang-Woo finds a kind of moral and spiritual direction with his grandmother in her ramshackle thatched cottage atop a rocky hill. Both films offer a stark contrast to the urban landscape in *Cherry Tomato*. The pastoral tradition in East Asia,

Figure 7.4. Screenshot from *Treeless Mountain*. Jin and Bin prepare food with their grandmother.

and in South Korea in particular, pervades contemporary cinema, although the best-known Korean example is probably *Welcome to Dongmakgol* (2005). Set during the Korean War, the film depicts an accidental meeting in the remote village of Dongmakgol of a handful of soldiers from the two Korean armies and an American pilot who went "missing in action." Dongmakgol appears to be an emanation of Shambhala, a legendary kingdom in Sanskrit and Tibetan texts that, as a Buddhist Pure Land, is as much a spiritual site as it is physical. The inhabitants of Dongmakgol exist outside time, living by subsistence farming, without any knowledge of modern technology or of any kind of violence. As a consequence, they are unaware that a war is raging across the peninsula. To preserve the villagers, all of the visiting soldiers sacrifice their lives to draw the focus of war elsewhere.

This version of Shambhala is the kind of setting that the children of *Treeless Mountain* and *The Way Home* enter. The houses have few, if any, modern amenities, and most of the food consumed is gathered from the land. In *Treeless Mountain*, Jin and Bin learn to take delight in picking and preparing vegetables, watching their grandmother roll out dough to make stuffed dumplings, eating sweet potato baked in the coals of the wood fire, and gathering wood for the fire (Figure 7.4).

Sang-Woo progresses from resenting his grandmother's requests that he thread a needle for her—her sight is too poor—to preparing a pincushion stuffed with threaded needles before his return to Seoul. The rural, pastoral landscape is explicitly presented as a refuge for Jin and Bin, and ultimately a place of solace and learning for Sang-Woo, who glimpses a pure and lovable quality not just in his grandmother but in the two older children he encounters. At the end of his sojourn, he is better equipped to grow into a more fully intersubjective way of life.

In both films, however, there are also reminders of the transience of happiness and of human mortality, so that the idyllic mood is tempered by the limitations of a simple life. There is beauty, of course, but does this compensate for the lack of modern facilities? The pervasive presence of ruined or dilapidated buildings further implies a meditation on time's relentless passage. When asked in an interview why she chose to shoot *The Way Home* in the remote mountain village of Jeetongma, director Lee Jeong-Hyang replied:

> All the houses are built with [mud-brick] and all the roads are old and curved, just like the life of the grandmother. The feeling I got from the land there resembled so much the character of the grandmother. The villagers [. . .] have spent many years so lonely in the mountains. At the time we made the movie, there were eight people living there. Now it is six people in the village because two have passed away because of old age.

As Lee implicitly acknowledges, the pastoral thus incorporates suggestions of temporality and temporariness. Before Sang-Woo returns home with his mother, he leaves behind some message cards for his grandmother to mail if she needs him. These cards, especially "I am sick," are visually embedded within an extended sequence of the grandmother climbing the long and difficult path from the valley to her house on the mountain. In conjunction, they presage ever-imminent tragedy, as viewers are reminded that the mountain, as in *Goryeojang*, is both the place of enlightenment and the place of death.

Treeless Mountain offers the most positive encoding of the interactions of youth and old age, in that the children bring new energy to their grandparents' subsistence farming, and a new joy to their grandmother in giving her the opportunity to pass on her knowledge to another generation. The children find pleasure in discovering a life closer to nature. Jin accepts that there will be no money to buy warm shoes for winter, and even presents their precious piggy bank—symbol of their hope that their mother will return for them—to her grandmother so that she can buy shoes without holes for herself. Pastoral literature has traditionally accepted vulnerability and loss, but in one of the final frames, the film foreshadows that the kind of loss depicted in *Cherry Tomato* may not be very far away, and their little farm and very existence may be swept away by agribusiness. The idealized natural setting will then no longer function as a refuge from the relentless forces of capitalist greed, intrigue, and modernization. The capacity of the grandmother to care for Jin and Bin may be suddenly swept away, so that the "urban" catastrophe of displacement and homelessness, as depicted in *Cherry Tomato*, may soon overwhelm this family too.

Conclusion

The formation of grandparent/grandchild family units in South Korea is not a new phenomenon, but in recent years it has notably been employed as a motif in film to explore changes in society that can be attributed to modernization and an increasing breakdown of family structures. Urbanization has both isolated older generations in economically depressed rural situations and, in a society that tends to limit social mobility, produced an urban poor class and urban slums. Park Goo from *Cherry Tomato* is one of the elderly urban poor, and, because of his age and lack of education, he finds it difficult to support himself and the granddaughter who has fallen into his care. The child abandonment that leads to such circumstances stems from social dysfunction, when a parent, like the mothers in *The Way Home* and *Treeless Mountain*, finds life difficult to manage after divorce or separation and consequently sends the children to live with her or his own parents, thereby removing the children from a technologically advanced urban life to a disadvantaged rural life, and potentially placing a burden on elderly people with limited resources. Jin and Bin (*Treeless Mountain*) may seem secure, but it is clear they will not receive even rudimentary education, and they are likely to fall into dire circumstances before they reach adulthood. The final image of the grandparents in each film depicts lives that will soon be swept away by inexorable time or economic "progress": the slow, hard climb up the mountain in *The Way Home*; the encroaching agribusiness in *Treeless Mountain*; and Park Goo sitting in desolation and despair beside a mechanical digger in the demolition site, with dead Da-Sung's backpack at his feet. The conceptual metaphor that children and elderly people are incomplete vessels functions in these films to consign these generations to the social periphery, since it assumes they lack any form of agency. Then again, the films also explore the possibility that the generations can complement one another through mutual support and affection, but their situation may be fragile as aspects of economic modernization continue to threaten the tenuous well-being of these vulnerable and liminal members of society.

Notes

1. When the thirty-six-year Japanese occupation of Korea ended in 1945, only 22 percent of Koreans were literate, so most people born in the early 1930s had missed at least the childhood learning years. Research undertaken by Alexandre Castro-Caldas et al. indicates that "learning to read and write during childhood influences the functional organization of the adult human brain" (1060).

2. The *Tripitaka Koreana* is "by far the most complete collection of Buddhist scriptures, laws, and treaties extant today" (UNESCO). It was the basis for the Japanese compilation of the *Taisho Shinsu Daizokyo* (1912–1926) and continues to be drawn upon in China and Taiwan. Short versions of "The Son Who Abandoned His Old Father in the Mountains" can be found in Zŏng In-Sŏb (186–187, collected in 1916) and Grayson (325–326, collected in 1921).

3. For a discussion of conceptual metaphors as a universal phenomenon, with particular reference to East Asian languages, see Neumann (2001), Shen and Aisenman (2008), and Yu (2003).

4. Unfortunately, a complete print of this film has not survived, as about twenty-four minutes of the video track have been lost. The complete audio track survives.

5. The average cost of a wedding in 2015 had reached around USD 198,000, of which 64 percent—including purchase of an apartment—was met by the groom's family ("Newlyweds'").

Works Cited

Films

Cherry Tomato. Directed by Jeong Yeong-Bae. Korea: Cinema Service, 2007.
Goryeojang. Directed by Kim Ki-Young. Korea: Korea Art Films Co. Ltd., 1963.
Treeless Mountain. Directed by Kim So Yong. Korea: Oscilloscope Pictures, 2008.
The Way Home. Directed by Lee Jeong-Hyang. Korea: CJ Entertainment, 2002.
Welcome to Dongmakgol. Directed by Park Kwang-Hyun. Korea: Show Box, 2005.

Other Works

Castro-Caldas, Alexandre, Karl Magnus Petersson, Alexandra Isabel Dias Reis, Sharon Stone-Elander, and Martin Ingvar. "The Illiterate Brain." *Brain* 121.6 (1998): 1053–1063.

Deloche, Gérard, Ligia Souza, Lucia Willadino Braga, and Georges Dellatolas. "A Calculation and Number Processing Battery for Clinical Application in Illiterates and Semi-literates." *Cortex* 35.4 (1999): 503–521.

Grayson, James H. *Myths and Legends from Korea: An Annotated Compendium of Ancient and Modern Materials*. New York: Routledge, 2012.

Hockey, Jenny, and Allison James. "Back to Our Futures: Imaging Second Childhood." *Images of Aging: Cultural Reflections of Later Life*. Eds. Mike Featherstone and Andrew Wernick. London: Routledge, 1995. 135–148.

Jeong, Cheol-Hwan. "One Out of Two Old People Lives in Extreme Poverty: The Life of the Elderly Is the Worst amongst OECD Nations." *Chosun Ilbo* (23 August 2011). http://news.chosun.com/site/data/html_dir/2011/08/23/2011082300194.html?Depo=twitter&d=2011082300194. Accessed on 9 September 2015.

Kim, Dong-Cheol. "Children Left to Grandparents' Care Due to Parents' Leaving Home or Divorce." *Kukmin Ilbo*, 21 November 2005. http://nowme.net/xe/93137. Accessed on 3 September 2015.

Kim, Jung-Wan, Ji-Hye Yoon, Soo-Ryon Kim, and Hyang-Hee Kim. "Effect of Literacy Level on Cognitive and Language Tests in Korean Illiterate Older Adults." *Geriatrics and Gerontology International* 14.4 (2014): 911–917.

Lakoff, George, and Mark Johnson. *Metaphors We Live By*. Chicago: University of Chicago Press, 1980.

Lee, Jeong-Hyang. Interview with Cindy Yoon: "Lee Jeong-Hyang Shows 'The Way Home.'" *Asia Society*, n.d. http://asiasociety.org/lee-jeong-hyang-shows-way-home. Accessed on 9 September 2015.

Lee, Sung-Ae. "Fairy-Tale Scripts and Intercultural Conceptual Blending in Modern Korean Film and Television Drama." *Grimms' Tales around the Globe: The Dynamics of Their International Reception*. Ed. Vanessa Joosen and Gillian Lathey. Detroit: Wayne State University Press, 2014. 275–293.

Lee, Sung-Ae. "Lures and Horrors of Alterity: Adapting Korean Tales of Fox Spirits." *International Research in Children's Literature* 4.2 (2011): 135–150.

Manly, Jennifer J., Desiree Byrd, Pegah Touradji, Danurys Sanchez, and Yaakov Stern. "Literacy and Cognitive Change among Ethnically Diverse Elders." *International Journal of Psychology* 39.1 (2004): 47–60.

Marx, Steven. "*Fortunate Senex*: The Pastoral of Old Age." *SEL* 25.1 (1985): 21–44.

Neumann, Christoph. "Is Metaphor Universal? Cross-Language Evidence from German and Japanese." *Metaphor and Symbol* 16.1–2 (2001): 123–142.

"Newlyweds' Average Wedding Expense." *Donga Ilbo* (16 February 2015). http://news.donga.com/List/3/all/20150216/69674371/2. Accessed on 9 September 2015.

Oró-Piqueras, Maricel. "Narrating Ageing: Deconstructing Negative Conceptions of Old Age in Four Contemporary English Novels." *Journal of Aging Studies* 27.1 (2013): 47–51.

Reis, Alexandra Isabel Dias, Maria de Sousa Guerreiro, and Karl Magnus Petersson. "A Sociodemographic and Neuropsychological Characterization of an Illiterate Population." *Applied Neuropsychology* 10.4 (2003): 191–204.

Shen, Yeshayahu, and Ravid Aisenman. "'Heard Melodies Are Sweet, but Those Unheard Are Sweeter': Synaesthetic Metaphors and Cognition." *Language and Literature* 17.2 (2008): 107–21.

UNESCO. "World Heritage List: Haiensa." whc.unesco.org/document/154150. Accessed on 16 May 2017.

Yu, Ning. "Synesthetic Metaphor: A Cognitive Perspective." *Journal of Literary Semantics* 32.1 (2003): 19–34.

Zŏng, In-Sŏb. *Folk Tales from Korea*. 3rd ed. Elizabeth: Hollym, 1982.

- 8 -

Mischief and Mayhem

A Cultural History of the Relationship between Children and Old People in the Contemporary Family Film

LINCOLN GERAGHTY

As this volume demonstrates, the romantic pairing of childhood and old age is a trope that has appeared in various media and genres in Western culture. It can take various forms: from more positive depictions, where children and the elderly are suggested to be ideal companions because both groups have the time to indulge in play and contemplate life's mysteries, to depictions that cast them as vulnerable members of society, unable to look after themselves or others because of physical frailty and lack of social status. In this chapter I look more closely at this pairing within the specific medium of the family film, and analyze to what extent children and the elderly are represented as both proactive participants in mainstream culture and marginalized citizens, outside the established norms of adult behaviour.

The basic conceptual metaphor (or root metaphor, to use George Lakoff and Mark Johnson's terminology) that "children are like old people, and vice versa" also appears in the contexts of international family film. I consider specifically *Charlie and the Chocolate Factory* (2005) and *Paddington* (2014), and argue that the relationships between young and old characters serve to emphasize the regenerative effects of the spirit of adventure and mischief in the elderly while children are valued for the imaginative contribution that play and youthfulness can make in everyday life. Charlie's Grandpa Joe accompanies him to Willy Wonka's factory, having been the only one in the family to support his wish to find a Golden Ticket. Joe develops a new lease on life as he experiences Wonka's fantasyland through the eyes of his grandson, while Charlie assumes adult responsibilities as he proves to Wonka that he is not a selfish child like the rest of the winners. As a young bear from the deepest and darkest jungle of Peru, Paddington follows a path to maturity as he is adopted by the Brown family in London. Childlike enthusiasm for the Tube, tea, and marmalade sandwiches symbolize youth and innocence in Paddington, while he also learns the importance of individual responsibility and family loyalty. The elderly Mr. Gruber befriends Paddington and relishes the company of the youthful bear, as it reminds him of his own childhood as an immigrant coming to England. Both these films, as well as pairing children and the elderly, also highlight the continued cultural fascination for nostalgia brought about through the adaptation of popular children's texts in the family film genre.

Global and Glocal Markets for Children's Literature

The repetition of this dynamic in the films can be understood explicitly in terms of two major themes: first, these films are part of a wider cultural history of childhood where changing representations of children and their relationships with the elderly have evolved alongside shifts in marketing, merchandising, consumer culture, and media broadcasting; and second, as adaptations of preexisting British literary texts, these films suggest that this specific childhood trope is intermedial and international as it moves across different but connected media platforms and international film markets (*Paddington* was cofounded by British and French studios, and *Charlie and the Chocolate Factory* was funded and released by America's Warner Bros.). Therefore, these two movies exemplify the historical trend in Hollywood film production where British literary texts are chosen for adaptation to attract as wide an international audience as possible while at the same time responding to criticism from those who continue to attack cinema as lowbrow and populist. Heyday, the UK studio that made *Paddington*, has a history of adapting British children's fiction for a global audience: titles range from the fantasy world of *Harry Potter* to the more somber *The Boy in the Striped Pyjamas*. The search for international audiences, however, does not imply that all audiences expect the same or are even familiar with other national literary traditions. For Maria Nikolajeva, "[t]he notion that there is a 'common' children's literature in all countries in the world is a misunderstanding. [. . .] With very few exceptions, children's literature in different countries has little in common" (*Children's Literature* 43). Even though we cannot speak of one type of children's literature (or, by extension, film adaptations), as this would simplify differing national contexts and modes of consumption, we can speak of an increasingly international flow for children's culture in all its forms—predicated on the growth of social media networks, the use of the Internet by children, and the global distribution and exhibition of Hollywood films in differentiated local markets using specialized marketing techniques.

The dominance of Hollywood within this international market is in many ways down to the ebb and flow of Disney's cultural and popular appeal through history—its success in animated movie output in the 1930s and 1950s, followed by television and music production in the 1980s and 1990s, and now mega franchise output like *Star Wars* and *Marvel*. Moreover, the adaptation of children's literature by Hollywood, sold to audiences around the world, highlights the problematic nature of both globalization and its refinement through glocalization (Robertson 30). Anna Katrina Gutierrez introduced the concept of glocalization to children's literature scholarship in her study of picturebook retellings of Philippine fairy tales. In recognizing this work I would argue that children's literature is inherently global in nature as stories circulate through filmic adaptations, then are blended, translated, and amalgamated with local traditions and frameworks to produce glocal iterations of the original. For Sung-Ae Lee, "a 'glocal' text [. . .] emerges when a culture appropriates a global text and localizes it by imbuing foreign elements with local flavor: glocalization exists as a dialectic between the pressure of uniformity and an affirmation of the local" (280). Also, while one might lay the blame for the dominance of Hollywood at the door of globalization or suggest that different national contexts for children's literature provide evidence of glocalization, we have to understand that all cultural texts, and characters within them, circulate across borders, generations, and time periods. So while Disney is often considered the primary exporter of children's media content, we might look to Asia and countries like Japan for a counterpoint to this dominance. Children's video game franchises like Pokémon and the anime studio Ghibli have become global media brands that are also leaders in international children's markets. In terms of the two literary works adapted to film discussed in this chapter, which are British stories reworked by French and American studios for international audiences, evidence of the global and glocal resides in the reworking of national stereotypes and the root metaphor of "children are like old people, and vice versa."

As I explore further in the next section, the family film is often considered to be mostly about profit. This generic construct was created in Hollywood during the Depression era to target a general audience, typically depicting scenarios and themes attractive to children (comedy, action and adventure), which are experienced by child characters alongside adult protagonists. Producers of family films are notorious for maximizing income through a strategy of school holiday release dates backed up by an aggressive marketing campaign focused on toys, merchandise, and consumer product tie-ins. This follows the strategy for Hollywood blockbuster releases that focuses on a film having specific components: "a pre-sold property (such as a best-selling novel or play), within a traditional film genre, usually supported by bankable stars (operating within their particular genre) and director" (Wyatt 78). However, for both Perry Nodelman and Karen Lury, films with children or based on children's texts are far more complicated than most critics would give them credit for. Lury argues that in many of these films, "the child and childhood, and indeed children themselves, occupy a situation in which they are 'other': other to the supposedly rational, civilised, 'grown up' human animal that is the adult" (1). This corresponds to Nikolajeva's concept of "aetonormativity," which describes how adult normativity has governed the production of children's literature and "othered" how children have been depicted in relation to the perceived normal behaviour of adults within that fiction. Children's literature is thus designed "to educate, socialize and oppress a particular social group" (*Power* 8). For the child protagonists in *Charlie and the Chocolate Factory* and *Paddington*, this "othering" is clearly apparent, yet in different tonal ways: for example, the mischievous children who disobey Willy Wonka's warnings are demonized and punished for gorging on candy, yet Paddington's childlike overexuberance is valued compared to the stiff-upper-lip approach to life displayed by Mr. Brown. Lury explains that the "othering" of the child coincides with changing conceptions of modern childhood in the West: "Set apart in terms of time and experience, the child and childhood became paradoxically other to adult human life—childhood was a special, if restricted, time period in which children were different from adults and should be treated accordingly" (24–25). Indeed, with respect to the two films I discuss in this chapter, it is not only the child that is "othered," but also the elderly, so that Nikolajeva's concept of "aetonormativity" (age-related normativity) can be seen as going both ways and is therefore broadened to include young and old. Each film features an older adult protagonist who is distinct from middle-age adulthood and side-lined from typical adult activities or actions due to perceived frailty or lack of usefulness or simply because they represent a supposedly bygone—and therefore outmoded—era.

This otherness depicted in film, and by extension literature, television, and other media for children, also works on a more abstract level. In discussing the metaphorical meanings of children's fiction, Perry Nodelman argues that stories

> possess a shadow, an unconscious—a more complex and more complete understanding of the world and people that remains unspoken beyond the simple surface but provides that simple surface with its comprehensibility. The simple surface sublimates—hides but still manages to imply the presence of—something less simple. (206)

So, for example, in the case of *Charlie and the Chocolate Factory*, what is a tale warning of the dangers of greed and gluttony can also be interpreted as a narrative of capitalist consumption, where the child's (Charlie's) relationship with adults (his parents), the elderly (Grandpa Joe), and an adult who acts like a child (Willy Wonka) is central to the processes of social identification and learning to grow up in a hierarchical society based on individual success and capitalism. Likewise, *Paddington*, a children's story about an orphan bear from Peru who loves marmalade sandwiches and gets into lots of awkward situations, is also a metaphorical tale of colonialism, conflict, and the end of empire. The encounters between Paddington and Mr. Gruber (an elderly antiques dealer) or Paddington and Mr. Curry (the nosy retired neighbour) reflect tensions in postwar Britain around nationhood, immigration, and fear of the foreign other. In both filmic examples there is a "doubling" effect that comes as a result of the child as "other," and this doubling is made implicit through the relationship between two extremes of life: childhood and old age.

Family and Children's Films

For many, the family film came to prominence in the 1980s, as a result of an increase in Hollywood output specifically targeting youthful audiences alongside a strategic shift in marketing and merchandising where children were positioned as consumers. However, scholars such as Noel Brown and Peter Krämer have argued that the roots of the family film stretch back to Disney and other animated features of the 1920s and 1930s. Crucial in the development of the genre was Hollywood's attempt to make films for all ages that conformed to the Hays Code. The Code, officially known as the Motion Picture Production Code, was published in 1930 in an effort to clean up Hollywood film content, determining what was appropriate and what was unacceptable for a public audience. Since there were no ratings for films at the time, all films were considered suitable for general audiences and thus had to conform to the guidelines of taste and decency published in the Hays Code.

Whatever starting point we might agree on, it is evident that Hollywood has devoted much attention and many funds to attracting a family audience, where parents can sit alongside their children and enjoy the movie in equal, but not necessarily the same, ways. Cary Bazalgette and Terry Staples describe the history of the family film in Hollywood as a reaction to the Depression, attracting adults and children to the cinema when financial times were tough (94). However, while the family film is a uniquely American genre, Bazalgette and Staples describe the children's film as an essentially European genre, where differences in casting child protagonists, emphasis on a child's point of view, and marketing to a niche audience separate it from its bigger and brasher North American cousin: "The consequence of these differences is that whereas the family film can be packaged as a commercial proposition because of the size and wealth of the intended audience, not only in the country of origin but also abroad, the children's film almost invariably looks on paper like a complete non-starter, confined within its national boundaries" (96). This last point is interesting, considering the global dominance of contemporary Hollywood film and the local markets of children's entertainment, which are discussed later in this chapter. However, the growth of the children's film "was not simply a matter of economics or even Anti-Americanness. It was a positive belief that children in the audience could only properly identify with children on the screen if they were recognisably from the same world as themselves" (Bazalgette and Staples 95).

Both *Charlie and the Chocolate Factory* and *Paddington* are examples of the contemporary Hollywood family film in that they come packaged for a wide international audience and can attract both children and parents in equal measure. Yet, following the definition of the European children's film offered by Bazalgette and Staples, we might also consider them examples of this niche form in that the central child protagonists (Charlie and Paddington) are "*not* desirable moppets" (95), but rather strong characters with their own distinct personalities: "Children's films can be defined as offering mainly or entirely a child's point of view. They deal with the interests, fears, misapprehensions and concerns of children in their own terms. They foreground the problems of coping with adults or coping without them" (96). Máire Messenger Davies clarifies this distinction between the American family film and the European children's film as the difference "between children *in* film, and film *for* children" (108). Elements of the more European tradition of the children's film can be seen in how Charlie deals with incredible poverty and how his desire for a better life for his family is symbolized by his dream of finding a Golden Ticket and meeting Willy Wonka. Similarly, through Paddington's point of view (although a young bear, not a young boy), we see how he deals with being far from home, alone in a foreign land, and has to cope with the strange and often quite mad habits of the adults with whom he lives. Linking this back to the trope of pairing childhood with old age, I would argue that the child protagonists in both films are forced to address deficiencies in the adults they encounter while at the same time the elderly protagonists are shown as more childlike in their quest to feel young again.

The family film attains its generic identity through a five-step, "non-textual" process outlined by Noel Brown: 1) the film is marketed to appeal to the family unit; 2) the ratings system ascribes a viewing recommendation based on age and the appropriateness of a film for a young audience; 3) critics and reviewers help form the generic classification of the film with reference to its intended audience; 4) merchandising is seen as an integral part of the marketing pre- and post-release, targeting youthful audiences with toys, games, and other licensed ephemera; and 5) television helps to frame the film as family viewing by screening it at holidays and during times of the day when children and adults tend to watch together, thus emphasizing notions of community and familial bonding (Brown 6–8). The films I discuss in this chapter largely conform to these characteristics, but more importantly, as I argue with reference to the representation of children and the elderly, they also highlight the continued cultural fascination for nostalgia brought about through the adaptation and reworking of older children's texts for a new audience. *Charlie and the Chocolate Factory* is both an adaptation of Roald Dahl's 1964 book and a remake of *Willy Wonka and the Chocolate Factory* (1971); and *Paddington* is based on Michael Bond's stories for children first published in the 1950s and adapted for the small screen in 1975 and 2011.

As well as taking into account the production contexts for the family film, we should recognize the centrality of the family unit as depicted in the genre. As Murray Pomerance argues, the family is where we learn to cope with the social world—where children can grow up and follow life lessons taught by elders. During the 1950s and 1960s, the American family was perceived to be under threat from social change and generational differences exacerbated by postwar malaise and the conformity of suburban living. Films of this period thus attempted to show the family as "the first bulwark against the entropic forces of anarchy and revolution that might threaten the newly secured hegemony of the postwar state" (Pomerance 2). The centrality of the family in Hollywood film increased as the genre became increasingly profitable. The image of the screen family became the ideal model to which we should all aspire: "Whether it is played for sentiment or for catharsis, for laughter or for mystification, the screen family is inevitably drawn as a glowing paragon to behold," writes Pomerance. The films "are relentlessly pedagogical, teaching us how to pose, think, behave, acquire, imagine, remember, fear and anticipate as members of families in real life" (8).

However, it is not just through the traditional bond between parent and child that we see the genre's pedagogical narrative at its strongest. In many family films children form strong ties with the elderly, particularly represented in the bond between grandchild and grandparent. For example, in the science fiction family films *Cocoon* (1985), *Cocoon: The Return* (1988), and **batteries not included* (1987), aliens are presented as bringing harmony and peace to humanity, through their encounters with children and senior citizens. If on the one level children represent a positive response to alien visitations because of their innocence and open-hearted acceptance of the fantastic, senior citizens represent a knowing wisdom and lack of prejudice. Furthermore, in these films, the alien effectively "brings out the child" in them. In *Cocoon* and **batteries not included*, an elderly or mature group of friends refuse to give up on life. In return for helping the aliens go back home, they receive a new lease on life. In *Cocoon* they even journey with the aliens to their planet, where they have the chance to live forever; and in **batteries not included*, the elderly protagonists—aided by their alien friends—succeed in stopping developers who want to tear down their old apartment building to replace it with a modern office block for the younger generation. Again, linking this to the pairing of childhood with old age, I would argue that child protagonists in the family film are forced to grow up quicker—be more adult than the adults. At the same time old age is celebrated as a chance to relive life and assume attributes of childhood in order to feeland in some cases, be—young again.

In these films the alien visitor allows humans to recover or discover their essential humanity: it is not only able to preserve or resurrect human life but also to enable those who feel estranged from society to rediscover the joys of life. Thus, while the aliens in *Cocoon* enable the elderly to live forever, they literally "change a swimming pool into a fountain of youth" and so "make children of senior citizens" (Grant 25). Furthermore, the story also concerns the grandson of one of the elderly residents. He not only helps the aliens to return home but, in so doing, demonstrates a childlike open-mindedness that is contrasted to the attitudes of his middle-aged parents, who believe that both he and his grandfather are suffering from delusions. As I have argued elsewhere about *Cocoon*, the senior citizens embody "all the qualities that these films associate with children—youthful exuberance, enthusiasm, curious innocence" (Geraghty 72).

This common narrative in the family film can be related to Robin Wood's observation that Hollywood tends to construct the viewer as childlike and therefore receptive to the wonder of cinematic illusion, a construction that is clearly related to the commercial success of George Lucas's *Star Wars* sequels *The Empire Strikes Back* (1980) and *Return of the Jedi* (1983) and Steven Spielberg's *Close Encounters of the Third Kind* (1977) and *E.T. the Extra-Terrestrial* (1982) (Wood 145; see also Krämer). However, the prevalence and popularity of the family film also signals, according to Estella Tincknell (88), "one of the central concerns of the post-war moment" in "that the future of post-war society depended on the inclusion of children within its conception of the social." Indeed, for Bengt Sandin, the history of childhood and child welfare in the first half of the twentieth century is marked by a change in social attitudes toward child labor and health, juvenile delinquency, and universal education. Western reformers believed that "[c]hildren's place was within the family or in an educational setting" (Sandin 54), so that society would benefit from proper child development—the young would grow into responsible adults. In the following discussion of *Charlie and the Chocolate Factory* and *Paddington*, I want to complicate these approaches to childhood and situate the contemporary family film in a broader cultural context. The pairing of children with the elderly in both films, the root metaphor being analyzed in this volume, serves to highlight the thematic importance of work and nationhood in the relationship between children and old people. *Charlie and the Chocolate Factory* and *Paddington* situate the main protagonists as active agents: the children behave like adults (assuming responsibility, even working to benefit the family), and the elderly have jobs to do, when traditionally they are supposed to withdraw from the workforce. In both cases nostalgia serves to frame how the children and elderly protagonists are represented and interact with other characters and scenarios: nostalgia for lost childhood or a childhood not lived in *Charlie and the Chocolate Factory* and nostalgia for home and a fantasy depiction of London in *Paddington*.

Work and Family in *Charlie and the Chocolate Factory*

The first of the two films to be analysed is described by Michael Duffy (153) as "an example of how to both benefit from and alter cultural perceptions of history and media." Like its two predecessors (the book and the 1971 film adaptation starring Gene Wilder), Tim Burton's *Charlie and the Chocolate Factory* is comical and garnered a cult audience a number of years after release. Yet it is an interesting film in its own right, not least because it plays with notions of childhood memory and intergenerational relationships. The film follows the original story quite closely; Charlie Bucket, played by Freddie Highmore, lives with his parents and four grandparents in a small, run-down house in the shadow of Willy Wonka's factory. Very poor and unable to even afford proper gifts for Charlie's birthday, his family scrimps and saves to buy him a chocolate Wonka bar every year. He shares a strong bond with his grandparents, particularly Grandpa Joe (played by David Kelly), who resides in a bed with the other three senior citizens. All grandparents are shown to offer advice and affection to Charlie, supporting his ultimate desire to find a Golden Ticket so he can visit the chocolate factory and meet Willy Wonka (played by Johnny Depp). Joe tells Charlie stories about how he used to work for Wonka, describing the factory as a fantasyland where childish desire and enthusiasm for candy made it the happiest place on earth. Grandpa Joe is the optimist of the family, compared with Grandpa George, who snipes and moans about everything. Joe is also the spriteliest, able to get out of bed and accompany Charlie on the tour of the factory. His youthful exuberance and memories of working at the factory help make his relationship with Charlie almost like that of father and son; indeed, Charlie's father is rather lackluster in his enthusiasm for the boy.

For June Pulliam, "Dahl's story is a non-sectarian morality tale" (103), and Burton continues this stance in his adaptation. The other children who find a Golden Ticket are greedy, spoiled, overconfident, and rude, whereas Charlie is thoughtful and extremely loyal to his family. Knowing that it is Charlie's dearest wish to see the factory, Grandpa Joe gives him the few coins he has in his purse so that he can buy another Wonka bar and thus have one last chance to find the remaining Golden Ticket. Yet in Burton's tale it is not just Charlie who wants to meet Wonka and see the wonders of the factory. It is Joe's secret wish to see inside his former place of employment one last time before he dies. Young and old are brought together through a sense of longing that is both utopic and nostalgic. When Joe is invited to go with Charlie after he finds the last ticket, he jumps out of bed and dances, as if youth momentarily returns to his feeble body. This "revitalization" is similar to that described in Elisabeth Wesseling's chapter in this volume, where music brings vitality to an elderly man in Hector Malot's *Sans famille*. Old Joe is shown to be more exuberant and childlike in his response to the good news than Charlie, who is more concerned with feeding his family.

In many ways Charlie is more adult than the adults, particularly compared to his dad, who barely makes enough money to feed the family and is made redundant at the beginning of the film. Charlie is even prepared to sacrifice his dream by selling the last Golden Ticket before the deadline. In the juxtaposition between father and son, Charlie seemingly occupies a higher status, because only he holds the power to change the fortunes of his family. In Burton's film Mr. Bucket works at the toothpaste factory, where he screws the tops on the tubes, until he is replaced by a machine. Redundancy not only puts the Buckets at further risk of starvation; it also cuts off the means by which Mr. Bucket supplies parts for Charlie's model of the Wonka factory, which is made of odd toothpaste tube tops. Let down by his father, Charlie is the real glue that holds the family together, and this is made overt when he becomes the adoptive father of Willy Wonka at the end of the movie, taking him into the Bucket family. This character arc serves to underscore the trope of children/elderly pairing as traditional roles are reversed. Charlie becomes the breadwinner, and Joe gets his wish to be young again for the day; Charlie's dad is ineffective and is not redeemed as head of the family by the end of the film.

The root metaphor is maintained throughout the film, particularly with Charlie, who consistently reacts against the other child protagonists, being more responsible and thus convincing Wonka to award him the prize of taking over and living in the factory. Even though Charlie refuses to leave his family to live with Wonka, it does not stop him from moving into the factory; in fact, the entire Bucket house is transferred indoors, and Wonka is shown joining them for family meals and to discuss the latest candy-inspired ideas with Charlie. In this case, the child is installed within the industrial system of chocolate making—Charlie has literally become part of the factory he merely dreamed of visiting at the start of the movie. In *The Queer Child*, Kathryn Bond Stockton sees this as "the quintessential insistence of create-in-order-to-destroy: the dream of manufacturing what you will profusely and on the spot consume, not as necessity but strictly as luxury" (238). Stockton argues that the ending of the film reflects a story of queer mentoring and inheritance where Wonka rejects adult masculinity and creates a lineage of boys who revel in the continued pleasure of making and consuming candy

(244). By making Charlie the boss, Wonka is able to enact his childhood fantasy to consume candy without the responsibility of managing the factory. Similarly, writing about the original book, Tim Morris describes the story as a "romance" with the "pairing of a boy with a suitable father" (102). However, I would argue that it is the childlike Wonka who is paired with the more adult and responsible Charlie.

Differing interprepations aside, it is clear that the film situates the child's relationship with his family and with Wonka within a capitalist system of production and consumption. Work is therefore central to the narrative. Abbie Ventura contextualizes this message in all three versions of the text (the book, the 1971 film, and Burton's adaptation) in a discussion of post-Fordism and economic globalization, the expansion of which "demands children as active citizen subjects more through their global participation as consumers than through particular national identities" (237). This assertion correlates with Sandin's history of child labor and welfare in Western society, where a large number of teenage boys and girls have entered the workforce in the early twentieth century, balancing school and paid work. He argues that the difference between children and adults has become blurred as a result of globalization: "In today's society, this creates an issue of how children's rights shall be negotiated between, on one hand, care and dependence, and on the other, adultlike independence and rights." As a result, "the notion of children as different has eroded; the same social rights are attributed to children as to adults" (Sandin 55). This links back to the root metaphor that "children are like old people, and vice versa," since work serves to make Charlie the responsible adult, while all the adults in his life either revert to childhood or lack the ability to "grow up" and fulfil their roles: Grandpa Joe no longer works but gets his wish of going back to the factory where he was once employed, Charlie's father is made redundant and then no longer needs to support his family, and Wonka passes responsibility for managing the factory to Charlie, so he can just concentrate on having fun inventing new candy.

In addition to Willy Wonka's relationship with Charlie, and Charlie's with Grandpa Joe, there is another father-and-son dichotomy at the heart of the film—one that Burton himself added, since it does not appear in either the original novel or the 1971 film adaptation. As a backstory to why Wonka devoted his life to making the world's greatest candy, and why he is perhaps the world's quirkiest businessman, we get to see Wonka's father (played by Sir Christopher Lee). As the town dentist, Wilbur Wonka prohibited his son from eating sweets and cast a dark shadow over his childhood. Authoritarian and emotionally distant Wilbur makes Willy determined to taste the pleasures of candy and eventually become the master sweet maker he is. In flashbacks throughout the film that follow the demise of each of the four aggravating children, Wonka's relationship with his father is revealed. Because of his unhappy past, it seems Willy is destined to live the childhood he missed due to his father's discipline; therefore, the competition to find a child to take over the factory in the most over-the-top fashion is his way of rebelling against traditional systems of familial inheritance. It is interesting that Wonka's childhood punishments are alternated with the punishments of the children who have lacked discipline. The literary and cultural norm of children being punished for their actions by adults is being upheld, while at the same time it is subverted through the childlike behavior of both Wonka and Grandpa Joe. The casting of Lee as Wonka's father is an interesting choice. Lee connotes a myriad of intertextual references to the gothic and horror genres (having played Dracula and Frankenstein's Monster in Hammer Horror adaptations of those famous novels) that adds another level of textual meaning to Burton's film. Moreover, and perhaps more importantly in light of the relationship between children and old people, Willy is clearly depicted as a child in the flashbacks, but Lee plays his own age (which at the time of the film's release in 2005 was eighty-three). This means that while Wilbur Wonka is a father (a role associated with middle age), he is also distinctly elderly. This perhaps underscores the notion that parenthood is the preserve of middle-aged adults and that the relationship between children and old age is more distinct; the two are more socially and culturally alike than child and parent. Moreover, unlike Charlie and Grandpa Joe's supportive relationship, Willy and Wilbur's connection is far more traumatic, because his father is the main reason why Willy remains like a child. His moment of rebellion came when he was young (eating the sweets he had been denied), and thus he cannot, or does not want to, grow up to be like Wilbur. Jeffrey Weinstock argues that "Wonka's social awkwardness is the product of misguided parenting" and that "the resistance of parents (especially fathers) to the child's unusual interests sets in motion the events of the film to follow" (18). Perhaps tellingly, after Willy witnesses the strong bond between Joe and Charlie during the tour, Burton has him return home to make peace with his father, and it is revealed that Wonka senior has actually been following his son's career with pride for years.

"As played by Depp, Wonka is more of a child than Charlie (Freddie Highmore). He is impulsive and amoral; perhaps even dangerous," argues Brown (213). As outlined above, the film thus reinforces certain age norms with regard to fatherhood. Burton's twist on the story is that generational roles are reversed and corrupted to underscore the absurdity of the factory and

Willy Wonka's personality. Indeed, Brown argues that the success of Depp's portrayal and the film at the international box office indicates "that there is substantial mileage in mainstream family entertainment which appears to eschew the obviousness and vulgarity of the lowest common denominator" (214). Weinstock lists several recurrent themes in his analysis of Burton as a director, including "the collision of worlds that restores a sense of wonder to the 'real' world, the disavowal of the finality of death, a privileging of the imaginative child or artist, [and] a drive toward the restoration of the family (sometimes nuclear, sometimes newly constituted" (23). In *Charlie and the Chocolate Factory*, the child is clearly privileged, and the family is restored by the end of the film: for example, Charlie gets his family out of poverty, Willy Wonka is "adopted" by the Buckets, and he makes peace with Wilbur. Weinstock states that the film fits neatly within the Burton tradition, because parents (in this case Wilbur) are "presented as disciplining forces of normalization that seek to straitjacket the child's imagination and sense of individuality" (17). We can see this happening in terms of the other ticket winners and their parents, who attempt to discipline their children because of their bad behaviour; however, the lack of success in controlling their children's selfish and greedy habits means the naive and obnoxious parents ultimately fail in parenthood, and the children are corrupted as a result. Grandpa Joe proves more successful as a father figure to Charlie, as he is able to both inspire and encourage Charlie's imagination and willingly takes part in the process of achieving his dream of visiting the factory.

From the textual I now turn to an analysis of the film's production context in order to understand its significance as children's film. *Charlie and the Chocolate Factory* was a transatlantic effort: based on a British novel, it was produced by Warner Bros., an American film company. It was directed by Burton and starred Depp; both are American. It was filmed in the UK and cast several British actors in major roles, including Lee as Wilbur Wonka. As mentioned earlier, Bazalgette and Staples draw out differences between the American family film and the European children's film, namely, in the scope of budget and the centrality of the child protagonist. Within *Charlie and the Chocolate Factory*, we can see the tension between American and European perspectives: it was made for $150 million and made almost $475 million,[1] clearly a blockbuster and, with its PG rating, evidently aimed at a family audience; but through Highmore's depiction of Charlie, we have insight into how children view the world, aspire to be a success in it, and judge the moral failings of those around them—thus more akin to the European-style children's film.

Nation and Nostalgia in *Paddington*

A similar argument could be made about the next film to be discussed, *Paddington*. Released in 2014 as a British-French coproduction and directed by British writer Paul King, the film was made by Heyday Films, the same British company known for producing the *Harry Potter* films. Based on Michael Bond's famous English series of children's books (1958–2014), the film was adapted for an international audience, casting popular and renowned actors from the United Kingdom, such as Hugh Bonneville, Julie Walters, Jim Broadbent, and Peter Capaldi, alongside Australian American Nicole Kidman. For its modest $55 million budget, it made $258.6 million at the box office.[2] Its main star, of course, is the computer-generated (CGI) Paddington Bear, voiced by the British actor Ben Whishaw, and it is through Paddington that we are introduced to the Brown family and the eccentricities of British society and culture. Naive and innocent, Paddington, like Charlie, offers a child's view of the world around him, aspires to a family life (similar to Stuart Little's desire to find a family), and often judges the moral failings of those adults who disappoint him in their actions and reactions (as revealed in Paddington's infamous "hard stare" aimed at Mr. Brown).

As in the books, Paddington arrives in London from the jungles of darkest Peru, but in the film we are first shown how his guardians, his elderly aunt Lucy and uncle Pastuzo, encounter the British explorer Montgomery Clyde. They are taught English, learn how to make marmalade, and are left a snow globe of London. Years later we see Aunt Lucy and Uncle Pastuzo raising their young nephew Paddington, passing on their love of marmalade sandwiches and the desire to travel to London and see the explorer again. Following an earthquake, Pastuzo is presumed dead, and Aunt Lucy sets Paddington on a voyage to England to find a new family, while she retires to a home for old bears in Lima. From the very beginning, Paddington is associated with older people (his aunt and uncle are clearly senior citizen bears), and once in London, Paddington frequently spends time with the elderly antique-shop owner Mr. Gruber, and the Browns' old housekeeper, Mrs. Bird, while he runs afoul of retired neighbor Mr. Curry. Through his relationships with these three, Paddington learns much about humans and teaches them something about themselves. This conforms to what Anne Royall Newman argues is typical of children's books with animal protagonists: they enable humans in the story to learn while at the same time acting as symbols of our more natural side. Getting in touch with this side "can be constructive, leading to natural wisdom, creativity, and spiritual truth when it is integrated as part of the total self." The bear is a perfect conduit for this, as it "stands for the instinctive side of man, it is complex enough to incorporate both the terrifying and comforting aspects of this natural side" (132).

Mr. Gruber, like Paddington, is an immigrant who came to the United Kingdom from Hungary as a child during the Second World War to escape the Nazis. Both see London as a utopic space, a refuge after the hardship in their respective countries. In the film Mr. Gruber runs an antique shop in Portobello Road, and Paddington visits because he needs help to investigate who the explorer was that came to Peru all those years ago. A scene combining live action and animation allows Mr. Gruber to talk about his childhood when he came to London, and this strikes a chord with Paddington, who himself is awestruck with wonder at all the items on display in the store. Mr. Gruber treats Paddington with respect, is interested in his stories about the explorer, and sees him as wise beyond his young years. The youthful energy of Paddington rubs off on Mr. Gruber, who revels in Paddington's adventures, and both feel a sense of kinship. The housekeeper, Mrs. Bird, has a similar relationship with Paddington; she uses his presence in the house to voice her dissatisfaction about Mr. Brown's being so boring and miserable. While she frowns upon Paddington's mishaps, she also celebrates how his moving into the house has brought a freshness and excitement to all, particularly Mr. Brown. Without Paddington the family would have continued to ignore Mrs. Bird's advice and guidance on family matters, but in her pairing with Paddington, she is able to contribute to the family and becomes one of them, just like the bear. In other words, the patriarchal hierarchy of the household, with Mr. Brown at the top, is destabilized as the oldest and youngest members assert their influence over the family. This transforms them and ultimately creates a happier home.

Unlike Mr. Gruber and Mrs. Bird, Mr. Curry is not fond of Paddington and serves as the stereotypical mean and miserly old man next door. He views Paddington's antics as troublesome and plots with a villainous taxidermist to capture him and return him to Peru. Depicted as a lonely bachelor eager to impress the sexy but unobtainable Millicent Clyde, played by Nicole Kidman, Curry is nosy and rude. His hatred of Paddington could be viewed as xenophobic—he objects to an illegal alien from South America living in the privileged surroundings of London's Notting Hill—and I would argue is meant to resonate with British audiences as a reference to contemporary political debates concerning immigration prevalent in the United Kingdom during the run up to the General Election and the rise of UKIP in 2014. Indeed, Kyle Grayson argues of the original books that they illustrate "how political theorising may take place in the vernacular space of popular culture" (391) and that the figure of Paddington as an immigrant works to unpack "liberal conceptions of identity, migration and tolerance while drawing attention to specific negotiations of difference" (378). Similarly, Angela Smith maintains that while the stories "are subtle in their articulation of racist and xenophobic discourses which [. . .] present the case for toleration and understanding towards immigrants," Paddington has to try to fit in just as "the immigrant conforms to the dominant culture's norms" (48). Therefore, the film is like the books in that Paddington represents a nonthreatening other who eventually wins over Mr. Curry and proves his worth to the Browns by bringing the family together.

The crotchetiness of Curry is further emphasized by the fact he is played by Peter Capaldi, who was cast as The Doctor on the BBC hit science fiction television series *Doctor Who* and is seen as being equally acerbic and prickly for younger audiences of that show. A contrast to Mr. Gruber, Curry is obviously mean-spirited, yet Paddington does not recognize this in him—which only proves to Curry that the bear is really up to no good, because he seems so relaxed and innocent in his company. Curry's presence in the film offers the most typical representation of old age in the family film genre, with the old character being an obstacle to the young protagonist. Nevertheless, by the end of the story, Curry mellows as he realizes how important Paddington has become to the Browns. Almost as a trade-off, the more the Browns are happy, then the more he might be included in their activities and thus be less lonely. Mr. Curry may, then, appear as a heartless old man, but his relationship with Paddington and his family, like Willy Wonka's with Charlie and the Buckets, transforms both him and them and brings resolution to the overarching journey seen in the two movies: finding somewhere to call home.

Both Paddington's and Mr. Gruber's search for a new place to call home can be considered nostalgic. Memories of Peru, living with his aunt and uncle, frame Paddington's initial reaction to the cold, unwelcoming city of London he now lives in. But finding solace in the words of another immigrant, Gruber, who has become part of a community of shopkeepers and city locals, inspires the bear to see how just at home he is with the Browns. This desire for a home is the epitome of nostalgia, whose rhetoric and experience is framed by a feeling of absence and longing: what Susan Stewart says "leads to a generalized desire for origin, for nature, and for unmediated experience" (24). Interestingly, it is in the mediation of this nostalgia for home, in documented film scenes of Peru shown to Paddington in Gruber's antique store, and the expositionary animation charting Gruber's flight to the United Kingdom, that we gain a greater understanding of the emotional connection between Paddington and Gruber (the child and the old man). Nostalgia, the longing for home, brings them together and helps drive the narrative forward to its upbeat conclusion—that home is anywhere when you are accepted and loved. Both Paddington and Gruber are in a constant state of longing for a home, remembering the past nostalgically, while making a new one in London.

Nostalgia is also linked with nation, and in *Paddington* we can see this connection in how London is represented through icons and stereotypes of Englishness: red double-decker buses, soldiers in front of Buckingham Palace, red telephone boxes, the English "bobby" policeman, rain, the city skyline (Houses of Parliament and Big Ben), tea drinking, English reserve and manners, the stiff upper lip of Mr. Brown, and a host of others throughout the movie. Indeed, for Margaret Meek in her study of English children's literature, a "thread" in the "texture of Englishness" is nostalgia (96). Linking back to my earlier discussion of the marketing of the international family film genre, the prominence of familiar icons of England and Englishness can be understood as part of the translation of an English children's story for an international audience—relying on well-known tourist images of the country to brand the film as English and using cultural stereotypes to add humor and emphasize Paddington's identity as stranger in a foreign country. However, more importantly, their use within the narrative exaggerates the sense of nostalgia that both Paddington and Mr. Gruber feel for home. For example, when Paddington sits looking at the London skyline from his attic room, he is seen writing to Aunt Lucy and remembering how much he misses Peru. Similarly, when Mr Gruber reminisces about leaving Hungary, he does so over a cup of tea and cake. It is perhaps the incessantness, the constant flagging (to borrow Michael Billig's term) of symbols of English nationhood and identity throughout the film's emotional high points, which in the end transforms the exiles (the bear child and old man) into adopted nationals—assimilated immigrants in a narrative of nostalgia, family, and nation.

Conclusion: Narratives of Being and Becoming

Throughout this chapter I maintain that the contemporary family film proves an interesting case study of the themes central to this volume: in the history of children's media, young characters have been routinely coupled and compared with old people, while old people have been depicted and treated as children. This conceptual metaphor is emphasized in how children and old people are physically represented onscreen: a young Charlie with his Grandpa Joe, a young Willy Wonka with his father Wilbur, and a young bear from Peru with Mr. Gruber and Mr. Curry. But also, in the two films discussed, the narrative implications of this conceptual metaphor are informed by cultural ideologies relating to family, work, nostalgia, and nationhood.

For example, family—and the importance of being in one—is central to the happiness of both Charlie and Willy Wonka, and Paddington and the Browns. However, in both films it is shown that becoming part of a family is achieved through hard work and emotional effort: Willy Wonka has to learn to like people, Paddington has to acclimate to living in England, and Mr. Brown learns to not take life so seriously so as to get closer to his children. These examples suggest that everybody, child and adult, has to put in an effort to make the family unit work. In terms of work, without Charlie, Grandpa Joe would be dismissed as a useless old man. Yet in going with him on the tour of the chocolate factory, he becomes like a young boy again—physically reinvigorated, or "revitalized," and useful in his advice and actions. Similarly, Charlie enters the world of work because of his desire for, and pursuit of, the last Golden Ticket. He puts in a lot of effort saving and searching for the lucky chocolate bar that might contain a ticket, but this only backs up the effort and interest he has put into learning about Willy Wonka and the factory, even making a model of it out of tops to toothpaste tubes. Moreover, in achieving his dreams by getting on the factory tour, Charlie becomes part of a global consumer society, ultimately owning the very company that educated him in the importance of mass production and consumption. Third, children and old people are important components of nationhood. In *Paddington* we see how a young immigrant (Paddington Bear) is assimilated into English culture and society; memories of Peru make him more determined to find a family and settle down. Likewise, through stories of childhood Mr. Gruber demonstrates the importance of nostalgia in the formation of a national identity. While becoming an important part of the local community in London, backed up by heartwarming stories of European children finding new hope when escaping Nazi oppression, he still feels a longing for the Hungary he left as a child during the war, as represented by visions of his family.

States of being and becoming are intrinsic to the narratives of these two films. The coupling of children and old people in both serves to underline the importance of the journey: moving from one state of being (a child or old person) and becoming another (more mature or like a child again). Indeed, the moving back and forth between states—most obvious in Charlie and

Willy Wonka growing metaphorically from child to adult and adult to child respectively—is symptomatic of modern society and the absence of adults and adulthood in contemporary culture noted by Susan Neiman. A narrative of being and becoming is not only central to the story of *Charlie and the Chocolate Factory* and *Paddington* but is characteristic of those themes of family, work, nostalgia, and nationhood discussed in this chapter: Grandpa Joe becomes a useful member of his family, while Charlie grows into being a worker and factory owner; both Paddington and Mr. Gruber become adopted immigrants as nostalgic memories of home inspire them to find a family or community in London. Nick Lee argues that childhood can be seen "as a journey towards a clear and *knowable* destination"—the journey towards adulthood (7). However, as argued throughout this chapter, Charlie and Paddington have to become like adults much quicker than biology allows (mirrored in how Grandpa Joe and Mr. Gruber are seen acting like children). This speeded process with its implied potential for reversion suggests that the metaphorical journey of being and becoming is less stable and defined than previously thought. Lee goes on to argue that more recently "global economic, political and social changes have begun to erode [. . .] standard adulthood and [. . .] the developmental state" (6). The family film appears to be picking up on this social uncertainty by depicting the child hero as more adult, and the elderly protagonist as more childlike; as a result, family hierarchies are blurred and roles reversed. The blend or reversal of roles throughout these two films creates happiness and bonding; it is not portrayed as problematic.

In both *Charlie and the Chocolate Factory* and *Paddington*, and in the family film genre as a whole, the central message is all about individual growth supported by the community—in other words, the family. That the relationships between Grandpa Joe, Willy Wonka, and Charlie Bucket and Mr. Gruber and Paddington are used to highlight this message shows just how important and versatile the basic conceptual metaphor of "children are like old people, and vice versa" is in children's literature and the wider contexts of popular Hollywood film. The metaphor appears to have multiple narrative purposes: while in some instances the bonding of young and old replaces the traditional nuclear family and excludes middle-aged adults, in others, like those discussed in this chapter, the relationship between child and old person primarily serves to strengthen and uphold the nuclear family.

Notes

1. See Box Office Mojo http://www.boxofficemojo.com/movies/?id=charliechocolate.htm.
2. See Box Office Mojo, http://www.boxofficemojo.com/movies/?id=paddington.htm.

Works Cited

Bazalgette, Cary, and Terry Staples. "Unshrinking the Kids: Children's Cinema and the Family Film." *In Front of the Children: Screen Entertainment and Youth Audiences*. Eds. Cary Bazalgette and David Buckingham. London: BFI, 1995. 92–108.

Billig, Michael. *Banal Nationalism*. London: Sage, 1995.

Bond, Michael. *A Bear Called Paddington*. London: HarperCollins, 1958.

Brown, Noel. *The Hollywood Family Film: A History, from Shirley Temple to Harry Potter*. London: I. B. Tauris, 2012.

Davies, Máire Messenger. *Children, Media and Culture*. Maidenhead: Open University Press, 2010.

Duffy, Michael S. "Charlie and the Chocolate Factory." *Directory of World Cinema: American Hollywood 2*. Ed. Lincoln Geraghty. Bristol: Intellect, 2015. 152–153.

Geraghty, Lincoln. *American Science Fiction Film and Television*. Oxford: Berg, 2009.

Grant, Barry Keith. "'Sensuous Elaboration': Reason and the Visible in the Science-Fiction Film." *Alien Zone II: The Spaces of Science Fiction Cinema*. Ed. Annette Kuhn. London: Verso, 1999. 16–30.

Grayson, Kyle. "How to Read Paddington Bear: Liberalism and the Foreign Subject in *A Bear Called Paddington*." *British Journal of Politics and International Relations* 15.3 (2013): 378–393.

Gutierrez, Anna Katrina. "*Mga Kwento ni Lola Basyang*: A Tradition of Reconfiguring the Filipino Child." *International Research in Children's Literature* 2.2 (2009): 159–176.

Krämer, Peter. "Would You Take Your Child to See This Film? The Cultural and Social Work of the Family-Adventure Movie." *Contemporary Hollywood Cinema*. Eds. Steve Neale and Murray Smith. London: Routledge, 1998. 294–311.

Lakoff, George, and Mark Johnson. *Metaphors We Live By*. Chicago: University of Chicago Press, 1980.

Lee, Nick. *Childhood and Society: Growing Up in an Age of Uncertainty*. Buckingham: Open University Press, 2001.

Lee, Sung-Ae. "Fairy-Tale Scripts and Intercultural Conceptual Blending in Modern Korean Film and Television Drama." *Grimms' Tales around the Globe: The Dynamics of Their International Reception*. Eds. Vanessa Joosen and Gillian Lathey. Detroit: Wayne State University Press, 2014. 275–293.

Lury, Karen. *The Child in Film: Tears, Fears and Fairy Tales*. London: I. B. Tauris, 2010.

Meek, Margaret. "The Englishness of English Children's Books." *Children's Literature and National Identity*. Ed. Margaret Meek. Stoke-on-Trent: Trentham Books, 2001. 89–100.

Morris, Tim. *You're Only Young Twice: Children's Literature and Film*. Urbana: University of Illinois Press, 2000.

Neiman, Susan. *Why Grow Up?* London: Penguin Books, 2014.

Newman, Anne Royall. "Images of the Bear in Children's Literature." *Children's Literature in Education* 18.3 (1987): 131–138.

Nikolajeva, Maria. *Children's Literature Comes of Age: Toward a New Aesthetic*. New York: Garland, 1996.

Nikolajeva, Maria. *Power, Voice and Subjectivity in Literature for Young Readers.* New York: Routledge, 2010.

Nodelman, Perry. *The Hidden Adult: Defining Children's Literature.* Baltimore: Johns Hopkins University Press, 2008.

Pomerance, Murray. "Introduction: Family Affairs." *A Family Affair: Cinema Calls Home.* Ed. Murray Pomerance. London: Wallflower, 2008. 1–10.

Pulliam, June. "Charlie's Evolving Moral Universe: Filmic Interpretations of Roald Dahl's *Charlie and the Chocolate Family.*" *Fantasy Fiction into Film: Essays.* Eds. Leslie Stratyner and James R. Keller. Jefferson: McFarland, 2007. 103–114.

Robertson, Roland. "Glocalization: Time-Space and Homogeneity-Heterogeneity." *Global Modernities.* Eds. Mike Featherstone, Scott Lash, and Roland Robertson. London: Sage, 1995. 25–44.

Sandin, Bengt. "Coming to Terms with Child Labor: History of Child Welfare." *The World of Child Labor: An Historical and Regional Survey.* Ed. Hugh D. Hindman. London: Routledge, 2009. 53–56.

Smith, Angela. "Paddington Bear: A Case Study of Immigration and Otherness." *Children's Literature in Education* 37.1 (2006): 35–50.

Stewart, Susan. *On Longing: Narratives of the Miniature, the Gigantic, the Souvenir, the Collection.* Durham: Duke University Press, 2007.

Stockton, Kathryn Bond. *The Queer Child, or Growing Sideways in the Twentieth Century.* Durham: Duke University Press, 2009.

Tincknell, Estella. *Mediating the Family: Gender, Culture and Representation.* London: Hodder Arnold, 2005.

Ventura, Abbie E. "Post-Fordist Nation: The Economics of Childhood and the New Global Citizenship." *The Nation in Children's Literature: Nations of Childhood.* Eds. Christopher Kelen and Björn Sundmark. New York: Routledge, 2013. 235–245.

Weinstock, Jeffrey Andrew. "Mainstream Outsider: Burton Adapts Burton." *The Works of Tim Burton: Margins to Mainstream.* Ed. Jeffrey Andrew Weinstock. New York: Palgrave MacMillan, 2013. 1–29.

Wood, Robin. *Hollywood from Vietnam to Reagan . . . and Beyond.* New York: Columbia University Press, 2003.

Wyatt, Justin. *High Concept: Movies and Marketing in Hollywood.* Austin: University of Texas Press.

- 9 -

Grandparents and Grandchildren in *The Simpsons*

Intergenerational Rupture and Prefigurative Culture

MARIANO NARODOWSKI AND VERÓNICA GOTTAU

> Lisa, in these crazy times who knows what's right or wrong?
> My gut's telling me: Bleed Gramps dry.
> BART SIMPSON (*THE SIMPSONS*, S2E20)

As a television series that has been running for over a quarter of a century, and that has family relationships at his heart, *The Simpsons* provides a unique case study to explore the connection between childhood and old age in American popular culture. In this chapter we interpret the intergenerational relationships in *The Simpsons*, specifically those between grandchildren and grandparents, as an instance of "prefigurative culture"—a concept introduced by Margaret Mead in her classic work *Culture and Commitment* (1970), where she contrasts it with so-called postfigurative culture, where cultural transmission runs from the older members of a given society to the younger, and where changes are gradual and slow. When the technological paradigm for subsistence tends to reproduce itself without significant changes over time, when the community is not under the control of another community with different rules, or when there are no drastic ecological changes, accumulated experience throughout the generations is validated as common knowledge for a specific society (Mead, *Culture* 76). As a consequence, power relations in such postfigurative cultures center on those who have the most accumulated experience and whose knowledge is hence associated with more legitimacy. Indeed, in postfigurative cultures, the oldest people, the elderly, are respected for the knowledge that has been gathered in their own, relatively long lives and accumulated through various generations. The more a society relies on spoken language to pass on its knowledge, the more it will depend on the memory of its old people to bring it up to date. In contrast, access to written sources makes it possible for anyone with the requisite political or reading competences to refer to past sources.

As such, Mead argues, in prefigurative cultures, the monopoly of knowledge no longer lies in the hands of the elderly. As stated by the author: "I believe we are on the verge of developing a new kind of culture [. . .]. I call this new style prefigurative because in this new culture it will be the child — and not the parent and grandparent—that represents what is to come" (Mead, *Culture* 69). Mead raises the expectation that in postfigurative cultures, the elderly are loved and revered. The old people, as adults who represent accumulated knowledge, are consulted and obeyed. An asymmetry arises that is not necessarily based on domination but rather relies on collective certainty. The young no longer want to be young: it is in adulthood and old age where the most exalted values are to be found. The first years are a phase marked by the perception of lack. Childhood, adolescence, and youth are defined by the absence of maturity, knowledge, and experience, among others; absences that the mere passing of time will solve. The children simply have to wait (and prepare themselves) to become adults. This does not mean that the power of the elderly cannot be questioned. In *Culture and Commitment*, Mead notes that at certain times, young people may try to displace the old people from their powerful position. However, due to the postfigurative nature of their own cultural background, these young people do not contribute elements (whether technological or political) that help solve the problems of the present more efficiently than the traditional way. They cannot separate themselves from the inherited traditions that they share with the old people who they try to supplant in the exercise of power. In this sense, such rebellions, in fact, consolidate the existing criteria of power and confirm that senior citizens are most competent to rule.

In postfigurative cultures, education is understood as intergenerational interchange in broad terms, not only schooling. Émile Durkheim defines education as

> the influence exercised by adult generations on those that are not yet ready for social life. Its object is to develop in the child a certain number of physical, intellectual and moral states which are demanded of him by both the political society as a whole and the special milieu for which he is specifically destined. (237)

As this definition makes clear, intergenerational transmission depends on the conservation of a tradition in which old people are active ambassadors and the young are passive recipients until they grow old and assume the position that their elders pass down. A problem arises when the asymmetric and lineal model that is characteristic of postfigurative cultures (including the theoretical educational models based on Durkheim's definition) is applied to cultural models where violent and constant technological development, ecological changes, and/or migration have led to a decline of the adult-centered monopoly of knowledge.

From Postfigurative to Prefigurative Cultures

Mead studies the cultural changes typical of big Western cities in the 1970s, a time when a relative decline could be perceived in the weight of traditions and the importance of the elderly as social models or regulatory figures. Young adults and even children and adolescents became operators of greater legitimacy, as youth was established as a counterculture that challenged the power of the adult. In other words, in the context of prefigurative cultures, youth becomes the generalized parameter of legitimacy, while the old are rejected. In societies where rapid changes can be effectively processed only by those that have been directly brought up in them, accumulated experience becomes an obsolescent burden. As a consequence, the outlook, sexuality, and body aesthetic of adolescence receive social preeminence. In the American culture analyzed by Mead, the 1960s and 1970s became the watershed moment in which the young's clothing, musical taste, and looks shifted from the margins to the center, from being residual to nuclear. In many societies, cultural icons such as the Beatles, the protesters of May 1968, the leaders of the Black Panthers, or Che Guevara stood out for their anti-authoritarian stance, and they appear to have gradually disseminated their young aesthetic in all the regions of their culture. In this vein, in *L'empire de l'éphémère* (1987), Gilles Lipovetsky describes the cultural scenario of the new culture: the generalized ideal of a body immune to the passage of time and the concealment of white hair and wrinkles. A carefree attitude has replaced the rigid and inflexible symbols of a tradition that did not adjust to the violence of the current changes.

In this new prefigurative context, "without models and without precedent" (Mead, *Culture* 7), the rejection of a straightforward intergenerational transmission of knowledge and skills from grownups to children leaves an enormous interpretive hole each time that adults know less than the children. The young appear as models to their seniors, and the queries that arise cannot be effectively solved by tradition. This new fabric disrupts, as expected, the traditional family scheme and, within it, the bonds between grownups (parents, uncles, aunts, grandparents) and minors (children, nephews, nieces, and grandchildren). These bonds are transformed according to the new prefigurative logic and are triggered by urban, domestic, and technological mutations.

The Simpsons: A Typical Modern Family

The place of the elderly, especially grandparents, in prefigurative times appears to be doomed to permanent revision. To gain a better understanding of how this idea is reflected in popular culture, we will analyze the intergenerational relationships in *The Simpsons*, a cartoon released in the United States in 1987 that still runs to date. Our selection of *The Simpsons* as an interesting case study is based on two arguments. The first is the family structure that is central to the series. The nuclear family consists of Dad (Homer Simpson), Mom (Marge), and three children: Bart (ten years old); Lisa (eight years old), and Maggie, a baby who crawls. The extended family includes Homer's father, the eighty-year-old Grampa Abraham, and two aunts. In addition, Homer's mother, Mona Simpson, who is divorced from Abraham, makes sporadic appearances. Marge's parents, Clancy and Jackie Bouvier, appear in only a few episodes. Since they are rarely mentioned, we will not consider them as part of our analysis.[1]

The family structure of *The Simpsons* is conservative and traditional: a couple on their first marriage that has been together a number of years, with three small children in a period of around ten years. They live in a classic American middle-class family house in Springfield. Homer appears to be the breadwinner of the family; however, the maintenance of the family with only Homer's salary seems quite tight. The division of tasks seems to be clearly defined, as Homer never gets involved in household chores. As regards free time, the main activity of the family is to watch TV from their living room sofa. Except for Lisa, the family rarely displays any interest in cultural activities or politics. The exception is Sunday church service; religion is at the core of the everyday life of the family (Lewis). As stated by Paul Cantor, contrary to other mainstream American series since the 1960s, *The Simpsons* seems to have glorified the stable and traditional nuclear family. *The Simpsons* combines traditionalism with antitraditionalism (Cantor 737): it continually makes fun of the traditional American family, yet it offers an enduring image of the nuclear family in the very act of satirizing it. It can be argued that *The Simpsons* is profoundly anachronistic, since it hauls back family and political traditions that have been massively surpassed by American society. Even if it is possible, as Cantor (745) argues, that this anachronism is in harmony with Svetlana Boym's aesthetic construction of postmodern and reconstructive nostalgia, an awareness of the constant interplay between traditional and antitraditional practices allows for a better understanding of the presence of Grampa Abraham as an ambassador of tradition, as opposed to the grandchildren, representatives of a revealing alternative that breaks with the past. The second reason for selecting *The Simpsons* as a case study is the duration and globalization of the series. Born first as part of another series of the North American television network FOX, *The Simpsons* has been independent since 1989, with more than five hundred episodes and a significant global impact. As a result, the series has been the subject of academic scholarship, with countless studies covering various areas of research (Blakeborough; Gray; Rhodes; Scanlan and Feinberg).

The Simpsons and Prefigurative Culture

Even though the Simpsons appear in the series as a now-dated nuclear family with clearly defined gender roles, the series does not freeze these features in all the characters but rather reserves them for the protagonists. The rest of the inhabitants of Springfield represent more diverse types of families. In the course of the series, the Simpsons' neighbor Ned Flanders becomes a widower and raises his two small children alone; Apu the shopkeeper, an Indian immigrant, enters into an arranged marriage and has eight children; Skinner, the school principal, is a middle-aged man living with his mother; the parents of Bart's friend Milhouse are divorced and constantly fighting over custody; Aunt Selma engages in a same-sex relationship, and so forth. In Cantor's view (1999), *The Simpsons* thematizes both the resistance and the endurance of a traditional family in a context that is increasingly breaking with traditions.

Is this ambivalence also reflected when it comes to age norms? Grampa Abraham is—paradoxically—part of the antitraditional stance of the nuclear family in *The Simpsons*. Grampa lives in a retirement home where he shares his life with other senior citizens and is assisted by medical and paramedical staff. In one of the earliest episodes of the series, Lisa makes clear that Grampa did not move there voluntarily, when she asks "Remember the fight he put up when we put him in the home?" (S1E5). The move is not motivated by a lack of room at the Simpsons' house (in fact, they host several long stays along the series), or by the absence of family members that can help in his everyday life. Nor is it the only form of rejection that Abraham suffers at the hands of his offspring: at the retirement home, he is constantly waiting for visits, which rarely occur. When Grampa goes and visits the Simpsons, the family openly expresses its annoyance and complains loudly about the old man. Grampa Abraham wants to participate in family life, but his attempts are systematically rejected, with total disregard for good manners. Instead, the old man is met with aggressiveness and peevishness.

The retirement home is portrayed as a dumping ground for old people, as a place of permanent confinement, which differs significantly from the nuclear family's home. This treatment of the elderly is an important element of the Simpsons' antitraditional stance: the postfigurative logic to the nuclear family gets aborted at the moment when the old man is no longer treated as an authority for the family, but rather as a heavy burden, which is eased only through the confinement to a specific and clearly differentiated habitat (Mead, *Culture* 79). This displacement of the old man to the retirement home signals a transition to prefigurative logic in terms of cultural legitimacy and valuation. This shift is illustrated when the family discusses Grampa Abraham on the way back from a rare visit to the home:

> BART: Grampa smells like that trunk with the wet bottom.
> LISA: He smells like a photo lab.
> HOMER: Stop it! Grampa smells like an old man, which is like a hospital hallway.
> MARGE: That's terrible! We should teach them to value the elderly. We'll be old someday.
> HOMER: My God, you're right! You kids won't put me in a home? Well . . .
> [Bart smiles sarcastically]
> HOMER: [worried] Er, Marge, what'll we do?
> MARGE: Well, I think we better set an example.
> HOMER: Absolutely! Our Sundays should be a pleasure. Where's a fun place we can take Grampa? (S2E17)

Marge and Homer's sympathy for Grampa mainly seems to stem from the realization that they too will be old one day (a pattern that resembles the

A-frame discussed in Sung Ae Lee's chapter in this volume), rather than from respect for the old man's knowledge or experience. In this context, and somewhat paradoxically, Grampa Abraham continues to act as the ambassador of tradition, despite the mockery and rejection. Many of his lines start with "In my times..." and are loaded with an enormous moral weight. The letter that he writes to a TV advertising company illustrates Grampa's "that is how it ought to be" stance:

> GRANDPA: Dear Advertisers, I am disgusted with the way old people are depicted on television. We are not all vibrant, fun-loving sex maniacs. Many of us are bitter, resentful individuals who remember the good old days when entertainment was bland and inoffensive. The following is a list of words I never want to hear on television again. ... (S1E5)

The quotation makes clear that the bitterness that results from having his experience rejected over again does not stop Grampa from insisting on the position of authority that the elderly hold in postfigurative cultures.

Grampa is not the sole major character in the series to represent his generation. Montgomery Burns, the owner of the nuclear plant that employs Homer, is of the same age. Both went through some similar experiences in their youth and share some features in senescence. Like Grampa, Burns's senility and general impotence represent a caricature of his old age, and the show frequently ridicules the way he perceives the past and articulates his memories. Unlike Grampa, however, Burns is not a grandfather and never raised a child: his son Larry grew up in an orphanage. He does not have family bonds but hardly ever appears without his docile personal assistant Waylon Smithers, who fantasizes about a sexual relationship with Burns. In this elderly dyad, Burns—as opposed to Abraham—is feared, respected, and desired: his whims tend to be satisfied, and his sometimes absurd perceptions of reality, similar to those of Abraham, are usually covered up. Neither Homer nor Bart dares laugh at the senile businessman in his face. Contrary to Abraham, Burns does not pontificate or rule, nor is he depicted as an ambassador of the past. On the contrary, his wealth and business position are enough to be obeyed. In essence, the two old men of the series represent parallel articulations of old age. Burns derives legitimacy from his socioeconomic status, but he has no offspring to whom he can impart knowledge or values. In contrast, Abraham has children and grandchildren, but he does not have the means to legitimate himself. Neither of the men is ultimately capable of leaving a legacy, or of transmitting the traditions they take pride in. In what follows, we will further analyze Grampa's prefigurative position in three paradigmatic situations of the series: the good babysitter, helping the grandchildren, and helping Grampa.[2]

The Good Babysitter

One of the roles attributed to Grampa is the care of the children when the parents go out or travel. This structure appears for the first time in the twentieth episode of the second season. There, Homer and Marge originally want to hire a babysitter, but the employee withdraws when she remembers the children's outrageous behavior. As a substitute, they call Grampa Abraham, which instigates a long process of denigration. The old man is required only as a last resort, and it is assumed that he is always available. Once he is occupied with the chore of looking after the grandchildren, they never stop mocking Grampa, to the extent that in the middle of a wild party, Milhouse summarizes the situation as follows (S2E20): "There is party at the Simpsons' house; the only adult is frail and old." When the party finishes, the house is in complete chaos, and Grampa is crying on the sofa, saying: "I tried to be a good baby-sitter, but I failed. I'm a feeb, a useless, old, worn-out . . ." Lisa and Bart then feel touched and start cleaning the house, after which Grampa laughs out loud, trying to hide from his grandchildren that he faked crying. This leads to a moment of triumph when the parents return (S2E20):

> MARGE: Oh, my, the house looks wonderful. Grampa, what's your secret?
> GRAMPA: Pretending to cry. [Chuckling] That's right. You heard me. Pretending to cry!
> LISA: Way to go, Grampa.
> BART: I'll never trust another old person.
> GRAMPA: I fooled you! So long, suckers! [Laughing]

It is noteworthy how Grampa and the grandchildren appear as equals trying to probe each other's limits. At no moment are feelings of care or protection expressed among them. In the end, the guilt that the grandchildren feel after Grampa's fake cry and pretended complaint is immediately betrayed by the cynical retort of their elder, whose only possible resource when facing the challenge of the children is to feign pain.

Helping the Grandchildren

Whereas the previous analysis lays bare the ageism related to old age in *The Simpsons*, the children are not immune to age-related prejudices either. In one episode (S4E19), Bart and Lisa present a script for an episode of *Itchy and Scratchy*, their favorite TV cartoon, but it is not accepted because they are not adults. Once again, Grampa's help is needed:

> LISA: Maybe he just doesn't take us seriously 'cause we're kids. Let's put a grownup's name on it.
> BART: How about Grampa? He's pretty out of it. He let those guys use his checkbook for a whole year.
> [When they arrive at the home, Grampa is writing a letter of complaint.]
> GRAMPA: When I read your magazine I don't see one wrinkled face or single toothless grin. For shame! To the sickos at *Modern Bride Magazine*.
> BART: Hey, Grampa, we need to know your first name.
> GRAMPA [gasps]: You're making my tombstone!
> LISA: No! We're just curious.
> GRAMPA: All right, let's see. First name. Well, whenever I'm confused I just check my underwear. It holds the answer to all the important questions. Call me Abraham Simpson.

The joint experience of age-related prejudices does not produce any connection between the children and their grandfather. In fact, ageist assumptions motivate Bart and Lisa to seek Grampa's help, as they assume he will be easy to fool ("He's pretty out of it"). This scene not only ridicules the old but also takes aim at political correctness. Grampa chooses an inappropriate target (*Modern Bride Magazine*) for his critique of the invisibility of the old in the media—a point of criticism that has been repeatedly raised in a more serious context (see, among others, ICAA; Klein and Schiffman; McClintock Greenberg). The scene reinforces the image of the elderly as being out of tune with reality. In order to become useful, Grampa needs to give up his identity—here symbolized by his name, which the children use as their alias. Throughout the episode, Grampa always gives his name unwillingly to his grandchildren and is critical of the cartoon's content. But his criticism goes completely unnoticed: complaints fall on deaf ears in a prefigurative context in which the figure of the old person is necessary only to sign a contract. To Bart and Lisa, none of his experience or opinions are worthy of consideration; neither are they incorporated in the task carried out by the children. It is the children who possess the monopoly of legitimate knowledge.

Helping Grampa

One of the most emblematic episodes regarding the relationship between Grampa and the grandchildren is entitled: *Raging Abe Simpson and His Grumbling Grandson in "The Curse of the Flying Hellfish"* (S7E22). The episode starts with Grandparents Day at Springfield Elementary School. All the children go with their grandparents.

> [Grampa Abraham Simpson spits on the floor.]
> BART [ashamed]: Grampa! I don't mind when you spit at home, but I have to work with these people!
> GRAMPA: Oh, jabber jacks! Schoolhouse don't put out spittoons, I ain't responsible.
> TEACHER: All right, seniors, we'd all love to share in your wisdom, experience. Let's start with Milhouse's grandfather.

Grampa then makes fun of those who are in the spotlight, and Bart feels ashamed. When it is his turn to go to the front, Bart does not want him to go. Grampa claims to have invented the toilet and once again puts his grandson to shame. Back at home, Bart tells everyone at dinner about the embarrassment at school and wonders why Grampa is always making up crazy stories.

> HOMER: Maybe it's time we put Grampa in a retirement home.
> LISA: You already put him in a home.
> BART: Maybe it's time we put him in one where he can't get out.
> LISA: Nooo. Old people deserve our respect. They are not second-class citizens.

In this case, as well as in others, Lisa represents the voice of political correctness: her statements are void, with only symbolic value and without any practical consequences. The episode both addresses and confirms the ageist stereotype of the old as useless and embarrassing. Grampa, however, reasserts his claim to wisdom and authority. In a later scene of the same episode, he shares with Bart his experiences as a soldier during World War II. He was part of the same squadron as Mister Burns: once again, we see the two elderly men appearing in a dyad. The squadron discovers a cache of valuable artworks and hides it with the agreement that the last member of the group (called Hellfish) would take possession of the fortune. Bart dismisses Grampa's story as fiction:

> BART: Great story, Grampa. Could've used a vampire, though.
> GRAMPA [sobs]: My own grandson thinks I'm a liar.

At that moment, Burns himself appears on the scene to force Abraham to confess where the treasure is hidden. Bart gradually realizes that Grampa's story is true and thinks he can keep the treasure himself. Finally, it is Burns who manages to achieve his goal. Bart gets trapped at the bottom of the sea, and Abraham submerges himself in the water to save him. The episode closes as follows:

> GRAMPA: Well, at least I got to show you I wasn't always a pathetic old kook.
> BART: You never were, Grampa.
> GRAMPA: Oh, I'd hug ya, but I know you'd just get embarrassed.
> BART: I won't get embarrassed. I don't care who knows I love my grandpa.

This is the only registered situation where Grampa and his grandson enter into an emotional relation of mutual understanding, protection, and care. However, to reach that attachment, Grampa had to show that he was a hero, could have been rich, and was able to save his grandson from death.

In contrast, in various episodes, the grandchildren are presented as helping Grampa resolve problems that require a youthful perspective, while remaining disdainful of the older person's experience. This prefigurative structure of the intergenerational link can be observed, for example, in an episode from the eleventh season, when Lisa gets the old people at Grampa's retirement home a Wii, a video game device (S21E11, "Homer the Whopper"). After the elderly initially complain that it is not a television, they start having fun playing tennis, which encourages them to be very active; the nurses, however, break the Wii on purpose, because, in their opinion, it stimulates the elderly too much. Once again, the old people are then placed in front of a television that emits only static images. The nurses claim that looking after old people is the worst job in the world, with a low salary and the constant presence of death. Lisa retorts that they should allow the senior citizens to have fun; the nurses sharply state that they should have had their share of fun before entering the retirement home.

The old people in the retirement home are portrayed as disempowered and infantilized by the middle generation, whom they are at the mercy of. Unlike the middle-aged, the young imagine new and unknown possibilities for the old, but they lack the power to change something for the better. Lisa, for example, may desire to break down institutional barriers, but she is as limited by her non-adult status as the elderly are by their old age. When the young and old connect in a way that empowers both, as in this episode, that bond is soon shattered by the middle generation, which appears only to care about its own needs. In spite of the humorous tone of the series, its criticism of institutionalized care for the elderly should not be dismissed as unserious. As Jenny Hockey and Allison James would argue, "age impacts very powerfully on the way we see ourselves—and are seen by others" ("Social Identities" 3), and, paradoxically, there is a growing tendency to attribute childlike characteristics to the elderly (*Growing Up* 10).

Beyond Parody

According to Albert Taylor (1998), grandparents may be the key agents in restoring a sense of continuity in their grandchildren's lives. In a traditional and postfigurative culture, as Mead confirms, grandparents are representations of continuity in that they have lived through and adjusted to more change than any generation in history. As "living repositories of change," Mead argues in "Grandparents as Educators" (1974), grandparents are best able to help adolescents and young adults know who they are. They do so by providing the young with direct connections to the past, a sense of continuity over time, and a sense of confidence for facing the future. Evidently, this is not the case in the relationships between Abraham and his grandchildren. The figure of Grampa may indeed represent a tenuous line of continuity to the past, but this link is completely delegitimized. As stated before, mockery and scorning of the old is customary, especially from Homer and Bart, a practice that tends to be highlighted through contrast with Lisa's politically correct language. Grampa no longer appears as a treasurer of experience that ensures the continuity with the past, but rather as a witness of times that are best forgotten, a connoisseur of obsolete certainties, a protagonist of phrases and attitudes that ought to be cruelly rejected, and the carrier of a worn-out, tired body that reminds the young of death. Ultimately, respect for the old person (Grampa Abraham or Burns) is portrayed solely as a by-product of material interests; it is feigned only so long as the older person can be used to advantage; and it is not undergirded by genuine feelings of care, admiration, or emotional reciprocity.

What is the logic or ideology that underlies these intergenerational interactions between the old man and the children who are tied by blood? What meanings can we attribute to the mockery, disdain, and cruelty that the old are subjected to in *The Simpsons*? It is clear that *The Simpsons* constitutes a television satire in which it is possible to corroborate the changes in contemporary ("global") societies: through a structure of reiteration, it depicts societies and their tendencies ironically. The parodic tone is sometimes evident; other times it is less overt, and often contradictory, argues Chantal Herskovic (2011). The deliberately grotesque representation of the grandfather can be interpreted as an exaggeration of qualities of the physical weaknesses and cultural obsolescence of the elderly, as well as the rejection of affection in American society's discourse on old age. *The Simpsons* parodies not only the typical American family but also, and especially, its televisual representations. As Jonathan Gray (2006) points out, "the force of its depiction of suburbia comes from its negation of depictions offered by countless other traditional family sitcoms. The family sitcom, suburban paradise, in good cliché style, like ball-games and hot dogs" (137).

The exact meaning of this parody has led to divergent views among scholars. On the one hand, Daniel Blakeborough (2008) supposes that while on the surface the show appears to mock older people, it criticizes, in fact, society's disrespectful view of the elderly, calling instead for a reevaluation. According to Jason Gillespie (2012), *The Simpsons* is unique in calling for a critique of established ageist stereotypes and opens the door for their possible subversion:

> While these familiar stereotypes exist within the larger social structure and are repeated ad nauseam in our cultural texts, there exists a means by which such representations can be historicized, contextualized, probed, questioned, undermined, and subverted: With the opening of a critical discourse through the satiric and ironic parodizations of such representations on *The Simpsons*, we can look into the ideology that drives these portrayals in the mass media and our culture. (16)

Then again, some other studies show that in the American cartoon tradition, the bonds between old and young people are far removed from the way they are represented in *The Simpsons*. For example, Hugh Klein and Kenneth S. Schiffman (2009), analyzing TV cartoons in the twentieth century, found almost exclusively positive portrayals of the elderly. Their study yielded that older people were usually portrayed as "good guys," had above-average intelligence, and did not differ from their younger counterparts in their level of physical attractiveness or prosocial and antisocial acts. As Gillespie (17) shows, television portrayals of older people in both primetime television and television programming intended for children follow a trend of under-representation but differ in their overall positive depiction of older people.

These trends and interpretations enable the inference that *The Simpsons* in fact parodies old series and sitcoms of American television in which old people had a central, harmonious, and balanced role within the expected limits of a postfigurative culture that admired and respected the elderly. This hyperbole, which magnifies the decline of the grandparents' authority in *The Simpsons*, suggests that the rise of prefigurative culture can explain contemporary society's incapacity to facilitate meaningful intergenerational links. Indeed, the connection with past traditions that the elderly might represent is buried under the cynicism and cruelty of the younger characters. More than a denunciation of stereotypes, *The Simpsons* is an ironic and disconsolate expression of the end of a culture in which grandparents guided their grandchildren in their growth. In line with Pierre Schoentjes's conception of irony in *Poétique de 1'Ironie*, we argue that it is a brutal closure of the old postfigurative lineage, which is replaced with a prefigurative model in which cultural legitimacy is held only by the new generations.[3] This can be observed in particular in the aforementioned "Raging Abe Simpson" (S7E22), where Grampa is depicted as being embarrassing to his grandchildren, and also in "Homer the Whopper" (S21E1), which shows institutionalized and infantilized old people playing with the Wii and at the mercy of young and middle-aged adults.

According to Naomi Bell Cornman O'Neil (2007), when grandchildren do not have a relationship with their grandparents, the younger generation lacks a cultural and historical sense of self. When young adults, with strong intergenerational ties, experience life events, O'Neil argues, they may recall how their own grandparents acted in similar situations or what their grandparents said to them. However, when the transmission of historical and cultural knowledge loses value, when intergenerational references are relegated to confined institutions, when the mere idea of sharing everyday life with an old person provokes resistance, this lack is no longer perceived as a weakness but rather as strength. Any attempt to reconstruct it seems only to provoke a brutal and ironic backlash that suppresses memory of an era already surpassed.

Notes

1. All these character profiles are vailable at *The Simpsons' Wikiaweb* page: http://simpsons.wikia.com.

2. We have checked all episodes from all seasons, and there is no record of any change in the bonds between grandparents and grandchildren throughout time. The paragraphs taken as examples are representative of similar scenes in the cartoon.

3. The narrative force of this displacement is so strong that it produces a feeling of nostalgia for the old forms of infancy and old age.

Works Cited

Blakeborough, Daniel. "'Old People Are Useless': Representations of Aging on *The Simpsons*." *Canadian Journal of Aging* 27.1 (2008): 219–236.

Boym, Svetlana. *The Future of Nostalgia*. New York: Basic Books, 2001.

Cantor, Paul. "The Simpsons: Atomistic Politics and the Nuclear Family." *Political Theory* 27.6 (1999): 1–22

Durkheim, Émile. *Education et sociologie*. Paris: Presses Universitaires de France,1968.

Gillespie, Jason R. The Portrayal of Older People in Marketing Materials for Senior Centers. Diss. Brigham Young University, 2012.

Gray, Jonathan. *Watching with* The Simpsons: *Television, Parody, and Intertextuality*. New York: Routledge, 2006.

Hockey, Jenny L., and Allison James. *Growing Up and Growing Old: Ageing and Dependency in the Life Course*. London: Sage, 1993.

Hockey, Jenny L., and Allison James. *Social Identities across the Life Course*. Hampshire: Palgrave Macmillan, 2003.

Herskovic, Chantal. "Chegando a Springfield: Humor e sátira na série Os Simpsons." *Revista USP* 88 (2011): 100–111.

ICAA. "Ageism: How Negative Stereotypes of Aging Impede an Inclusive Society." *US Department of Health and Human Services* (29 May 2013). http://health.gov/paguidelines/blog/post/Ageism.aspx. Accessed on 21 April 2016.

Klein, Hugh, and Kenneth S. Schiffman. "Underrepresentation and Symbolic Annihilation of Socially Disenfranchised Groups ("Out Groups") in Animated Cartoons." *Howard Journal of Communications* 20.1 (2009): 55–72.

Lewis, Thomas. "Religious Rhetoric and the Comic Frame in *The Simpsons*." *Journal of Media and Religion* 1.3 (2002): 153–165.

Lipovetsky, Gilles. 1987. *L'empire de l'éphémère: La mode et son destin dans les sociétés modernes*. Paris: Gallimard, 1991.

Mead, Margaret. *Culture and Commitment: The New Relationships between the Generations in the 1970s*. Garden City: Anchor Press, 1978.

Mead, Margaret. "Grandparents as Educators." *Teachers College Records* 76.2 (1974): 45–52.

McClintock Greenberg, Tamara. "The Invisible Years: Thoughts on Why the Elderly Become Invisible." *Psychology Today* (11 August 2009). https://www.psychologytoday.com/blog/21st-century-aging/200908/the-invisible-years. Accessed on 21 April 2016.

O'Neil, Naomi Bell Cornman. Socialization of Grandchildren by Their Grandparents about Attitudes and Beliefs of Love and Marriage. PhD diss. Ohio State University, 2007.

Rhodes, Carl. "D'Oh: The Simpsons, Popular Culture, and the Organizational Carnival." *Journal of Management Inquiry* 10.4 (2001): 374.

Scanlan, Stephen J., and Seth L. Feinberg. "The Cartoon Society: Using 'The Simpsons' to Teach and Learn Sociology." *Teaching Sociology* 28.2 (2000): 127–139.

Schoentjes, Pierre . *Poétique de 1'Ironie*. Paris: Seuil, 2001.

The Simpsons. FOX. 1989–2015.

Taylor, Alan C. Perceptions of Intergenerational Bonds: The Comparison between Grandfathers and Their Grandchildren. Diss. Virginia Tech University, 1998.

- 10 -

Sustaining and Transgressing Borders

The Relationship between Children and the Elderly in Mad Men

CECILIA LINDGREN AND JOHANNA SJÖBERG

Children and the elderly are, in various contexts, portrayed as ideal companions and positioned as "others" in relation to the more powerful generation in between (Hockey and James 2–5; Joosen 128, 136–138;). In children's literature, for example, the relationship between the two age groups tends to be romanticized, featuring their mutual interests in nature, animals, fantasy, and storytelling. In this chapter we explore how the two categories meet in the award-winning drama TV series *Mad Men*. The aim is to scrutinize the link between childhood and old age, by analyzing how the relationships between a young girl, Sally Draper, and her elderly relatives are played out. Exploring key scenes, we show how the companionship between children and the elderly is constructed as rewarding for both parties, yet as provocative and challenging rather than romantic and harmless.

Mad Men is produced by Matthew Weiner and was originally broadcast by the US channel AMC. Since then, it has been featured in at least three dozen countries across America, Europe, the Middle East, Asia, and Australia (Edgerton xxi). It premiered in July 2007, and the seventh and final season was aired in 2015. *Mad Men* centers on a fictional Madison Avenue advertising agency in the 1960s and '70s, featuring the working lives and personal relations of men and women at the office. The series has been praised for its production and accuracy in period detail. It has also received criticism for stereotypical depictions of, among others, cigarette and alcohol consumption and for implicitly approving sexism (Ferrucci, Shoenberger, and Schauster 93). Researchers from several fields have found *Mad Men* worthy of scholarly study.[1] Even though time, age, and intergenerational relationships are central to the plot, only a few studies (Baruah; Dole; Marcovitch and Batty) draw attention to these aspects.

Mad Men pays great attention to period detail and integrates significant historic events in its storyline, yet most scholars agree that the series is not, and should not be read as, a historic reconstruction of the period in which it is set (Batty 192; Beail and Goren 4, 22; Black and Driscoll 190; Goodlad, Kaganovsky, and Rushing 2; Polan 36, 48). Rather, the series uses historical fiction to say something about our present and to address issues that are ever so urgent, such as sexism, racism, family relations, and child-rearing (Baruah 13; Batchelor 70; Colton Josephson 272; Wilson and Lane 77). Linda Beail and Lilly Goren (2015) argue that *Mad Men* tells stories "that illuminate our continuing political dilemmas of freedom, identity, inclusion, consumption, and authenticity" (4), and they point out that the show's creator, Matthew Weiner, has described it as science fiction set in the past. Telling stories that take place in the 1960s, however, also serves to challenge popular and idealizing narratives about this period. *Mad Men* subverts nostalgia and destabilizes romantic notions of life, and specifically family life, in the postwar era (Baruah 3–13; Colton Josephson 261–263).

Julia Wilson and Joseph Lane (2012) read the series as a text about family and child-rearing, portraying a family that constantly fails to live up to both past and present expectations. They conclude that "Mad Men operates to invoke our idealizations of family life and then to collapse them" (83). The children in the series serve as identification points and offer a moral corrective, and Sally Draper in particular has been put forward as a key to understanding the series' perspective and relationship to the past (Baruah 8; Batty 196, 202; Beail and Goren 21, 24; Dole 185; Marcovitch and Batty xii). As Nancy Batty (2012) so elegantly puts it, however, the *Mad Men* children are often excluded from the adult world and are "either viewers of the adult dramas enacted around them or exiled to their rooms, left to ponder what the future will hold for them" (203).

In the course of the series, the characters grow older and evolve. Intergenerational relationships are brought to the fore as several characters experience difficulties with their parents, in-laws, or children. Moreover, generational gaps between older and younger professionals at the agency are one of the show's central themes (Baruah 9–10; Miggelbrink 8). Dafna Lemish and Varda Muhlbauer (165–166) point out that media images travel around the world in a profit-driven market. Representations of gender and age categories in television and film are thus influential and should be subjected to critical analysis (Lepianka 1096). We argue that studying children and the elderly, and so-called intergenerational bonds (Taylor 12), in *Mad Men* can deepen our understanding of how the two age categories are constructed and presented in visual media for an international audience.

Visual Representations of Children and the Elderly

Chronological age and age categories shape most societies. Age norms, akin to a socially constructed clock, constitute expectations about appropriate times and ages for particular achievements and transitions in life. Hence, age is socially constructed (Krekula, Närvänen, and Näsman 83), and so are the borders for childhood and senescence. Being classified as a child or an old person carries with it various expectations and prejudices (Fineman 3). The result is an order that is not natural or neutral, but culturally constructed and hierarchical. The construction of age is, similar to constructions of gender and ethnicity, closely connected to relations of power (Fineman 56–57; Krekula, Närvänen, and Näsman 83).

Visual media studies on age are rare, compared to studies on gender or ethnicity. There are studies focusing on, for example, the dissonances between the proportion of elderly people in society and their visibility on TV. Media researchers Tim Healey and Karen Ross (105–106) and Lemish and Muhlbauer (166–167) argue that the television landscape mostly comprises younger adults, that is, the middle generation, and that older people are generally underrepresented. They are typically cast to play secondary characters in supporting roles and are represented in a stereotypical manner. Aging is furthermore often negatively constructed and characterized by the absence of good health and mental clarity, and as a period of helplessness, physical vulnerability, dependency, meanness, bitterness and lack of productivity (Lemish and Muhlbauer 166; Lepianka 1108). Representations of the elderly on television hence support the dominant "decline narrative" of growing old (Gullette 6–7). Particularly underrepresented and negatively stereotyped in media are older women. The powerful female image of motherhood is replaced by the controlling and nagging old mother or mother-in-law. Older women are less likely than older men to be presented as authority figures, for example at a workplace, and their bodies are often displayed as objects of ridicule rather than as sexual bodies of desire. Consequently, they suffer from the double marginalization of age and gender (Lemish and Muhlbauer 169–171).

Children too are an underrepresented category, yet they are seen in a range of visual imagery (Holland). Karen Lury (2010) has studied children in films produced for an adult audience. Taking an interest in how children are seen to participate in the adult world, she examines whether and how children's subjectivity, emotions, experiences, and thoughts can be represented, and questions whether it is possible to identify and represent the "childish-ness of the child" (10). Lury argues that, from a filmmaker's point of view, the children's contribution is to allow for different types of reflections and filmic worlds. Anne Higonnet (1998) has argued that contemporary pictures and art showing children indicate a turning point in how children are visually defined. Although most images are romantic, showing innocent children, a "knowing child" is portrayed more and more frequently—a child who understands more about the adult world than the notion of the innocent child would allow. The "knowing" child is not presented as easily accessible or controllable, or as an object for visual pleasure. Instead of being placed in their own protected world, children are subjects in a multifaceted existence. These children are, however, also potentially appalling, since they do not easily fit the norms of childhood (Higonnet 12, 207). In her analysis of the mediation of family and childhood in popular culture, and especially in film and on TV from the 1950s onward, Estella Tincknell (2005) observes a greater flexibility in how children are presented. She argues that the idea of childhood is currently being challenged and that rigid divisions between knowledge and innocence, and between adulthood and childhood, are destabilized (Tincknell 98–101).

To find studies specifically dealing with the relationship between children and the elderly in fiction, one can turn to research on children's literature. In her study on contemporary children's books and young-adult fiction, Vanessa Joosen (128) finds that a relationship with an older person is portrayed as beneficial for children and their development, in that it fosters their imagination, agency, and emotional strength. She addresses the trope of "the wise old mentor," an elderly person who "guides the young to knowledge and understanding" (131). Even though this entails a positive image of the elderly, it has been criticized for being one-dimensional. Because wisdom is typically associated with balanced reflection, it tends to exclude strong feelings, such as anger or passion, and the elderly are depicted as having no needs of their own (131).

Family Relations in *Mad Men*

The characters in *Mad Men* are numerous and complex. Due to experimental storytelling techniques (Miggelbrink 2–4), some of them occur frequently, while others are present in only one episode or season, never to return again or to stay absent for a long time. Most characters are men and women in their twenties, thirties, or forties. They live busy lives at work, and/or they function as parents and housewives in the city and the local community. Don Draper (Jon Hamm) is the leading character in the show. He is a creative genius, a businessman, and also an army deserter, a womanizer, and a fraud (Falklof 31–32). Together with Betty (January Jones), he has two boys and a girl.

Sally Draper (Kiernan Shipka), born in 1954, is the oldest of Don and Betty's three children and represents the American "baby boomer generation." As Nancy Batty (194–196) illustrates, some viewers may have memories and experiences that through Sally can be reevaluated. It is, however, important to point out that most viewers, from various countries and age groups, do not have any personal connections to the time, place, or lifestyle portrayed in *Mad Men* (Batty 192). Sally has been described as one of the most vexed characters in the series (Polan 50). She is also the most prominent of the children in the series, becoming more central to the storyline as she grows older (Baruah 8; Beail and Goren 21). Don, who is described as having a genuine love for his children, does not live up to the image of the good father, as he is portrayed as selfish, often drunk, and preoccupied with work, constantly failing his promises to the children (Falklof 39–41). Housewife Betty is not portrayed as an ideal parent either (Davidson 141), coming across instead as narcissistic, immature, and dissatisfied (Tudor 337). Parents, and the middle generation at large, expect Sally and other children to obey adults; in return they are cared for and protected, which often means being excluded from actions and information (Batty 203).

Betty's father, Gene Hofstadt, a widower in his seventies, is portrayed as having a close relationship with his granddaughter Sally. In the third season, he starts showing signs of dementia and moves into the Drapers' house. Later in the same season, he passes away. Compared to other elderly characters, such as the protagonists' parents and in-laws, and particularly the young-at-heart advertising boss Bertrand Cooper, Gene is a stereotypical weakened old man. After Betty remarries in season four, the children are, to Sally's dislike, sometimes left in the care of their new step-grandmother, Pauline Francis, a corpulent housewife in her sixties or early seventies. Pauline, who has a peripheral role in the series, is constructed as a firm and in some respects bitter lady.

Sally, Gene and Pauline represent two age groups, children and the elderly, that are excluded from the busy professional sphere where the main plots in the series are played out. They are primarily seen in the domestic sphere, at times assigned only to each other. In such scenes, "intergenerational bonding" is brought to the fore. Predominantly, Mad Men reproduces the middle generation as the powerful norm, while children and elderly are set aside as "others," bound to act their age. Some interesting scenes in the series take place when the young and the old interact together, escaping the supervision of the parents or other adults.

Analyzing Key Scenes

By analyzing key scenes we aim to scrutinize the roles and relationships ascribed to children and the elderly. Emphasis is put on the visual material itself, as we explore how Mad Men as a visual form of meaning making constructs specific views of the social world (Rose 146–147). Consequently, we do not analyze the production site or study how the series is interpreted by its audiences. Our analyses of how the relationship between children and the elderly is constructed do not aim to test the series' representation in relation to research about family life and family norms in the United States in the 1960s. Instead, when scrutinizing how borders of childhood are sustained, stretched, and transgressed, we refer to age norms established within the series itself. There are several examples of how Sally's parents, and especially Don, set limits for what children should do and know about, and thereby define borders of childhood: children should not know about politics (S1E12), attend funerals (S3E5), watch upsetting news (S3E12; see also Batty 203), or do things that are "too dangerous," such as horseback riding (S2E1). Children should not wear women's boots or makeup (S5E7), and they should definitely not be smoking (S2E12) or exploring their sexuality (S4E5). Furthermore, grandparents are expected to respect these boundaries and, for instance, not let children know too much about war or death (S3E4). The parents' obvious ambitions to keep childhood and adulthood separate make the relationship between children and the elderly in the series particularly interesting.

The analysis focuses on two episodes in which the relationship between the old and the young is brought to the fore: "The Arrangements" from the third season, and "Mystery Date" from season five. The material consists of five scenes where children and the elderly spend time together. Two scenes focus on Sally and her grandfather, and another three on her and her step-grandmother. Our analysis will concentrate on verbal and visual actions that construct age relations between the child and the elderly. What characteristics and actions are ascribed to the child, Sally, and what to her grandfather and step-grandmother, Gene and Pauline? How are the roles of children and the elderly negotiated and contested? For analytical purposes, the scenes were transcribed, with a left column describing the course of events, nonverbal actions and camera angles, and a right column accounting for audible dialogue. The two were matched according to the timing of the sequence. In the following, we include print screen images, descriptive text, dialogue extracts, and two-column excerpts to present the analyzed material.

In the analysis we make use of the concepts of "gatekeeper" and "enabler" to characterize what goes on between the characters and what roles they take on in relation to norms of childhood and grandparenthood. These concepts have previously been used in various fields of study, such as psychology, medicine, informatics, sociology, and education, and with different meanings depending on the context (Barzilai-Nahon; Ehmann et al.). Here, we use "gatekeeper" to describe a person whom one has to pass to enter certain territories (literally or symbolically), to do certain things or to get certain information. The gatekeeper has the power and means to prevent someone else from doing something or from accessing information. We use "enabler" to describe a person who allows for something to happen or who makes it possible for someone to do something that he or she would not be able to accomplish without help or support.

An Empowering and Challenging Companionship

In the episode "The Arrangements," Sally is about eight or nine years old and spends quite a lot of time together with her grandfather Gene, who now lives with the Draper family. The two contrasting scenes to be analyzed here illustrate how the child and the old person can be ascribed very different roles in the same setting—going to school by car.

"You Got to Really Pay Attention"

The first scene starts with Sally, Bobby, and Gene leaving the house, walking toward a parked car. In the next cut the viewer sees Bobby in the backseat

Figure 10.1. Sally drives (*Mad Men*, "The Arrangements," 00:59).

while hearing Gene's voice commenting on the houses they drive by: "I don't care if it's windy or rainy. There's no reason for a shake roof to fail if it's laid right. Except for that one. No flashing around the chimney. That's gonna cost them."

Cut and camera movement first prevent the viewer from seeing where Gene and Sally are placed in the car. Therefore, it takes a few seconds to realize that Gene, who becomes visible in the front passenger seat, is not driving, as would be expected. Instead, it is Sally, dressed in a stiff white shirt and checked jacket, who drives the car (Figure 10.1). She looks concentrated, while Gene is relaxed. He starts shouting at a car honking at them from behind: "GO AROUND!" They seem to be moving too slowly. Gene turns to Sally and says: "Now I'm gonna push it up to 25 miles an hour. That's what we're allowed to do here." Sally does not reach the pedals, but Gene presses the gas with his left foot from the side. He controls the pedals while she steers the wheel. Bobby, in the backseat, looks relaxed. Both Sally and Gene look straight ahead, their eyes on the road. In an encouraging voice, Gene says to Sally, "You got to really pay attention." As she keeps going along the road, she starts smiling.

In this scene Sally is positioned by Gene as an adult. He lets her do something that is not allowed for a child her age, and he is also talking to her as an adult, about the construction of roofs in the neighborhood. Nevertheless, her inability to reach down to the pedals, which means that she needs help to drive, signals that she is in fact a child. She is a child doing what adults do. At first her facial expression reveals that she is out of place, but then her smile says that she accepts the role of a child visiting the adult world, and that she enjoys it.

To do what adults do, Sally is, however, dependent on Gene in several ways. For her to drive the car he must give permission, and he must operate the gas and brake pedals. In this scene, Gene acts as an enabler, making it possible for Sally to transgress the borders of childhood. He also lets her do something that is obviously not allowed, that could be dangerous, and that her parents would certainly not approve of. So, is Gene portrayed as a senile old man who cannot act responsibly? Not necessarily. He appears to know that Sally cannot really drive, and while letting her do so, he informs her how fast they are allowed to go and stresses that she must pay attention. Hence, when helping Sally to transgress the borders of childhood, and the law, he also acts as her guide into the adult world.

That Gene's behavior has a pedagogical purpose, and he is not simply confused, is supported by another scene in the same episode where they eat ice cream together and Gene tries to boost Sally's self-esteem. When he asks her if she remembers her grandmother Ruth, she replies that Grandma once gave her a ukulele. When Gene asks her if she learned how to play, and she says no, he says to her: "You can, you know. You're smart. [. . .] You can really do something. Don't let your mother tell you otherwise." Gene challenges Betty Draper's authority, assuring Sally that she can accomplish things. In fact, when letting her drive the car he defies not only her parents' authority, but any authority that postulates what children can do, and he lets her experience that she can do things she did not know she could. Gene thus helps Sally to transgress the borders of childhood and lets her have a foretaste of adulthood. If we assume that parents do not expect grandparents to let children do potentially dangerous or illegal things, Gene can also be said to transgress the borders of grandparenthood.

To summarize, in this scene the positions of the child and the old man have been, literally as well as symbolically, unsettled. The old man does not fulfill the role of a responsible, caring adult, but instead he is the enabler who lets the child visit the world of adults, and who acts as her guide and educator. The child takes the position of an adult but is still dependent on her guide to do so. In the car they have changed places, but they actually meet in driving (managing the steering wheel and the pedals respectively), and together they break the law as well as challenge the normative borders of childhood and old age.

Figure 10.2. Gene drives (*Mad Men*, "The Arrangements," 30:29).

"Don't Keep Me Waiting"

In the second scene the setting is the same, with Gene taking the kids to school, but the roles of the child and the grandfather, and the relationship between them, are played out in a different way. The car appears again, driving in the middle of the road. The next cut shows Gene driving and Sally sitting beside him in the passenger seat. Bobby is in the backseat, eating a sandwich. Gene says in a firm and harsh voice: "What the hell is that?" Bobby replies "It's an English muffin," and Gene says: "The hell it is. Put it away. You can eat at school." Sally turns toward Gene and says, "I already ate my breakfast." She smiles and looks content. Gene looks back at her with love. Then his face turns serious, and he says: "Don't keep me waiting this afternoon. I want you dressed and ready for ballet at 3:00 on the button. No dawdling." "Okay," Sally says chipperly. Gene tells them he is going to buy fruit and asks what they want. Sally answers, in a childish, lisping voice "Peaches, please." When Bobby protests by saying, "Peaches give me a rash," Gene yells at him, "Your sister likes them!" Gene looks moody, and Sally a bit insecure.

In this scene Gene and Sally are back in their expected positions, both literally and symbolically. Gene talks to her and Bobby in a disciplinary voice, showing he expects them to obey. He keeps watch over what they eat and when, and requests Sally to be in time for afternoon activities. At the same time he shows willingness to meet the kids' wishes (at least Sally's, who is clearly favored) by asking them what fruit to buy. He hence acts according to what would be expected from a grandparent, namely, to be a supervising and responsible caregiver who may spoil the children a little. Sally, in turn, is given, and takes, the role of the child. She relates to Gene as an adult authority, trying to please him by saying she has had her breakfast properly at home and by gladly accepting his lecture about keeping time. Her position as a child is also consolidated by the way she is dressed, in a girly pink dress and white blouse with a red waistband, and by her childish lisping voice (Figure 10.2). Here, no borders are challenged or transgressed.

The analysis of these two scenes makes clear that the roles of the child and the grandfather, and the relationship between them, are not fixed but rather explored and stretched in interesting ways. In the very same setting—the routine of going to school—the grandfather acts as the enabler who lets the child transgress the normative borders of childhood, but also as the disciplining adult who sees to it that the children do what they are expected to. The child, Sally, acts as a child but also as an adult. With her grandfather's blessing and help, she does things that are not considered to be an appropriate part of childhood. Her different positions are emphasized by the way she is dressed: in a strict white shirt and checked jacket when she drives the car, and in a sweet pink dress when she sits beside Gene acting like a good girl (Figures 10.1 and 10.2).

From these scenes in the car, we can conclude that the pairing of childhood and old age in *Mad Men* is not constructed in a straightforward way. Gene and Sally are portrayed as ideal companions, at least from their own perspectives, and their relationship is implied to be rewarding for both parties. It is worth pointing to Wesley Colbath's interesting analysis of the function of cars in *Mad Men* as "the site for major changes in interpersonal relations of power and privacy" (133). Here, in the car, Gene and Sally escape the supervision of Don and Betty, and both gain power in relation to each other. With Sally, Gene regains his position as an adult in charge, which he seems to have lost in his everyday life. To her he is not a confused old man who needs to be taken care of, but a competent adult who can guide and educate the younger generation. Sally, for her part, gets a lot of positive attention and responsibility from Gene. She is not just a child that needs to be raised but also a companion and a friend, and she is believed to be competent. Their relationship is thus constructed as empowering but also as provocative in relation to what children and grandparents can be expected to do. Sally and Gene both challenge the normative borders of their age groups and roles, and, when transgressing the borders of childhood and grandparenthood, they do potentially dangerous things.

An Unholy Alliance

In "Mystery Date" from season five, Sally is twelve years old, and the news about the Chicago murders is all over the papers and on everybody's lips. The episode refers to an actual event in 1966 when a man raped and killed eight student nurses. A ninth girl hid under a bed and survived. In this episode Sally and her brother are left in the care of their new step-grandmother, Pauline, while their mother and her husband are out of town. In a series of three scenes, the relationship between Sally and Pauline evolves in an interesting way, as both take on different roles.

"Some Things Are Not for Children"

In the first scene Sally, Bobby, and Pauline are sitting at the kitchen table. Sally looks bored, and she has not touched her sandwich. Pauline is reading the newspaper. She tells Sally to eat her sandwich, but Sally replies she is not hungry. Pauline focuses on her reading, and as she makes some comments, Sally becomes interested (see Table 10.1 for scene transcript).

In this scene, Sally tries to get information about the news, which she seems to understand is really horrifying. Symbolically, she attempts to move beyond the scope of childhood and look into the adult world. She wants to know what is happening, but she is dependent on Pauline to let her. Throughout the scene, however, Pauline refuses to let her in. She instead fulfills the role of gatekeeper and makes sure that the door to the adult world is kept shut, and the borders of innocent childhood upheld.

Through a series of utterances and gestures, Pauline pins Sally down to the role of a child: she explicitly refers to her as a child ("Some things are not for children"), slaps her, refers to her "behavior," which her mother would not approve of, and makes her eat the food she does not like. When Sally tries to breach the limits of childhood, Pauline pushes her back. She consequently restores their conversation to one between a child and an adult, until she marks the end of that conversation by unfolding the newspaper again.

Pauline holds the newspaper as as barrier between Sally and herself, and also, symbolically, as a barrier between what children are allowed to know and what she as an adult knows. Pauline thus shuts Sally out, leaving her with no more information than the newspaper's headline "NATION HUNTS MASS KILLER" (Figure 10.3). Ironically, she thereby protects Sally from information while still flashing the abridged gruesome facts at her. Here, we see no closeness or companionship between the generations, but rather

Figure 10.3. Pauline reads (*Mad Men*, "Mystery Date," 12:38).

Table 10.1	
Pauline, in a low voice, when reading:	P: Oh, my lord. Those poor souls. S: What? P: Nothing.
Sally leans over to see the newspaper. Pauline slaps her hand. Pauline rivets her eyes on Sally. Sally rubs her hand. Sally, in a vague and hurt voice: Pauline looks angry. In a firm voice:	S: Aww P: Some things are not for children. S: Mommy lets me watch the news. P: You *demanded* tuna salad, so you're gonna sit there until you eat it.
Sally, grimacing: Pauline, quickly: Pauline shakes her head and returns to the newspaper. Sally looks as if she is ready to cry. Looks intensely at Pauline. Pauline puts the newspaper down slowly and puts her hands on the table. Pauline in a controlled, somewhat strained but soft voice:	S: It has relish in it. P: You haven't even tasted it. S: You hurt my hand. P: Well, I shouldn't have done that, I'm sorry, but you have to be respectful. I know your mother has other rules.
Sally shakes her head:	S: She doesn't have rules. P: I don't believe that. (sigh) But I believe that she may be distracted. And I'm sure she would be *sick* if she knew how you were behaving.
Pauline, resolutely: Pauline picks up the newspaper and continues reading.	P: Now you're gonna *finish* that sandwich, crusts and all! I don't care if it takes all day.

distance and confrontation. A struggle is established that continues in the next scene.

"How Old Are You?"

In this scene Sally lies on the sofa in front of the TV. Pauline sits in the same room, talking with someone on the phone. When Sally hears Pauline discussing the murders and the ninth girl who survived, she sits up and listens. Pauline says in a low voice: "Oh, that poor thing. Paralyzed with fear while he opened that door eight times. And dragged another one out. And then ..." When Pauline notices that Sally looks at her and listens, she interrupts herself in mid-sentence and changes the conversation. In a loud voice she explains to the person on the other end that even though she wants to, she cannot make any plans as long as she is taking care of the children. She hangs up and turns toward Sally.

Table 10.2	
Pauline, slow and firm: Sally, without taking her eyes off the TV: Pauline takes the remote control and turns off the TV.	P: You need to take out the trash. S: Right now? P: Take out the trash or you can go to bed right now, watch the sun set from your bedroom window. It's the saddest thing in the world.
Sally looks at Pauline.	S: If I take out the trash, will you tell me about the murder? P: *No!* I will not bargain with you.
Sally grimaces. Pauline puts away the telephone.	S: How *old* are you? P: That's something we girls keep to ourselves. S: Was your mom strict? P: No, but my father was, and I'm a better person for it. S: I know you don't think so, but I'm a good person. P: Sally, I just think someone in your world needs to discipline you, so you can start acting like an adult. . . .

Sally is eager to find out about the murders, to get some information about the events that the adults read and talk about. Just as in the previous scene, however, Pauline pushes her back and positions her as a child. We see a struggle between the child acting like a challenging teenager, wanting to enter the adult conversation, and the old woman acting as a gatekeeper, trying to sustain the borders of childhood. This conflict is played out almost like a duel. When Sally eavesdrops, Pauline closes her phone call. She orders Sally to take out the trash and threatens to punish her if she does not obey. Sally tries to negotiate and suggests an exchange of favors. Pauline's refusal makes clear she would never bargain with a child. Sally's question "How old are you?" implies that Pauline is old and square, and that her standards are obsolete. Yet again she tries to reason with Pauline, saying she is a "good person," but the woman insists on talking to her, and treating her, as a child. In her world, discipline rather than inclusion is what turns children into adults.

In this scene too, the step-grandmother, Pauline, fulfills the role of a strict adult authority, rather than a companion or confidant. As a gatekeeper, aiming to maintain the borders of childhood, she does not tell children things they are not supposed to know, and she definitely does not negotiate with them. Sally does not accept being positioned as a child. In trying to stretch the limits set up by her step-grandmother, she alternates between questioning her adult authority and trying to negotiate with her to get what she wants. Even though Pauline refers to them both being "girls," the distance between them is consolidated and manifested through Sally's utterance "How old are you?" In the last scene to be analyzed, however, they take on new roles, and the relationship between them changes in an interesting way.

"You're Old Enough to Know"

In a very short cut, preceding the scene transcribed below, Sally lies in bed under a blanket with a flashlight, reading the newspaper. The headline says "Nurses' Slayer Eludes Dragnet," and Sally, who now realizes that the murderer is still on the loose, looks terrified. A few minutes later the show returns to Pauline sitting in the dark living room in a nightgown, reading a book and eating snacks. Sally turns up in the doorway, dressed in a short, frilly nightgown, holding the flashlight in her hand. Pauline, who does not see her at first, gets startled (see Table 10.3 for scene transcript).

Whereas in the previous two scenes, Sally took the position of a soon-to-be teenager wanting to know about the adult world, she now acts out the role of a child. She is portrayed as a little girl who has learned about things she cannot handle, and her "childness" is emphasized by the girly nightgown that leaves her legs bare. She comes to Pauline to seek company and security, but Pauline is also afraid and has brought a knife for protection. In this situation their relationship, and their way of communicating, takes a new

Table 10.3

	S: I'm sorry. I can't sleep.
	P: Well, you can't sneak up to someone my *age*, especially in this house.
	S: I'm scared. Can I sit with you?
Pauline puts away her book.	P: Only for a bit.
Sally comes into the room and sits down beside Pauline.	
Sally points down to the space between them at the sofa.	S: What's that for?
Pauline picks up a big knife lying there and moves it to her other side.	P: Why are you scared?
	S: I read the newspaper.
Pauline, in a compassionate voice:	P: Oh honey. Did you pull it out of the trash?
	S: Why did that man do that?
	P: Well, probably because he hates his mother.
	S: I don't understand what happened.
Pauline, slowly and clearly:	P: What happened? Those girls got ready for bed, and there was a knock on the door. And a handsome man was there. And maybe one of them knew him. But probably not. Because he was probably just watching them from afar. All those young innocent nurses. In their short uniforms. Stirring his desire.
Sally listens wide-eyed.	
	S: For what?
	P: What do you think? You're old enough to know.
	S: Why didn't they run away?
	P: Because they were scared. They probably thought, He can't rape nine of us.
	S: Why not?
	P: You just can't. They didn't know it was going to be worse than that. Hmm. They didn't know what was in store for them.
	S: Now I'm really scared.
	P: It's not going to happen. Not while I've got my burglar alarm.
Pauline picks up the knife.	
Sally looks at the knife.	
Sally looks concerned.	S: How am I going to sleep?
Pauline reaches for something. With soft voice:	P: Get the water.
Sally reaches for a glass of water on the table.	
Pauline brings out a pillbox and tips a pill into her hand.	S: What is that?
	P: It's *Seconal*.
Pauline bites the pill in two. She chews one half and keeps the other half between her fingers.	P: Do you know how to take a pill?
Sally nods.	

Figure 10.4. Sharing a sleeping pill (*Mad Men*, "Mystery Date," 36:06).

direction. It is almost as if they meet on neutral ground, vulnerable in their nightgowns in the dark house, where they take on new roles. Pauline is now kind and compassionate. She lets Sally stay with her, even though she should be in bed. When Sally silently admits to having pulled the newspaper from the trash, she does not get angry. Instead she says, "Oh, honey," and starts explaining what happened. Consequently, she finally resigns from her post as a gatekeeper and lets Sally through, to explore the horrors of the adult world. In doing so Pauline assumes the role of an enabler: she is still the one in charge, not by means of discipline but because of her knowledge, and Sally continues to be dependent on her. Pauline turns into Sally's guide and educator, and together they challenge the borders of childhood.

The ultimate transgression happens when Pauline lets Sally take the sleeping pill (Figure 10.4). In that moment she, just like Gene, oversteps the normative boundaries of a responsible grandparent. This also becomes evident later, in a scene where Sally's mother and stepfather come home to find Pauline passed out in the living room. When they cannot make contact with her, they get worried and start looking for the children. They do not spot what the TV viewer can see, that Sally is lying on the floor underneath the sofa, mirroring the position of the ninth girl, who escaped the murderer by hiding under the bed.

In the series of scenes analyzed above, Pauline's transition from gatekeeper to enabler corresponds with Sally's transition from a challenging soon-to-be teenager to a scared little child. It is not until Sally accepts and acts out the role of an innocent child that Pauline lets her into the adult world. This seems like a paradox. When Sally was eager to know about the murders, Pauline's answer was, "Some things are not for children." When she is scared and shows her ignorance by asking a child's questions about sexual desire, Pauline says, "You're old enough to know." Apparently, Pauline does not see her as an innocent little girl, after all. How can we understand this? Why does Pauline suddenly seem to enjoy telling Sally this gruesome story, making her even more scared? When rereading the previous scenes with these questions in mind, one possible interpretation is that Pauline was careless, throwing the newspaper in the trash and then asking Sally to take it out. Yet another, more plausible interpretation would be that she actually arranged for Sally to find the newspaper. It is worth noticing that when Sally comes to her for comfort, Pauline immediately knows she has found the paper in the trash. It is then not surprising that she does not get angry, but willingly tells Sally everything.

This interpretation sheds new light on the role ascribed to Pauline as a step-grandmother, and her relationship to the child in her care. In front of Sally, and implicitly also in front of Sally's parents, Pauline upholds the act of the supervising adult, disciplining the child and maintaining the borders of childhood. Behind the scenes, however, she takes the role of the enabler who secretly helps the child to stretch those borders. In doing so, she gets the satisfaction of being an expert, teaching her disciple about the world without having to defend her actions if questioned. This may also seem to be a way for Pauline to manage her own fears. Pauline thus artfully maneuvers between what grandparents could be expected to do and not do.

Just as in the scenes with Sally and Gene, the relationship between the child and the grandparent is not simple and straightforward, but indeed complex. Sally's relationship with Pauline, however, is quite different from that with Gene. Sally and Pauline are *not* ideal companions. The relationship is *not* rewarding to either party. Pauline claims that she cannot go out because she has to watch the kids, and Sally is forced to spend time with someone she thinks is not only old but also old-fashioned and rigid. Nevertheless, they both get something out of it: Pauline (sees to it that she) gets the satisfaction of being the expert, introducing a young novice to the events of a spectacular crime, and Sally gets the information she wants. Consequently, both are empowered by their forced relationship, and together they stretch the borders of childhood and grandparenthood. This challenge is manifested as Pauline shares with Sally her sleeping pill, a pill that is the privilege of the knowing adult but that serves to escape the anxiety and fear that could follow from that knowledge.

Conclusion

The scenes from *Mad Men* that we have analyzed show that the roles of children and the elderly are constantly negotiated and fluid—they can be fixed in a certain situation but not in the relationship as such. The elderly take on the roles of both gatekeeper and enabler in relation to the child. When they act as gatekeepers, they see to it that the kids eat properly and are on time for their activities. They also discipline them and make sure they behave as children are expected to. The gatekeeper hence sustains the borders of childhood. The enabler, in contrast, lets the child explore the adult world, to know and to do things that may not be considered suitable for a child. The enabler is the guide when entering forbidden territory and hence helps the child to stretch the borders of childhood.

The child, in this case Sally, also takes on different roles in relation to the grandparents. Sometimes she accepts being positioned as a child and complies with what is expected of her; at other times she resists. She also evolves in the course of the series, as she grows older. In the first scenes analyzed (from season three), Sally is portrayed as wanting both to be a good girl and a young woman learning how to drive a car. Later, in season five, we see a soon-to-be teenager who resists being treated and disciplined like a small child. She tries to move beyond the scope of childhood to be included in adult conversation. When she succeeds, however, she has difficulties handling the information she has gained, and she takes the position of a little girl who needs comfort and protection. When the elderly are portrayed as enablers, they make it possible for the child to transgress the borders of childhood, and as such they themselves transgress the borders of grandparenthood. When Sally and Gene change places in driving the car, and when Sally and Pauline share the sleeping pill, they also challenge the power and authority of the middle generation. Consequently, their relationship is not primarily harmless or preservative but challenging and subversive.

We can hence conclude that the *Mad Men* portrayal of children and the elderly, and the relationship between them, is indeed complex. In general, the elderly may be represented according to ageist stereotypes, as dependent and weak, as confused like Gene, and as bitter and controlling like Pauline (Lemish and Muhlbauer 166; Lepianka 1108). In their relationship with the child, however, they step out of the stereotypes. In Sally's company, Gene gains strong and confident authority, and Pauline finally becomes the confidant and expert to whom the child wants to listen, instead of the aloof and dismissive step-grandmother she despises. Furthermore, the age gap between Sally and Pauline is bridged when they, as females, join in their fear of the Chicago rapist and murderer. This does not mean, however, that the elders are constructed instead as "wise old mentors" (Joosen 131). They do guide the young girl to knowledge and understanding, but they come across neither as mild and wise nor as having no needs of their own. On the contrary, as mentors they let the child explore the horrors of the adult world and do potentially dangerous things. Consequently, in their interaction with children, these elderly figures are constructed neither in accordance with a "decline narrative" (Gullette 6–7) nor as one-dimensional old people that are only sensible and kind.

Sally, for her part, personifies, in her relationships with Gene and Pauline, both the romantic "innocent child," the sweet little girl who needs protection, and "the knowing child" who, thanks to the elderly, stretches and transgresses the borders of childhood and becomes part of a more complex adult world. The knowing child, who drives the car, learns about rape and murder, and takes a sleeping pill to manage her fears, does not fit the norms of childhood (Higonnet 12, 207). The portrayal of Sally thus illustrates the destabilization of the division in film and on TV between innocence and knowledge, and between childhood and adulthood, which Tincknell has observed (98–101).

Mad Men has been described as a period drama series that subverts nostalgia and dispels romantic images of family life in the 1960s and today. It reminds us, Wilson and Lane argue (77–79, 83–84, 88), that we should meet any idealized narrative with skepticism. Our analysis shows that *Mad Men* also serves to destabilize the romantic pairing of childhood and old age. The companionship between children and the elderly is constructed as rewarding for both parties, but as norm-breaking and potentially dangerous, rather than idyllic and harmless. Together, they stretch the borders of childhood and grandparenthood and challenge the authority of the generation in between.

Notes

1. The topics that have been scrutinized include visual style and sound (Anderson; Butler; Yacovar), narration (Lavery; Miggelbrink; Newcomb; O'Sullivan), representation of the past (Baruah; Beail and Goren; Black and Driscoll; Tudor), masculinity (Falklof; Lair and Strasser; Witzig), gender roles (Akass and McCabe; Ferrucci, Shoenberger, and Schauster; Haralovich; White), women and family (Marcovitch and Batty), and femininity and race (De La Torre).

Works Cited

Akass, Kim, and Janet McCabe. "The Best of Everything: The Limits of Being a Working Girl in *Mad Men*." *Mad Men: Dream Come True TV*. Ed. Gary Edgerton. London: I. B. Tauris, 2011. 177–194.

Anderson, Tim. "Uneasy Listening: Music, Sound, and Criticizing Camelot in *Mad Men*." *Mad Men: Dream Come True TV*. Ed. Gary Edgerton. London: I. B. Tauris, 2011: 72–85.

Baruah, Debarchana. "Remembering through Retro TV and Cinema: *Mad Men* as Televisual Memorial to 60s America." *COPAS-Current Objectives of Postgraduate American Studies* 15.1 (2014): 1–19.

Barzilai-Nahon, Karine. "Gatekeeping: A Critical Review." *Annual Review of Information Science and Technology* 43.1 (2009): 1–79.

Batchelor, Bob. "Spin the Carousel: *Mad Men*, Nostalgia and the American Dream." *Lucky Strikes and a Three Martini Lunch: Thinking about Television's* Mad Men. Eds. Danielle M. Stern, Jimmie Manning, and Jennifer C. Dunn. Newcastle: Cambridge Scholars Press, 2014. 60–70.

Batty, Nancy. "*Mad Men's* Epoch-Eclipse: Marking Time with Sally Draper." *Mad Men, Women and Children: Essays on Gender and Generation*. Eds. Heather Marcovitch and Nancy E. Batty. Lanham: Lexington Books, 2012. 191–206.

Beail, Linda, and Lilly J. Goren. "*Mad Men* and Politics: Nostalgia and the Remaking of America." Eds. Linda Beail and Lilly J. Goren. *Mad Men and Politics: Nostalgia and the Remaking of Modern America*. London: Bloomsbury, 2015. 3–33.

Black, Prudence, and Catherine Driscoll. "Don, Betty and Jackie Kennedy: On *Mad Men* and Periodization." *Cultural Studies Review* 18.2 (2012): 188–206.

Butler, Jeremy G. "'Smoke Gets in Your Eyes': Historicizing Visual Style in *Mad Men*." *Mad Men: Dream Come True TV*. Ed. Gary Edgerton. London: I. B. Tauris, 2011. 55–71.

Colbath, Wesley. "Sex, Privacy, and Relations of Power: The Role of Automobiles in *Mad Men*." *Lucky Strikes and a Three Martini Lunch: Thinking about Television's* Mad Men. Eds. Danielle M. Stern, Jimmie Manning, and Jennifer C. Dunn. Newcastle: Cambridge Scholars Press, 2014. 133–141.

Colton Josephson, Rebecca. "Tomorrowland: Contemporary Visions, Past Indiscretions." *Mad Men and Politics: Nostalgia and the Remaking of Modern America*. Eds. Linda Beail and Lilly J. Goren. London: Bloomsbury, 2015. 259–275.

Davidson, Diana. "'A Mother Like You': Pregnancy, the Maternal, and Nostalgia." *Analyzing Mad Men: Critical Essays on the Television Series*. Ed. Scott Frederick Stoddart. Jefferson: McFarland, 2011. 136–154.

De La Torre, Miguel A. "Mad Men, Competitive Women, and Invisible Hispanics." *Journal of Feminist Studies in Religion* 28.1 (2012): 121–126.

Dole, Carol M. "Bishops, Knights and Pawns: Mad Men and Narrative Strategy." *Mad Men, Women and Children: Essays on Gender and Generation*. Eds. Heather Marcovitch and Nancy E. Batty. Lanham: Lexington Books, 2012. 173–189.

Edgerton, Gary R. "Introduction: When Our Parents Became Us." *Mad Men: Dream Come True TV*. Ed. Gary Edgerton. London: I. B. Tauris, 2011. xxi–xxxvi.

Ehmann, Falk, et al. "Gatekeepers and Enablers: How Drug Regulators Respond to a Challenging and Changing Environment by Moving toward a Proactive Attitude." *Clinical Pharmacology & Therapeutics* 93.5 (2013): 425–432.

Falklof, Nicky. "The Father, the Failure and the Self-Made Man: Masculinity in *Mad Men*." *Critical Quarterly* 54.3 (2012): 31–45.

Ferrucci, Patrick, Heather Shoenberger, and Erin Schauster. "It's a Mad, Mad, Mad, Ad World: A Feminist Critique of *Mad Men*." *Women's Studies International Forum* 47 (2014): 93–101.

Fineman, Stephen. *Organizing Age*. Oxford: Oxford University Press, 2011.

Goodlad, Lauren M. E., Lilya Kaganovsky, and Robert A. Rushing. "Introduction." *Mad Men, Mad World: Sex, Politics, Style, and the 1960s*. Eds. Lauren M. E. Goodlad, Lilya Kaganovsky, and Robert A. Rushing. Durham: Duke University Press, 2013. 1–34.

Gullette, Margaret Morganroth. *Aged by Culture*. Chicago: University of Chicago Press, 2004.

Haralovich, Mary Beth. "Women on the Verge of the Second Wave." *Mad Men: Dream Come True TV*. Ed. Gary Edgerton. London: I. B. Tauris, 2011. 159–176.

Healey, Tim, and Karen Ross. "Growing Old Invisibly: Older Viewers Talk Television." *Media, Culture & Society* 24.1 (2002): 105–120.

Higonnet, Anne. *Pictures of Innocence: The History and Crisis of Ideal Childhoods*. London: Thames & Hudson, 1998.

Hockey, Jenny, and Allison James. *Growing Up and Growing Old: Ageing and Dependency in the Life Course*. London: Sage, 1993.

Holland, Patricia. *Picturing Childhood: The Myth of the Child in Popular Imagery*. London: I. B. Tauris, 2004.

Joosen, Vanessa. "Second Childhoods and Intergenerational Dialogues." *Children's Literature Association Quarterly* 40.2 (2015): 126–140.

Krekula, Clary, Anna-Liisa Närvänen, and Elisabet Näsman. "Ålder i intersektionell analys." *Kvinnovetenskaplig tidskrift* 26.2–3 (2005): 81–94.

Lair, Daniel J., and Daniel S. Strasser. "*Mad Men's* Mad Men: Multiple Masculinities and the 'Masculinity-in-Crisis' Narrative." *Lucky Strikes and a Three Martini Lunch: Thinking about Television's* Mad Men. Eds. Danielle M. Stern, Jimmie Manning, and Jennifer C. Dunn. Newcastle: Cambridge Scholars Press, 2014. 177–189.

Lavery, David. "'The Catastrophe of My Personality': Frank O'Hara, Don Draper and the Poetics of *Mad Men*." *Mad Men: Dream Come True TV*. Ed. Gary Edgerton. London: I. B. Tauris, 2011. 131–146.

Lemish, Dafna, and Varda Muhlbauer. "'Can't Have It All': Representations of Older Women in *Popular Culture*." *Women & Therapy* 35.3–4 (2012): 165–180.

Lepianka, Dorota. "How Similar, How Different? On Dutch Media Depictions of Older and Younger People." *Ageing and Society* 35.5 (2015): 1095–1113.

Lury, Karen. *The Child in Film: Tears, Fears and Fairytales*. London: I. B. Tauris, 2010.

Mad Men. Executive producer Matthew Weiner. Lionsgate Television, Weiner Bros, AMC, 2007–2015.

Marcovitch, Heather, and Nancy E. Batty. *Mad Men, Women and Children: Essays on Gender and Generation*. Lanham: Lexington Books, 2012.

Miggelbrink, Monique. "Serializing the Past: Re-evaluating History in *Mad Men*." *InVisible Culture* 17 (2012): 1–13.

Newcomb, Horace. "Learning to Live with Television in *Mad Men*." *Mad Men: Dream Come True TV*. Ed. Gary Edgerton. London: I. B. Tauris, 2011. 101–114.

O'Sullivan, Sean. "Space Ships and Time Machines: *Mad Men* and the Serial Condition." *Mad Men: Dream Come True TV*. Ed. Gary Edgerton. London: I. B. Tauris, 2011. 131–146.

Polan, Dana. "Maddening Times, *Mad Men* in Its History." *Mad Men, Mad World: Sex, Politics, Style, and the 1960s*. Eds. Lauren M. E. Goodlad, Lilya Kaganovsky, and Robert A. Rushing. Durham: Duke University Press, 2013. 35–52.

Rose, Gillian. *Visual Methodologies*. London: Sage, 2007.

Taylor, Alan C. *Perceptions of Intergenerational Bonds: The Comparison between Grandfathers and Their Adult Grandchildren*. PhD diss., Virginia Polytechnic Institute and State University, 1998.

Tincknell, Estella. *Mediating the Family: Gender, Culture and Representation*. London: Arnold, 2005.

Tudor, Deborah. "Selling Nostalgia: *Mad Men*, Postmodernism and Neoliberalism." *Society* 49.9 (2012): 333–338.

White, Mimi. "Mad Women." *Mad Men: Dream Come True TV*. Ed. Gary Edgerton. London: I. B. Tauris, 2011. 147–158.

Wilson, Julia C., and Joseph H. Lane Jr. "Is This the Traditional American Family We've Been Hearing So Much About? Marriage, Children, and Family Values in *Mad Men*." *Mad Men, Women and Children: Essays on Gender and Generation*. Eds. Heather Marcovitch and Nancy E. Batty. Lanham: Lexington Books, 2012. 77–90.

Witzig, Denise. "Masculinity and Its Discontents: Myth, Memory, and the Future on Mad Men." *Mad Men and Politics: Nostalgia and the Remaking of Modern America*. Eds. Linda Beail and Lilly J. Goren. London: Bloomsbury, 2015. 175–205.

Yacovar, Maurice. "Suggestive Silence in Season One." *Mad Men: Dream Come True TV*. Ed. Gary Edgerton. London: I. B. Tauris, 2011. 86–100.

- 11 -

Representations of Intergenerational Relationships in Children's Television in Turkey

Inquiries and Propositions

GÖKÇE ELİF BAYKAL AND ILGIM VERYERİ ALACA

As contemporary populations age in developed countries, and as the diversity of age groups leading active and productive lives increases, the construction and performance of age, as a constituent of social identity, becomes more varied and complex. Indeed, scholars such as Nick Lee (2001), Anne Davis Basting (1998), and Susan Neiman (2015) argue that in postmodern societies, there are almost unlimited ways of experiencing and conceiving of age. Unsurprisingly, the design of content and texts in media, which plays a critical role in introducing children to a range of age-related imaginary material, reflects these demographic and cultural shifts. In Turkey, for instance, the percentage of elderly people is expected to double from 10 to 20 percent by the year 2050, while children aged fourteen and below currently make up a quarter of Turkey's population.[1] These numbers indicate an increasingly elderly population, which suggests that intergenerational relationships will acquire greater significance in children's lives. In this chapter we investigate how these relationships are portrayed in Turkish cartoon series on children's television, with a particular focus on depictions of fictional elderly characters. According to Carl DiSalvo (2009), media design can facilitate the growth of pluralistic public discourse, if its characters encourage inclusion and pluralism (48). This study seeks insight into this process, analyzes the degree to which it is occurring in contemporary Turkey, and explores possibilities for the future.

Our research builds on recent literature that discusses the specific function of children's media in constructing such pluralistic discourse. Frequently, it is through the representation of interactions between diverse age groups that these media achieve an inclusive effect. Vanessa Joosen (2015), for example, highlights the potency of examining intersections between children's literature studies and age studies. Sandra Beckett (2009), Roberta Seelinger Trites (2014), and Patricia Crawford and Sharika Bhattacharya (2014) confirm that children's literature often includes representations of older characters who are diverse in terms of their narrative roles and cultural backgrounds. On a related note, Máire Messenger Davies contends that "one of the primary ways in which children and culture are linked is through media" (15). Inclusive children's television programs might thus serve as powerful agents to encourage bonds between children and the elderly, creating a variety of forms of complementary and progressive alliances. Alan Prout (2008) stresses that children must be seen and treated as active agents in the construction and determination of their own social lives. Similarly, we observe that intergenerational bonds are not limited to members of different ages within a society but can also refer to a person's relationship with his or her future self. Furthermore, exchanging information and knowledge between different age groups is not a one-directional phenomenon; on the contrary, adults learn a great deal from children, especially in the contemporary world.

In contemporary Turkish children's fiction, the elderly are often cast in secondary roles as grandparents who share similar visual characteristics and secondary traits. This practice contributes to a sense of uniformity among elderly identities. As a result, it appears that their typological status corresponds to Maria Nikolajeva's (2003) view that contemporary characters "tend to become more like 'real people,' appearing on low mimetic and ironic levels" (47). Following Northrop Frye, she argues that unlike high mimetic, fairy-tale, or romantic heroes, low mimetic characters display traits that are neither superior nor inferior to other humans' while negotiating ordinary situations in their search for identity (26). In this respect, elderly people are not designed to be role models for children; rather, their subjectivity is portrayed as equal to that of children, which Nikolajeva argues is a recent development in modern children's literature (37). Despite the purported realism of these depictions, however, it is debatable to what degree they correspond to readily observable facts about "real people" in Turkey. Indeed, there is evidence to suggest that the idealized family relations represented in Turkish cartoons, which serve a primarily didactic purpose, diverge from the lived experience of Turkish people. It is thus fruitful to consider whether, and to what extent, they reflect and meet the interests of contemporary audiences.

In line with the theoretical model that David Buckingham (2008) has outlined for analyzing the multiple conceptual dimensions of children's media (224), this chapter pays particular attention to producers, texts, and audiences in order to understand how intergenerational relationships are presented in Turkish children's television. Our approach to analyzing fictional portrayals of the elderly and children is twofold. First, we briefly analyze past and present production strategies for representing youth and senescence in Turkish animated cartoons, in comparison with patterns from abroad. Second, we explain the results of a survey on intergenerational relationships, which captures grandparents' and grandchildren's views of each other, in order to provide insight into these key segments of the Turkish audience and to identify a gap between the contemporary "realistic" typology of characters and the features of a sample of real-life contemporary Turkish audiences.

Demographic Shifts in Turkey

As in most Western countries, the growing proportion of older people is part of a general slowing of population growth, which has led to a shift in the characterization of certain demographic groups in Turkey. Both children under fifteen and adults older than sixty-five are considered to be groups that produce less than they consume. While our findings, and those of others (for example, Tufan; see below), partially challenge such assumptions, it is true that these two groups often spend more time at home than do others and thus have an increased chance of interacting with each other. The European Foundation for the Improvement of Living and Working Conditions declared 2012 to be the year of "active ageing and solidarity between generations" in Europe.[2] The aim was to reformulate the concept of old age as the working-age population declines. It is necessary to raise a similar awareness in Turkey through pursuing active aging strategies to realize various opportunities that present themselves as part of life in the twenty-first century.

Turkish gerontologist İsmail Tufan (2015) has recently pointed out that the increasing life span and processes of modernization have shifted prescribed roles for age groups, as older generations continue to participate in economic life after retirement. They not only continue to work and be a source of income but also maintain their social lives. It is thus important to recognize that future increases in the number of older members of society supply a unique opportunity, which should be fostered by social and economic policies. By implementing strategies of lifelong learning and related services, older people can be encouraged to improve their skills, including their technological abilities, thus optimizing employment opportunities (European Training Foundation, *Lifelong Learning*). According to a 2012 report from the Turkish Industrialists' and Businessmen's Association (TÜSİAD), there is little evidence or research regarding resources used by the older generation in maintaining their lives in Turkey. Given the limited social security services offered for the retired, it does not make much sense to consider the elderly a burden on the economy, argue Tufan and Suzan Yazıcı (2009). Instead, they should be recognized for their potential to contribute to society.

Characters in media are "the primary vehicles for revealing meaning in narrative" in media programs (Scholes and Kellog 104); thus, we argue that the portrayal of rewarding intergenerational relations can serve to promote different forms of quality time that can be shared between young and old people. Buckingham (2008) emphasizes that like all cultural products, the content produced for children's media is closely linked to the surrounding political economy and cultural practices and is constituted by a "collaborative process that evolves over time, within specific institutional and political settings" (224). Childhood, aging, and intergenerational dialogues are attracting rising awareness, due to their affiliation with the political economy of the twenty-first century. We draw attention to the influence of representations of interplay between young and old in children's television and also consider how audiences may respond to them.

Turkish Children's Television and Animated Programs

The concept of children's television as a niche broadcasting service is a relatively new phenomenon in Turkey when compared to other Western countries. Başak Ürkmez's review of the animation industry in Turkey reveals that animated cartoons were not produced for children until the 1980s. In that decade television became widespread in Turkey, but the Turkish Radio Television Institution (TRT), founded in 1964, was the only investor in children's programs. TRT typically commissioned adaptations and retellings of epic and folkloric stories from Turkish culture, such as *Dede Korkut* and *Evliya Çelebi*, in which old and wise male heroes played the major roles. An exception was another TRT broadcast, the animation series *Karınca Ailesi* (The ant family). Its anthropomorphized animal characters signaled a new approach for the period, unlike other productions, which usually used prominently featured elderly characters to promote morally and culturally oriented themes.

In the United Kingdom, which played a pioneering role in children's television worldwide, broadcasting for the young dates back to 1946; since 1950 the BBC has had a specific children's department (Herbert Art Gallery and Museum 4). The first thematic children's channel in Turkey was Maxi TV, founded in 1997. Yumurcak TV has been broadcasting since 2007 and was the second-largest investor in children's programming in Turkey until recently. Today, TRT Çocuk (the national public channel for children), which started broadcasting in 2008, is the largest investor in domestic cartoon productions for children in Turkey. TRT Çocuk was launched with the particular aim of preserving local cultural images of age, gender, and family, as well as folkloric characters. Before its establishment, almost all television shows for children that aired on Turkish channels were international cartoons. As a national channel, TRT Çocuk can therefore be regarded as the leading actor in defining the conventions and trends in Turkish television for children, yet it is regulated by prevailing governmental policies.

It is important to note that today TRT Çocuk has a centralized role and is the highest-ranked children's television station in Turkey, as reported by the Radio and Television Supreme Council (RTÜK). It has a 39.5 percent viewing ratio across all children's television channels in the country, a rating followed by Yumurcak TV, which has a 36.6 percent viewing ratio (2013). Given the low rate of preschool attendance in Turkey (27 percent, according to OECD reports from 2014), it is plausible that TRT Çocuk also plays an important role in the daily care and early education of children. Both TRT Çocuk and Yumurcak TV were established with the aim of incorporating cultural and occasionally religious elements in the production of content and thus play a significant role in presenting certain kinds of images, or performances, of childhood and adult—child relationships. Numerous questions emerge in the context of a strategy that aims to sustain and preserve the authenticity and tradition of Turkish cultural values: How well do native children's programs in Turkey attract the interest and reflect the voices of today's children? How diverse are they in their representations of people, intergenerational relationships, and topics related to the contemporary world? These questions will be addressed in a brief analysis of children's programs broadcast on TRT Çocuk and Yumurcak TV.

Analysis of Turkish Children's Television Cartoons

A comparative analysis of Turkish and foreign children's television programs helps demonstrate the scope of artistic approaches. We are particularly interested in postmodern trends expanding visual and literary perspectives in children's media that have yielded new possibilities in terms of narrative techniques, settings, and characters. The sampling of the television shows in this study consists of television cartoon series that are broadcast in Turkey and that feature at least one human or nonhuman old-age character in either minor or major roles. Our identification of old-age characters is based on a set of subjective criteria gathered by Tom Robinson, Mark Callister, Dawn Magoffin, and Jennifer Moore (2007) in their extensive review of literature on the portrayal of older people in the media:

1) an appearance of retirement
2) extensive gray hair
3) wrinkles of the skin
4) extensive balding
5) trembling voice
6) use of an aid such as a cane or wheelchair
7) evidence of grandchildren (Robinson et al. 205)

According to this set of criteria, we can define two types of animated television series that employ old-age characters in Turkish children's television programs. One category consists of adaptations of early folk literature that have been recommissioned by TRT Çocuk, such as *Keloğlan* (Egghead, TRT Çocuk, 2009—present), *Nasreddin Hodja*, and *Dede Korkut*. None of the features listed above, except "extensive gray hair," were present in folktales they were based on. The more recent fictional adaptations have also maintained the original patterns of these folkloric heroes, without pursuing postmodern narrative interpretations, but focusing instead on the technical innovations of the animation.

The second type is newly created domestic productions that mirror present-day narrative design approaches in Turkey, which avoid challenging the expectations of the audience and present idealized human relations in harmonious lifestyles. Particular emphasis is thus placed on the latter. This group also divides into two categories of representations of performing old-age and intergenerational relations: (1) series in which Turkish family norms are portrayed in low mimetic narrative, where the old-age characters present almost all the criteria listed above, and (2) series that feature relatively controversial features of old age, while casting ordinary, realistic characters in high mimetic, mythic narratives. Three of the five Turkish shows selected for this research fall into the first category: *Pepee* (TRT Çocuk, 2008–2013), *Can* (Yumurcak TV, 2013–2015), and *Niloya* (Yumurcak TV, 2014–2015). In contrast, *Köstebekgiller* (The Family Talpidae, TRT Çocuk, 2012–present) and *Cille* (TRT Çocuk, 2009–present) offer a new perspective in terms of character and narrative development.

Pepee, *Can*, and *Niloya* are family fictions that present similar patterns of grandparenthood in linear narrative structures, whereas *Köstebekgiller* is composed of two parallel and interwoven narratives: to distinguish them, the program switches from animation to live-action shooting, as a family of animated moles tries to find its way out of the house of a nonanimated human family. The show represents age in interesting and diverse ways: the old-age mole character is depicted as being a curious adventure enthusiast, while one of the human characters, Grandpa Aslan, is the primary caregiver to his grandson. In *Cille*, there is also an energetic elderly character, Müdrik, who signifies wisdom and patience yet also engages in adventures.

With the exception of *Cille*, the old-age characters in all of the selected shows above are featured as grandparents, and not in alternative roles such as friend, neighbor, worker, boss, or villain. In contrast, in early Turkish folk literature, the relationships between the elderly wise heroes and the children do not depend necessarily on family bonds, but rather on friendship: old and young characters are simply presented as people enjoying a conversation. For instance, one of the most prominent old characters in Turkish literature, Nasreddin Hodja, is well known for his funny stories and anecdotes that encourage children to use critical reflection to solve problems, while challenging standard ways of thinking. John Stephens and Robyn McCallum (2013) explain that an oral narrative, such as a Hodja tale, can be appealing because it operates at an abstract level.

> This is what determines that a particular narration has value because it offers a patterned and shapely narrative structure, expresses significant and universal human experiences, interlinks "truth" and cultural heritage and rests moral judgments within an ethical dimension. (7)

In this respect, Nasreddin Hodja is an important example for producing narrative structure in Turkish children's media: this folklore tradition praises an old character's intellectual capacities and incorporates his controversial and nonconformist acts, such as riding a donkey backward.

The elderly in recent Turkish cartoon representations are recurrently frail, conservative, and, when compared to Nasreddin Hodja (a witty philosopher) and Evliya Çelebi (a vigorous traveler), lacking in distinctive individual characteristics. Indeed, their roles are mostly defined in terms of their family bonds. Grandparents in *Can*, *Niloya*, and *Pepee* are characterized in similar ways: they wear old-fashioned dress, rely on didactic verbal expressions and gestures, speak in quavering voices, and display exaggeratedly slow movements—all stereotypical features of old age. Cartoon grandparents are depicted as far older and more vulnerable than the elderly whom most contemporary Turkish children interact with in their daily lives.

As Nancy Signorielli (2001) explains, "television programs with limited time to devote to character development resort to stereotypes that are usually conventional and standardized images or conceptions, typically lacking in originality, and which often appeal to people's emotions rather than to their intellects" (345). The formulaic children's television shows in Turkey involving intergenerational relations reveal repetitive patterns of certain visual symbols (dress codes, personality traits, family types, lifestyles, gender roles) and thematic elements that are strongly associated with spiritual values and cultural codes. In light of the revival of traditional and predominantly Muslim values in the last decade in Turkey (Rankin, Ergin, and Gökşen), related symbolic elements have become more visible in the media. This trend also affects the construction of old age.

Jack Zipes (2002) emphasizes that texts and images of childhood play a role in the social construction and socialization of children in ways that serve the hegemonic interests of adults, rather than the children themselves. The stories of *Niloya*, *Can*, and *Pepee* all build upon an idealized image of the extended family living in a detached house with a garden, which is not in fact very common in Turkey. According to the Turkish Statistical Institute, 76.8 percent of the population reside in cities, yet most of the cartoons studied for this chapter do not depict urban scenes, skyscrapers, shopping malls, cinemas, or traffic. The construction of the characters radiates similar nostalgic idealism. The child figures are depicted as being at the center of family life, while the adults are portrayed as complete and independent human beings. For instance, the dinner scenes in each cartoon illustrate how the settings, gender representations, and relationships between characters are constructed according to a standard hierarchy. For instance, a male character (usually the grandfather) is seated at the head of the table. The knowledge transfer that frequently occurs between adults and children is presented as unidirectional: the adults share knowledge with the child, but not vice versa. Lee (2001) criticizes the sense of certainty that is created from standardized lifestyles and family models (16). He finds that the ideal of standardized adulthood restricts the endless experience of becoming, especially for children who grow up in an age of uncertainty (6). He finds the expectation for children to pursue a standardized adulthood to be underrating the value of becoming through experience in this age of pluralism (6).

Furthermore, especially in *Can* and *Niloya*, the conversations between grandparents and grandchildren mainly reveal the sense that traditional and cultural values are something directly transmitted from older people to the young, rather than something actively constructed and experienced in bidirectional interaction. In one of the episodes of *Niloya*, "Fındık Zamanı" (Hazelnut harvest time, 2014),[3] little Niloya surprises her grandmother by presenting her with a baby doll made from harvested hazelnut leaves, an action that revives her grandmother's childhood memories. The motivation behind this act is presented as little Niloya's desire for reinstalling the old practice of making dolls by hand and for soothing the grandmother's yearning for her younger days when she sees a newer-style doll. Thus, the young and the old rejoice in reviving the past together. Helle Strandgaard Jensen distinguishes between different types of nostalgia conveyed in children's literature:

> the quality of the items argued to be "classics" is believed to bridge a gap between past and present by bringing part of the past into the present through their revitalisation. This can be motivated by a feeling of nostalgia, a longing for a time when children were believed to experience the world in a different way.

In a similar sense, the grandmother's longing for a handmade baby doll and yearning when seeing a new one reveals the detachment from change and the present world. We argue that the type of nostalgia displayed in "Fındık Zamanı" is reactionary and fails to bridge the gap between two generations. As Nikki Gamble (2001) points out, "change is also evident in the representations of fictional families which generally reflect a trend towards more liberal attitudes and subversion of the traditional values. However, this development is not smoothly linear but punctuated by periods of progress and reaction" (1). Indeed, Niloya's episode reveals that there are two conflicting structures of nostalgia active in children's programs today: one that is conservative and reactionary to change, and another that promotes transformative relationships between generations.

Pepee, an adaptation of *Pocoyo*, was originally developed in Spain, broadcast by Clan TVE, and subsequently modified by Düşyeri Animation Studios for Turkish audiences. *Pepee* differs from *Pocoyo* primarily in that the former introduces parents and grandparents into the narrative. This inclusion of parental figures in *Pepee* suggests that the subjective experience of being a child is believed to involve protection by parents and grandparents. In this sense, the adaptation appears to correspond to Çiğdem Kağıtçıbaşı's model of emotional interdependence in traditional obedience-oriented Turkish families. She contrasts the Turkish model of child-rearing with Western practices, which are more oriented toward developing autonomy and self-reliance. The Spanish production *Pocoyo* is a clear example of the Western model in showing that a four-year-old character can cope with various situations on his own, without the visual appearance or intervention of parental characters. The accompanying male voiceover that converses with Pocoyo is the only adult presence that can be detected—this is a narrative feature that contributes to a congenial interaction between (quasi) adult and child. Despite introducing parental interventions, *Pepee* deserves credit for reaching beyond stereotypes in terms of the personal traits, interests, and abilities that it attributes to old characters. For instance, the grandfather travels with a hot-air balloon as a part of his everyday activities. Grandmother is competitive when playing hide-and-seek and solves mathematics problems with her grandchildren; and even when she is tired, she is able to engage in a robust hug with her energetic grandchildren.

Challenging ageist stereotypes in children's media is not a new phenomenon in Turkey. For instance, Mammy Yokum in *Li'l Abner* (Al Capp's famous comic strip that ran from 1934 to 1977) can be regarded as one of the toughest old female characters in the history of character design that was accessible in Turkey. Such challenges have, however, gained additional importance in recent international children's media. The British CBeebies comedy drama, *Grandpa in My Pocket* (Nottingham Playhouse, 2013), for example, stages younger and elder family members together as ideal companions and, in an effort to break down rigid categorizations of chronological age, presents a grandfather who is even naughtier than his grandson. Astley Baker Davies's *Ben and Holly's Little Kingdom* (Nickelodeon UK, 2012) has also attracted audiences from several continents by representing people from different age groups in a supernatural setting that deconstructs a sense of certainty about adulthood. Another international animation that has achieved cross-cultural

Figure 11.1. Meçi Meçi, created by Özgün Zümrüt (2011).

success is *Sarah & Duck* (CBeebies, 2013). Its central relationship involves a preschool-aged girl and a forgetful old lady, who are companions in adventures that force them to combine imagination and problem-solving skills. It primarily targets preschool viewers, yet it remains relevant to adult audiences, because of its novel ways of representing the experience of old age.

The dynamic structure of animation provides great opportunities for the art of storytelling to tap into children's fantasy worlds. Irony, slapstick, and metaphoric narrative styles are all elements that can contribute to transgressing the boundaries of common sense. The use of slapstick produces laughter across cultures, especially among eight-to-twelve-year-olds (Götz et al.). In depicting family life, however, current Turkish animation projects focus heavily on idealized life patterns, even when they do not align well with reality, and tend to refrain from drawing on magical characters or techniques that might appeal to the audience's sense of humor. Günseli Oral's research (2006) indicates that Turkey's rich creative resources are not always utilized, because of social pressure and traditionalism.

Meçi Meçi (Figures 11.1 and 11.2), for example, was a project in which the story and characters were designed in an effort to challenge customary images, conventional roles, and standardized intergenerational relations. In this program, an old captain teams up with a little girl for several fantastical scenarios and journeys. The project was submitted to TRT Çocuk in 2011 but was not accepted, due to its inconsistency with authentic representations of Turkish culture, despite the fact that its visual design quality and narrative structure could capture transcultural interest. It is evident that TRT Çocuk

Figure 11.2. Meçi Meçi, created by Özgün Zümrüt (2011).

gives priority to authenticity and cultural heritage over experimental and progressive design techniques. In the second part of this chapter, we question how the information and ideology conveyed through the pictures in Turkish animation meet the expectations of its audiences.

Hearing the Voices of the Turkish Children's Media Audience

Participants and Procedure

As Buckingham (2008) notes, the study of audience reception is relevant to producers of media programming as well as to cultural and media studies scholars. When it comes to intergenerational relationships, to include participants of various age groups in a reception study can help address issues of stereotyping. Since the majority of new productions deal with family patterns in their stories, our sample group consisted of fourteen grandparents who were between fifty-three and seventy-five years old, and ten grandchildren of between five and twelve years old (Tables 11.1 and 11.2). The socioeconomic and educational backgrounds of the sample group as well as their gender were evenly selected in order to gain insight into the variety of cross-cultural relationships that operate in the Turkish context.

The sample of this study consists of individuals who were born and raised in Turkey, who are currently living in Istanbul, where one-fifth of the Turkish population lives, and who are in contact with or see their grandchild

(GC) or grandparent (GP) at least once a week. We conducted face-to-face interviews individually in order to avoid influence from other participants. We prepared two sets of open questions to understand how grandchildren and grandparents view each other in their real lives within their own cultural environments, and to find out how they respond to the intergenerational relations reflected in contemporary Turkish cartoons.

The first set of questions was designed to investigate everyday relationships between older and younger members within Turkish families, that is, their shared activities in everyday life. The data collected ranged from personal profiles of the grandparents and grandchildren (including age and occupation) to the experiences of shared moments. We asked them, among other questions, to tell us about their favorite or least favorite shared activities, about games they play together, and about the feelings and ideas they associate with various basic concepts such as places, belongings, or clothes. Our findings provide insight into the character of daily interactions between Turkish grandparents and grandchildren, and the visual and sentimental representations with which they perceive each other. The second set of questions focused on how the participants' perception of old-age characters might be adequately captured in fiction. We asked them in particular to share how they would envision old age if they were to design cartoon characters themselves. To evaluate how they combine their imageries of reality and fiction, we encouraged them to think about the strengths, weaknesses, and aims of a character of their own creation and to construct figures that they thought would help them tell their own stories (Tables 11.2 and 11.3).

Results

The participants in our survey had lower middle and upper middle socio-economic backgrounds. In terms of education, all the ten grandchildren we interviewed were attending primary school. Two of the fourteen participant grandparents were illiterate, while ten of them were university graduates. All grandparents had houses separate from their children and grandchildren and lived independent lives, and all (except one) had regular incomes of their own. As noted above, Robinson, Callister, Magoffin, and Moore's list of stereotypical features used to signal old age includes glasses, grey hair, wrinkles, extensive balding, cracking voices, and the need for a cane or wheelchair; yet these characteristics rarely appear in the descriptions that the children gave when they were asked to define their grandparents (Table 11.1). In fact, an eight-year-old grandson (GC 1) reported wearing glasses as a similarity between himself and his grandfather. Notably, a headscarf occurs in only one response, whereas in all Turkish cartoons selected for this study the grandmothers wore one, while the younger female characters did not. When invited to think about their grandfathers, the children referred most frequently to cardigans and electronic devices. In the case of grandmothers, the children mentioned dresses, cooking materials, and perfume. Two grandparents (GP 7 and 10) reported that the love and affection between family members in *Pepee* resembled their own relationships. The rest of our respondents did not find much similarity between their real-life intergenerational relations and the cartoon representations in Turkish productions.

The responses of participants (Table 11.1) show the variety involved in intergenerational relations in everyday life: indeed, the range is so broad that the data barely fit a recognizable pattern. As discussed in previous sections, Turkish cartoon series depict an idealized and stereotypical relationship between grandparents and grandchildren that is largely free of conflict, a depiction that places their respective subjectivities on unequal footing. Our eighteen participants testified to having occasional disagreements or arguments in real life. It seems that from a child's perspective, defining the rules of a game can be a source of disagreement. Still, both generations define playing together as their favorite shared activity.

Most of the children (GC 1, 3, 5, 7, 8, 10) articulated in their spontaneous speeches that they saw their grandfathers as more distant than their grandmothers and gave less information in describing the former. Likewise, three out of five grandfathers reported that the first thing that came to mind when playing with their grandchildren was their wives' presence. This suggests that Turkish grandfathers tend to build indirect relationships with their grandchildren. This observation corresponds to the male's traditional role as a figure of authority. It also reveals the fragmentary process of modernization in Turkish society, where many fixed gender roles are hard to unsettle, as Bekir Onur (2009) has shown. In this respect, *Köstebekgiller*, which casts a grandfather as a child's main caregiver, challenges both aging and gender stereotypes of Turkish male figures. Grandfathers appeared to be perceived as distant and passive in the children's responses. We suggest that cultivating the idea that grandfathers and grandchildren can make good teams together, as presented in *Grandpa in My Pocket* or *Köstebekgiller*, is one issue to be considered in local productions.

When we asked our participants to think about the types of cartoon characters that would represent intergenerational relations, grandparents were more likely to recall the names of characters from their childhood, such

Table 11.1

Favorite activities together	Causes of disagreement	Items peculiar to him/her	Significant outfit	Places that remind him/her
• Playing make-believe, toy, card games, hide-and-seek, football (GP 1,2,4,5,6,8,13, GC 3,4,6,7,10) • Just watching her playing with her grandmother (GP 2,8,11) • Traveling or visiting other places (GP 1,2,3, GC 1,2,10) • Chatting and spending time together (GP 7,8,10, GC 3,8,10) • Cooking (GP 4,6,9, GC 2) • Solving math problems or riddles (GP 6, GC 4) • Buying ice cream (GP 2, GC 2) • Storytelling (GC 4) • Knitting (GC 3) • Watching news on TV (GC 3)	• Struggles about eating, doing homework, taking a shower, getting dressed (GP 1,5,6,7,9,10,11,13,GC 1,2,3,7,8,10) • None (GP 2,3,4,8,12,14, GC 6,9) • Making noise (GP 10, GC 5) • Describing game rules (GC 4) • Not liking the nickname that the grandparent uses (GC 7)	• Toys (GP 1,2,5,6,11,12,13) • Computer, television, or mobile device (GP 3,4,8,9, GC 1,2,5,12) • Perfume (GC 1,2,3,5,7) • Armchair (GP 10,, GC 4,5) • Knitting needle (GC 4,8) • Meal (GC 6,9) • Frying pan (GC 4) • Pills (GC 6) • Prayer beads (GC 7) • Red hair (GC 5) • Vase (GC 10)	• Dress (GP 10, 14, GC 1,8,9) • Glasses (GP 7, GC 1,2,4,8) • Cardigan (GP 12, GC 3,5,7) • Sportsuit (GP 5,6,8,9,) • T-shirt (GC 5,8,10) • Short pants (GP 3,4,13) • Fantasy clothes for playing make-believe (GP 1,11) • Neckscarf (GC 5,3,10) • Headscarf (GC 6) • Pajamas (GP 7) • None (GP 14)	• Home (GP 1,2,3,6,10,11,12,13, GC 2,3,4,5,6,7,8,9) • Park, seaside (GP 4,7,9,14) • Cinema, theater (GP 1,10) • Restaurant, shopping mall (GP 5,8)

Table 11.2
Grandparents' view of self

	Age/gender	Strength	Weakness	Aim
GP 1	66/female	Bringing family together	None	Travel the world
GP 2	75/male	Being expeditious	none	Be strong and loving
GP 3	53/female	Being dominant	Easily angered	Tidy up everywhere
GP 4	67/female	None	Being introverted	Travel the world
GP 5	73/male	Being handsome	None	Travel the world
GP 6	76/female	Tidying up everywhere	Easily angered	Bring equality to world
GP 7	60/female	Being a good cook	Don't know	Travel the world
GP 8	67/male	Being helpful	None	Improve the world
GP 9	62/female	Being a good soother	Becoming speechless when disappointed	Be a good role model
GP 10	60/female	Being determined	Being unable to resist noise	Bring family together
GP 11	70/male	Having high cognitive and motor skills, good at using tools	Being easily persuaded	Construct a house on an island
GP 12	54/female	Being a good explorer	None	To graduate from school
GP 13	64/male	Willing to learn new things every day	Being moved to tears easily	To find truth behind nature

as Heidi and her grandpa, or Pinocchio and his woodcarver father-figure Geppetto, rather than contemporary and domestic ones. Among Turkish productions, the characters that most commonly occurred in the responses of grandchildren were Pepee and his grandparents (GC 4, 7, 8) and Keloğlan (Egghead) and his grandpa Bilgecan (GC 5, 6). However, our participants stated that they do not find any similarity between themselves and these characters, as they are too childish (GC 4, 7, 8) or have different lifestyles than their own (GP 1, 2). The children did identify some other resemblances in international characters, such as Phineas's imagination in *Phineas and Ferb* (GC 4), Ben10's tendency to fight with his cousin (GC 2), and Frank's skill in setting traps in *Scooby Doo* (GC 1). The children older than ten years of age (GC 4 and 7) claimed that they were not interested in television shows featuring elderly characters. One ten-year-old participant (GC 4), however, admitted to liking SpongeBob and added that SpongeBob's grandmother resembles his own, because they both have wrinkled skin.

Table 11.3			
Grandchildren's views of grandparents			
(*) Age/gender	Strength	Weakness	Aim
GC1 8/male	GM: traveling, multitasking GF: traveling, using computer	none	GM: go on a holiday GF: go on a holiday
GC2 8/male	GM: talking fast, humor GF: being witty	none	GM & GF: help other people
GC3 8/female	GM: cooking great GF: being mighty	GM: noise GF: computer errors	GM: turn off the TV GF: sit less, travel more
GC4 7/male	GM: cooking, problem-solving GF: playing football, witty	GM & GF: coping with new technology	GM & GF: bring goodness to the world
GC5 10/male	GM: cooking great GF: gardening	None	GM & GF: save the world, sleep longer
GC6 12/female	GM: hugging tight, humor	None	GM: hugging tight all the time
GC7 5/female	GM: making me angry GF: drinking tea	GM & GF: me being angry at them	GM: make me angry GF: read his newspaper
GC8 7/female	GM: cooking great GF: none	None	GM & GF: save the world
GC9 6/female	GM: sewing and knitting	none	GM: a painter
GC10 12/female	GM: helping people, and problem-solving	GM: getting tired easily	GM: saving lives
GC, GM, and GF are abbreviations for grandchild, grandmother, and grandfather			

Tables 11.2 and 11.3 pertain to the subjects' fictional constructions. Grandparents were asked to imagine a version of themselves, while children were asked to imagine their grandparents as fictional characters. The data reveal how the two groups express themselves differently on the subject. Since designing a character involves developing the strengths, weaknesses, and aims of that character, we thought this task would also help to yield information about how participants identify and perceive the state of being a grandparent.

The grandparents' self-portrayals as fictional figures reveal realistic associations between their perception of strength and the social roles or duties expected from them. Their stated aims in an imagined cartoon world, however, demonstrate that they do not limit their future actions on the basis of their age; apparently, they want to enjoy the endless experience of becoming. Moreover, six of them claimed that they do not have any weakness, which indicates a vigorous internal spirit.

The children's responses express a more modest perception of aims, basing their analysis on the individual peculiarities of their grandparents' habits. In contrast, their perception of strengths focuses on the skills that they enjoy and appreciate in their grandparents' idiosyncrasies. When they were asked to ascribe a special superpower to their grandparents, most of the children associated their grandmothers with strong, practical, and well-trained female characters. Three children (GC 3, 5, 9) suggested that their grandmothers might have the skill of throwing fire, because of their talent for cooking. Another grandchild (GC 10) imagined her grandmother as having a brain with a biologically integrated and searchable Internet; the respondent said this idea was inspired by her grandmother's curiosity and desire to learn new things on a daily basis. As with the previous set of questions, traditional masculine models emerged in the children's imagined cartoon versions of their grandfathers. Most of the children associated them with brawny characters such as the Hulk or Thor, or with running fast (GP 2, 3, 5).

Conclusion

Embracing plurality in children's media would benefit children in multiple ways, because it facilitates the strengthening of existing relationships with the elderly, prepares them to construct their future selves in meaningful ways, and encourages them to view differing subjectivities as equal. We suggest that television programs can be powerful instruments for promoting solidarity between generations, if they utilize new forms of narrative and character design and include suitable content that is supported by research on audience reception.

When Turkish television shows for children involving elderly figures are closely examined, it becomes clear that even different production companies are influenced by the standardization of family patterns, dress codes, and gender roles in character design. They reflect a traditional form of childhood that can be interpreted as anachronistic or inconsistent, given the contemporary realities of both young and elderly segments of the population. The gap between Turkish television characters and their audience is confirmed by the fact that young audiences in Turkey find international cartoon characters more attractive and representative of their experience than native ones. Children's survey responses are a valuable resource in determining what topics attract their interest: an ordinary grandmother equipped with extraordinary skills could be more appealing to a young audience than a more traditional one. At the same time, it might challenge the child's expectations and biases regarding old age.

Our analysis is not intended to undermine the importance of preserving the intangible elements and values of cultural heritage, especially those norms that are threatened by global capitalism. Moreover, it is important to recognize that national productions play an important role in introducing young audiences of the twenty-first century to traditional, culturally specific intergenerational relationships; having said that, it is also necessary to stimulate a dialogue on the subject of the conditions of contemporary relations. Rather than simply repeating idealized family patterns that do not surprise the audience, it can be fruitful to incorporate unconventional, and even controversial, age-related representational strategies. In this sense, progressive television could contribute to the construction of equitable alliances between generations. This is especially relevant today, as the extent to which grandparents learn from their grandchildren is greater than ever before. They are willing and able to gain new skills such as using new technologies. Using children's media to stimulate active aging strategies, lifelong learning, and divergent thinking skills in an age-integrated context would bolster solidarity and also assist children in constructing their future selves.

Notes

1. There are more than 19 million children (between zero and fourteen years of age) living in Turkey, making up 24.3 percent of the overall population (TÜİK 2014). Although the United Nations defines children as people between zero and seventeen years of age, the Turkish Statistical Institute (TÜİK) uses demographic data categories that are related to active participation in economic life (0–14, 15–65, and 65+). The ratio of those aged 65+ to the overall population in Turkey is 8 percent (TÜİK 2014); however, it is expected to rise to 17.3 percent by 2050 (TÜSİAD 2012).

2. See www.eurofound.europa.eu/europeanyear2012/index.

3. This episode was produced by Bee and Bird Animation Studio for Yumurcak TV. The timecode for this episode is 00:50–01:30.

Works Cited

Beckett, Sandra L. *Crossover Picturebooks: A Genre for All Ages*. New York: Routledge, 2013.
Buckingham, David. "Children and Media: A Cultural Studies Approach." *The International Handbook of Children, Media and Culture*. Eds. Kristen Drotner and Sonia Livingstone. London: SAGE, 2008. 219–236.

Crawford, Patricia A., and Sharika Bhattacharya. "Grand Images: Exploring Images of Grandparents in Picture Books." *Journal of Research in Childhood Education* 28.1 (2014): 128–144.

Basting, Anne Davis. *The Stages of Age: Performing Age in Contemporary American Culture*. Michigan: University of Michigan Press, 1998.

Davies, Máire Messenger. *Children, Media and Culture*. Berkshire: Open University Press, 2010.

DiSalvo, Carl. "Design and the Construction of Publics." *Design Issues* 25.1 (2009): 48–63.

Eurofound. "Living Longer, Working Better: Active Aging in Europe." *European Observatory of Working Life 2012*. http://eurofound.europa.eu/resourcepacks/activeageing. Accessed on 31 August 2015.

European Training Foundation. *Promoting Lifelong Learning in Turkey*. http://www.etf.europa.eu/web.nsf/pages/EV_2014_Promoting_Lifelong_Learning_in_Turkey_putting_the_LLL_Strategy_in_practice?opendocument. Accessed on 31 August 2015.

Gamble, Nikki. "Introduction: Changing Families." *Family Fictions*. Eds. Nicholas Tucker and Nikki Gamble. London: Continuum, 2001. 1–47.

Götz, Maya, Firdoze Bulbulia, Shalom Fisch, Dafna Lemish, and Máire Messenger Davies. "Is That Funny Anywhere Else? An International Comparison of Humour in Children's Programmes." *Children, Humour, Television, Televizion, 19/2006/E*. Ed. Maya Götz. Munich: IZI, 2006. 35–40.

Herbert Art Gallery and Museum. "The Story of Children's Television from 1946 to Today." *Herbert Touring—Exhibition Touring Pack* 2005. http://goo.gl/EvyCAL. Accessed on 31 August 2015.

Jensen, Helle Strandgaard. "Making Children's Classics, Making Past Childhoods: Children's 'Classics' as Sites for Memory Politics and Nostalgia." *Reinventing Childhood Nostalgia*. Ed. Elisabeth Wesseling. United Kingdom: Routledge, 2017.

Joosen, Vanessa. "Second Childhoods and Intergenerational Dialogues: How Children's Literature Studies and Age Studies Can Supplement Each Other." *Children's Literature Association Quarterly* 40.2 (2015): 126–140.

Kağıtçıbaşı, Çiğdem. "Autonomy and Relatedness in Cultural Context Implications for Self and Family." *Journal of Cross-Cultural Psychology* 36.4 (2005): 403–422.

Lee, Nick. *Childhood and Society: Growing Up in an Age of Uncertainty*. Buckingham: Open University Press, 2001.

Neiman, Susan. *Why Grow Up? Subversive Thought for an Infantile Age*. New York: Farrar, Straus and Giroux, 2015.

Nikolajeva, Maria. *The Rhetoric of Character in Children's Literature*. Lanham: Scarecrow Press, 2003.

Nottingham Playhouse. *Grandpa in My Pocket—Teamwork! Insight Pack, 2013*. http://www.nottinghamplayhouse.co.uk/whats-on/family/grandpa-in-my-pocket-teamwork-2013. Accessed on 31 August 2015.

OECD (The Organisation for Economic Co-operation and Development). "Social Policy Division: Directorate of Employment, Labour and Social Affairs." *PF3.2 Enrolment in Childcare and Preschool*. 2014. http://www.oecd.org/social/family/database. Accessed on 31 August 2015.

Onur, Bekir. *Türk Modernleşmesinde Çocuk*. İstanbul: İmge, 2009.
Oral, Günseli. "Creativity in Turkey and Turkish-Speaking Countries." *The International Handbook of Creativity*. Eds. James C. Kaufman and Robert J. Sternberg. New York: Cambridge University Press (2006): 337–374.
Prout, Alan. "Culture-Nature and the Construction of Childhood." *Children, Media and Culture*. Eds. Kristen Drotner and Sonia Livingstone. London: SAGE, 2008. 21–35.
Rankin, Bruce, Murat Ergin, and Fatoş Gökşen. "A Cultural Map of Turkey." *Cultural Sociology* 8.2 (2014): 159–179.
Robinson, Tom, Mark Callister, Dawn Magoffin, and Jennifer Moore. "The Portrayal of Older Characters in Disney Animated Films." *Journal of Aging Studies* 21.3 (2007): 203–213.
RTÜK. *Türkiye'de Çocukların Medya Kullanma Alışkanlıkları Araştırması*. Ankara: Children's Foundation Publications, 2013.
Scholes, Robert, and Robert Kellogg. *The Nature of Narrative*. London: Oxford University Press, 1966.
Signorielli, Nancy. "Television's Gender Role Images and Contribution to Stereotyping." *Handbook of Children and the Media*. Eds. Dorothy G. Singer and Jerome L. Singer. Thousand Oaks: Sage Publications, 2001. 341–55.
Stephens, John, and Robyn McCallum. *Retelling Stories, Framing Culture: Traditional Story and Metanarratives in Children's Literature*. New York: Routledge, 2013.
Trites, Roberta Seelinger. *Literary Conceptualizations of Growth: Metaphors and Cognition in Adolescent Literature*. Amsterdam: John Benjamins, 2014.
Tufan, İsmail. *Türkiye'de Yaşlılığın Yapısal Değişimi*. İstanbul: Koç University Publishing, 2015.
Tufan, İsmail, and Suzan Yazıcı. "Intergenerational Relations in Old Age." *Toplum ve Sosyal Hizmet* 20.1 (2009): 47–52.
TÜİK. "Population of Selected Age Groups by Scenarios" *Population and Demography*, 2014. http://www.turkstat.gov.tr/UstMenu.do?metod=temelist. Accessed on 31 August 2015.
TÜSİAD. *2050'ye Doğru Nüfusbilim ve Yönetim: İşgücü Piyasasına Bakış*, 2012. http://www.tusiad.org/__rsc/shared/file/Isgucu-Piyasasina-Bakis-.pdf. Accessed on 31 August 2015.
Ürkmez, Başak. "The Animation Journey in Turkey: A Contemporary Reflection of the Karagöz Shadow Play." *Animation in the Middle East: Practice and Aesthetics from Baghdad to Casablanca*. Ed. Stefanie van der Peer. London: I. B. Tauris, 2017.
Zipes, Jack. *Sticks and Stones: The Troublesome Success of Children's Literature from Slovenly Peter to Harry Potter*. New York: Routledge, 2001.

- 12 -

"It's Disgusting!"

Children Enacting Mixed-Age Differences in Advertising

ANNA SPARRMAN

The concept of age is entrenched with cultural and moral values, Stephen Fineman stresses (26). It is therefore important to make sense of cultural age categories like old, elderly, childhood, youth, and what it means to act your age, or being too young for something. To theoretically investigate "age culture," or as Margaret Morganroth Gullette puts it, being "aged by culture," means conducting research that focuses on systems producing age in diverse situations. This is done, she argues, by deconstructing and redefining age beyond numbers and chromosomes. A cultural take on age emphasizes that age is performative (Fineman 26). How old a person feels does not necessarily correspond to his or her chronological age, and specific situations may require or evoke different age performances. Both Gullette and Fineman point out in theory that age is always socially and culturally situated. Similar issues about the understanding of age have been raised more specifically in relation to children and childhood. It could be argued that culturally speaking, children materialize age in a way that is similar to the way elderly people personify age.[1] Children's lives, just like elderly people's, are, for example, often "aged" in terms of their perceived (in)abilities and knowledge.

Childhood researcher Virginia Morrow (2013) argues that as far as children are concerned, Western cultures are focused on age as a numerical order. This strong tradition becomes evident when it is contrasted with the Majority World,[2] where many children do not know their numerical age. In these situations, children's social capabilities and accomplishments matter more than numbers. Morrow uses the term "functional age" for thinking about age as a social qualification overruling numerical age. Not everything in the Western World, however, is organized according to numerical order. In an argument that partly mirrors Morrow's, Anne Solberg launches the concept "social age." As an example, she refers to Norwegian children who at ten or twelve years (an early age according to Norwegian standards) have to take responsibility for domestic housework, such as cooking family evening meals on a regular basis (129–133). Solberg argues that the demands and expectations placed on the children do not change their biological age but can make the child grow older socially, in the sense that the children with increasing housework responsibilities may also acquire more autonomy than other children of the same age.

Solberg's concept of social age slightly differs from Morrow's notion of functional age. Functional age is focused on abilities regardless of numerical age, while social age usually suggests a transgression of culturally established expectations that are still related to numerical age. Both concepts approach the ages of childhood as fluid and negotiated in practice. Age, as Morrow stresses, always also varies with gender, culture, religion, and wealth (154) and intertwines with normative ideas of "right" and "wrong": what is, for example, the right age to get married, have a baby, or leave school? In this chapter I explore how age is enacted—being made—in and through situated practices of focus group discussions with children. Children aged nine to twelve years old look at and talk about two visual advertisements launched by the Danish shoe company Bianco Footwear (see Figures 12.1 and 12.2). The analyses focus on how age—young and old—is enacted by the children when looking at, talking about, and responding to the two visual advertisements. The overall question that I address is: how are young age and old age enacted, negotiated, and sustained as social and cultural norms in practice?

The Enactment of Age

Sexuality is a good example of the notion that the young and elderly are "aged" in relation to perceived (in)abilities and knowledge. Both young children and the elderly are frequently associated with asexuality, even though sexuality is perceived to be central to life in general or, as Barbara L. Marshall stresses, is even the force of life (177). Jenny Hockey and Allison James (142) point to an increased "sexual quietude" around people the older they get (especially after the age of sixty-five). In a similar vein the discourse of the asexual child is still pervasive, as are ideas that young children should be kept sexually ignorant (Egan and Hawkes 309–311). Marshall stresses that to be treated as asexual is disempowering, as it implies a loss of control of one's own body.

Recent research both within child studies and age studies has, however, challenged the notion of the innocent, asexual child and the sexually quieted elderly. Since the 1970s, the elderly have become an increasingly important market segment. In the United States, they are perceived to be controlling, as Anne L. Balazs says, "the majority of the nation's wealth" (28). Part of the market segmenting is a sexualization of the third age (Marshall 169): sexiness has become an active third-age capacity. Contemporary research in childhood studies, as pointed out by Emma Renold, Danielle R. Egan, and Jessica Ringrose, shows that children are complex sexual subjects actively negotiating notions of sexuality in their everyday lives (1). In this chapter young children (aged nine to twelve) look at and talk about sexualized advertisements picturing mixed-age heterosexual couples. The point of departure is that both sexuality and age are enacted in and through practice. When they intertwine, or as Sara Ahmed expresses it, stick to one another, complex norms, values, and objects of emotions are generated (Ahmed, "Affective Economies" 120).

Ahmed considers emotions to be relational in a way that resembles my approach to age and sexuality as enacted. The concept of enactment derives from science and technology studies. Enactment, as argued by both Annemarie Mol (33, 41, 44) and John Law (56), pushes social constructivism a step further. Instead of arguing that the world is being socially and culturally constructed once and for all, enactment theory emphasizes that "reality" constantly multiplies and that an enactment is a powerful productive consequence of practice-based activities. Law argues that an enactment is more open than a performance, as the latter has a tendency to favor human behavior, while enactment comprises both the human and the material (54–58). As I have pointed out in earlier research (Sparrman, "Body" 126–127), this means that material objects like images are "being done" by and through relations in practice. By combining the theory of affective economy with enactment theory, it becomes possible to investigate *how* age and sexuality are being made up—enacted—and in what ways someone or something is "aged" or sexualized in and through the relational work of material and nonmaterial entities in practice. This also includes feelings.

Ahmed's focus on what emotions *do* rather than what they *are* aligns well with enactment theory. "How do emotions work to align some subjects with some others and against other others?" she wonders, and: "How do emotions move between bodies?" (Ahmed, "Affective Economies" 117). Ahmed argues against treating emotions as "psychological dispositions," arguing instead that "we need to consider how they work, in concrete and particular ways, to mediate the relationship between the psychic and the social, and between the individual and the collective" (119). Accordingly, the alignments and attachments *between* objects and subjects are crucial. Or, to be more exact, what matters is *how* objects and subjects, as Ahmed puts it, "stick" together and how that process creates collective coherence (Ahmed, "Affective Economies" 119). She argues that through the circulation of objects and subjects, passionate attachments are generated (Ahmed, "Affective Economies" 118). In this process of linking and sticking, emotions can accumulate affective value over time, so it can seem as if emotions reside inside objects and subjects. However, her idea is that feelings like hate, disgust, and joy do not simply reside in a given person, subject, object, or word. They are affective outcomes of circulations. Ahmed calls this the "affective economy" of emotions, the "cultural politics of emotions," or the "sociality of emotions" (Ahmed, "Cultural Politics" 8, 10). The study of the sociality of emotions in the making draws attention to how people, in this case children, stick things together.

The concept of affective economy is here used to understand the non-residency and emotional dimension of images. In her study of theatrical celebrity photography in the United States (1915–1930), Marlis Schweitzer argues that photographs can play an important role in forming close affective bonds between celebrities and fans (204–236). She shows that the more the celebrity photographs circulated, the more affectively loaded they became and generated feelings associated with the modern (206–207). Schweitzer's text has inspired me to approach images as active parts in the circulation and creation of affective economies. I will focus on how details in images stick together and enact emotions in social practice. Considering children's social practice, my approach challenges Ahmed's focus on the emotionality of text ("Cultural Politics" 12–16) as well as Ahmed's and Schweitzer's lack of attention to children. My combination of enactment theory with affective economy and the sociality of emotions is aimed at understanding how material as well as nonmaterial entities enact age. What happens when the concept of affective economy is mobilized to investigate social interaction between children in practice rather than in text and photography? Can it help us to understand what components become important when enacting age in practice? The specific case study—a discussion of two visual advertisements for Bianco footwear—leads to a set of additional questions, which will also be addressed: how are young and old age enacted in relation to each other by children? How do children enact their own ages when looking at and talking about the advertisements? In what ways can age be understood as enactments?

Bianco Footwear

Bianco Footwear was launched in Denmark in 1987 under the name Bianco sko (Bianco Shoe) and is now an international footwear brand. The campaign discussed in this chapter dates back to the spring and fall of 2003 and was called "How to afford the whole collection."[3]

The campaign consists of a series of images depicting older and younger men and women together. The advertisements came with different catchphrases, for example: "Young girl marries rich old guy—the only way to getting the whole shoe collection . . ." or "How about young guy marrying rich older woman—guys need shoe collections too."[4] The text points to heterosexual love relationships. The campaign was highly debated in Sweden. Two images from the campaign presented here (Figures 12.1 and 12.2) were reported by private persons to the self-regulating board of Sweden's Trade Ethical Council against Sexism in Advertising (ERK).[5] The board condemned the campaign and the company for not living up to the International Chamber of Commerce's advocacies, codes, and rules of social responsibility and ethics in marketing.[6] ERK argued that the advertisement campaign was gender stereotyping both women and men, and promoting the idea that young people choose partners for financial advantages, while old people choose partners for looks.[7]

This is not the only advertising campaign by Bianco Footwear combining sexuality, money, gender, and shoes. In 2008 their campaign was called "How to double your collection," suggesting costumers should get a same-sex boyfriend or girlfriend in order to double the number of shoes in their wardrobe. It seems simple enough, but should you choose your partner based on shoe size? In 2009 the campaign read "Orgasm for your feet." The company explains the slogan as follows: "We lift the duvets and ask the consumers what turns them on? Whatever [sic] it is a classic style, sexy stilettos or colorful pumps . . . shoes are an orgasm for your feet."[8] Over the years, Bianco Footwear has repeatedly combined consumer commodities with notions of sexuality and money. The 2003 campaign is particularly interesting for this volume, as the images depict age-mixed couples.

It can be argued that in this campaign, Bianco Footwear appeals to what is described as "the senior market." According to Balazs (27), this market segment consists of an aging group that includes the so-called new old, sixty-five seventy-five-year-olds with access to good finances (27). The older characters in the advertisement campaign are visualized and labeled as resourceful and sexy rather than pitiful. Yet Bianco Footwear Sweden AB states that the

Figure 12.1. Bianco Footwear: "How to afford the whole collection." Copyright @ Bianco Footwear

Figure 12.2. Bianco Footwear: "How to afford the whole collection." Copyright @ Bianco Footwear

brand mainly targets young adults with their campaigns, and not the elderly or children.[9] The slogan "How to afford the whole collection" makes that clear: it is written from the perspective of the young, attractive person, not from the affluent, older person. Although Bianco Footwear's advertisements are not primarily targeting children, children do see and consume a large amount of advertising that is aimed at adults. If we want to understand how they invest in the social and cultural norms of a society, we need to study how children relate to cultural products available in the public sphere, even when they are not mainly produced for them.

Analysis

The empirical analyses derive from a larger research study of young people and visual consumption, which focuses on love, sex, relationships, and gender in visual media.[10] In total, twenty-three children (aged nine to twelve years) from the United States and Sweden participated in focus group discussions on the topic. Two were conducted in the United States and four in Sweden.[11] The American children had one single session per group, while the Swedish met twice, and one group three times at their own request. The Swedish children were also invited to make a scrapbook diary over a period of one week. All the discussions took place inside the children's schools, either during regular school hours or during after-school hours. All sessions were video-recorded to enable a review of which image was being discussed and when. Moreover, all groups were gender mixed. This was a conscious choice, as I wanted to find out how boys and girls approached the topic of sexuality together (see also Sparrman, "Access" and "Seeing").

In the first focus group sessions, sixteen images were discussed,[12] all of which had been reported to Sweden's ERK for being sexist or gender stereotyping. In 2008 all these images were available on the ERK's homepage. The campaigns chosen for the project advertised technology, food, and clothing/underwear. Accordingly, even though the focus group discussions were framed as being partly about sex, I as a researcher had not selected what I thought were sexy or sexualizing images, nor had I planned to talk about age in relation to the Bianco Footwear ads. In the focus groups, considerable time was spent on articulating whether and why the images looked sexy. The two Bianco Footwear advertisements (Figures 12.1 and 12.2) were the only pictures where the children raised age and sexuality in tandem. A more general and recurring topic, which I have discussed elsewhere, was the intertwinement of sexuality and disgust (Sparrman, "Access").

During the focus group discussions, the Bianco Footwear advertisements were presented to the children as a pair or as part of a theme (fashion). The simultaneous introduction of the images affected, as I will show, how age was discussed. The main empirical example to be analyzed in this chapter was picked from the first focus group meeting with group 5B. The group consisted of two boys (Allan and Jens) and two girls (Fia and Moa) between the ages of ten and twelve.[13] The children were from the same school and already knew one another prior to the focus group discussions. The sample from 5B illustrates the main topics of concern in all the focus groups when discussing the images. I selected the second empirical example for its uniqueness, as that was the only time the children mentioned their own ages. This sample was picked from the first focus group meeting with group 5AB, which consisted of only two girls (both eleven years old). They attended the same school, in parallel classes. They also knew each other before the focus group discussions.

On being shown the two images, a common and shared response in all of the focus groups was confusion. The children struggled to decide what the ads were promoting. One group (3B) suggested they were about "home design," "advertisements for mums and dads," for "clothes" or "love." Someone claimed not to understand them. Another group (3AB) suggested they promoted housing. Group 5B suggested that the advertisements were for "clothes," "houses and interior objects like paintings," or more specifically "floors." One group focused more on the advertisements' incomprehensibility, while another suggested the advertisements were for "Boobs" and also touched on the issue that "the girl seems to be trying to get something from him [the older man in Figure 12.1]" (SD 1).

In my analysis, I treat children, images, verbal accounts, concepts, text, emotions, gazes, and bodies all as equal agents in the interaction. This is important both in enactment theory and in order to capture, as Ahmed puts it, how subjects and objects are sticking to each other and how the process of sticking circulates values: how do age and sexuality stick to each other? When, where and how does age become emotional? In what ways do the children's own ages stick with the ages depicted in the advertisements? And how does this enact age?

An Old Gaffer, an Old Hag, and The Young: Children Enacting Age-Mixed Relationships

When presented with the two ads, group 5B directly starts commenting on the age difference of the people in the images. It is not until the end of the discussion that they actually raise the question of what is being promoted. They mention clothing, followed by housing, floors, and paintings. At this point, they also figure out that "How to afford the whole collection" means that one can financially afford to have a collection of something. When they find out that the images advertise shoes, they blurt out expressions like: "You are joking," "Hello?" and "Where are the shoes?" The children are not convinced at all.[14] The children's initial comments on age raise the question how they enact the depicted age differences. What affective qualities become important when young and old age are related to each other? What social and cultural norms about young and old age are enacted by the children? And how?

Example 1[15]

Bianco Footwear: Group 5B, Sweden, Focus group discussion 1[16]
Focus group participants: Allan (age 11, soon 12), Fia (age 11), Jens (age 11), Moa (age 10, soon 11), and Anna (focus group leader, age 44)
Focus: Talking about two Bianco Footwear advertisements from 2003

1. ANNA: What's that?
2. ALLAN: Let's see let's see
3. GIRL?: An old gaffer and x
4. ALLAN: And an old hag and a young guy and an old gaffer and a
5. FIA: I don't like it, I think they would fit better together and they would fit better
6. ALLAN: Yeaah
7. X?: Why are they standing so far down?
8. ALLAN: Can you see where his hand is, right?
9. ALL: Heh-heh
10. ANNA: Where is it, does he have it
11. ALLAN: On the butt
12. ANNA: Ah, on her bum
13. JENS: (giggles)
14. ANNA: What did you call it?
15. ALLAN: Ass
16. JENS: He-he
17. ANNA: On her ass
18. ANNA: Okay should we
19. ALLAN: But wait, he's not just holding it like, he really
20. ?: (Giggle) Yeah
21. MOA: He's grabbing it
22. ALLAN: Yeaah
23. JENS: Heh-heh
24. FIA: But, like, it's sort of disgusting 'cause she's an old lady, and he's like kind of young
25. JENS: Yeaah
26. FIA: Then, then it would be better if it was those two and those two
27. MOA: Young and old

28. ANNA: Why is that?
29. ALLAN: 'Cause it x
30. FIA: 'Cause it looks more normal
31. MOA: Yes
32. FIA: Yes, it looks more natural
33. ALLAN: Yes
34. JENS: Yes
35. MOA: The other looks more sexy
36. ANNA: What, did you say sexy, what do you mean that it looks more?
37. ALLAN: Xxx you might think xxx
38. MOA: Right, but it's disgusting to have an old gaffer and a young girl
39. X: Yeaah
40. JENS: xxx

When the two Bianco Footwear images are presented to group 5B, one of the girl's firstverbal account concerns age: "An old gaffer xxx" (turn 3). Age becomes relevant straight away. The way old and gaffer stick together creates a slightly disparaging view of being an old man. This view is strengthened by Allan, who continues to define one of the women as "an old hag" (turn 4). He sticks old hag to "and young man" before Fia interrupts him, declaring by pointing at the images that the young man and the young girl, as well as the old man and the old woman, would make a better combination (see Figures 12.1 and 12.2).

Fia's comment shows how emotions enter the discussion. She verbally expresses her dislike by saying, "I do not like" and "would fit better" (turn 5). Her visual as well as verbal process of sticking different ages to one another enacts normative ideas of how dissimilar ages should (not) be entangled. As none of the other participants responds to her, Fia both takes a distance and raises her input in turn 24. She distances herself by first withdrawing from the "I" presented in turn 5, making instead a more general comment with "it is": "it is sort of disgusting." She raises the stakes by sticking the word "disgusting" together with the description of the woman as "an old lady" and the man as "kind of young" (turn 24; Figure 12.2). Fia enacts disgust as yet another shared feature important to the discussion. The connection between disgust and age involves still another little word, "'cause," with which Fia enacts the relation between heterosexually gendered old and young age as an established disgusting consistency.

The way Fia sticks old, young, man, woman, and disgust together creates an intense emotional attachment that shows how signs of age and the ways they are connected create values not resident in either of the concepts.

The value of age is rather located, as argued by Ahmed, in the circulation of verbal accounts and feelings expressed by Fia. She also offers a solution to avoid feelings of disgust, pointing at the two images and saying that: "it would be better" (turn 26) if the two young people and the two old people were together. After this comment Fia gets attention from both Moa and the focus group leader. Moa pulls together Fia's comments into two age concepts: "young" and "old" (turn 27). I then challenge Fia and Moa by asking why that combination would be better. At that point, a new concept is presented that advances the word "disgust": "normal." The combination of two young and two old people "looks more normal" (turn 30). Or, as more strongly expressed by Fia: it looks "more natural" (turn 32). Both Allan and Jens now agree.

The use of "natural" relates age to essentialism and biology. To stick similar age groups to one another enacts similar-age couples to stand out as the original and normal combination. The naturalness of homogeneously matching ages is strengthened by Moa, who mobilizes a negative attachment by saying that "the other [i.e., the age-mixed couple] looks more sexy" (turn 35). Moa introduces the verbal account "looks sexy" to the conversation and sticks it to age. When sexy is related to the old man and the young woman, on the one hand, and to the old woman and the young man on the other, it strengthens the argument of the unnaturalness of the ages mixing. As none of the children defies Moa, they have together enacted what makes age-mixed couples unnatural. It is not age mixing as such, but rather how it relates to "looks more sexy." From this it follows that sexiness is enacted in opposition to what is natural.

When the children are asked how one can see that it looks "more [sexy]" (turn 36), the word "disgusting" reappears. Moa specifically marks the age difference between "the gaffer" and the "young girl" as disgusting (turn 38) and is supported by the other children (turns 39–40). The way disgust, old gaffer, and young girl are related to one another makes the man stand out as more disgusting than the girl. The word "gaffer" enacts oldness. Still, the children stick the words "old," "sexy," and "young girl" to "gaffer." This circulation of words enacts (sexual) age difference as disgusting, with old age being less desirable than young age in the age mixing.

All the focus groups displayed difficulties attributing an age to the young girl. She was described to be a "young girl" (3B, SD1), "gal" (3AB), "twenty, thirty something" (5B), "young lady" (SD1), "really, really young girl," and a "young lady" (SD2). Maybe one reason for this imprecision is her light pink and very short dress. If one looks closely at her face, one can argue that she looks more like a young woman than a girl. The way the pink color of the dress sticks to the shortness of the skirt,[17] and to her straightforward look at the beholder, enacts her as simultaneously innocent and challenging. She looks like what Valerie Walkerdine would call a "girl-woman" (155, 165). This contradiction might make it difficult to establish a shared understanding of her age. The age of the young man does not receive the same attention. He is called "boy" once (3B), "young guy" (5B), and "young man" (SD2).

To get a better grip on the children's enactment practices, I challenged their versions of enacting age by asking whether the young girl could be the daughter of the older man. Example 2 is taken from the same focus group discussion as example 1.

Example 2

41. ANNA: But isn't she just his daughter?
42. JENS: It looks like he kind of
43. MOA: Nah, you don't really cling like that on
44. ALLAN: Yeah but look, if it's supposed to be, if it's supposed to be her, what's it called, son
45. FIA: Heh-heh
46. MOA: And she like
47. ALLAN: Then, she's standing like this kind of and he's kneeling down and x
48. JENS: He-he, on his mother (laughter)
49. MOA: Heh-heh
50. ANNA: So then that's not proper?
51. ALL: NOO!
52. ANNA: Okay, so then there's something between these two anyway?
53. FIA: Yeaah, I think it's bad, I mean what is it, well I guess it's an ad for, it's an ad for clothes, isn't it?

Moa is quick to respond to the challenge by explaining that "you don't really cling like that on [a father]" (turn 43). The way she verbally accounts for the physical relations between the pictured gendered bodies enacts the postures as socially and culturally normed. At this moment, Allan breaks into the discussion, returning to the image of the older woman and the younger man (Figure 12.2), which he, Jens, and the rest of us have talked about earlier. It turns out that the way the concepts daughter, son, and mother, as well as the physical contact between the depicted characters, sticks to one another creates collective emotions like laughter, giggles, and titters within the group. Even though the verbal interaction is full of unexpressed words and understatements (turn 45–48) and filled with laughter, it seems the children share an understanding of how physical touch, age, and notions of family should or should not be linked together.

As a result, the children seem to agree that there are no family relations between the couples in the images. The words "cling" (turn 43) and "grabbing" (turn 21) in the way they define the physical touch in the images enacts the age relation between the couples as sexual. This is confirmed by Fia, who agrees that "there's something between these two" (turn 52–53), and that "something" is, according to Fia, "bad" (turn 53). Fia sticks to her initial idea that mixing age differences among heterosexual couples stands out as wrong, disgusting, unnatural, and bad. It is vital to point out, though, that none of these qualities reside either in the images, the depicted people, their clothing, or the children. Age is enacted and made in practice through the process of sticking different attributes to one another.

Children's Age Differences in Practice

As mentioned previously, the age of the children in the focus group ranged from nine to twelve years. So far I have focused on how the children enact young and old age as related to one another while looking at and talking about the two advertisements. But it is important not to assume that children's sense of their own age is straightforward. So, an important question is whether children also enact their own ages during the discussion. To answer this question, I return to the first example and reflect on how the words "I," "they," "his," "her," and "those two" and laughter (turns 5–26) are used in the interaction. These words are used to distance the spectators from the characters in the images. In this process, the children and the focus group leader enact themselves as a "we." Not only the verbal accounts but also the shared and allowed laughter help reinforce this "we." The question is what kind of a "we" is being enacted? Is it a same-age "we," as in "we the children"? Or rather, "we here in the focus group"? Could we perhaps understand these "we's" arising from the kind of sticking together suggested by Ahmed? As implicit as the "we's" are, the children never talk about themselves as being younger or older than the depicted people, nor do they mention whether they feel young or old.

Do the children's comments about the images tell us something about how they enact their own ages? The only verbal account with explicit reference to the children's own age appears in the first focus group discussion with group 5AB. This group consists of two eleven-year-old girls and the focus group leader. Just before the example below, the group has discussed the age difference between the depicted couples in the two advertisements. The girls, Hedda and Rut, have talked about who in the images is in love with whom. These two girls have a somewhat more complex take on age differences than does group 5B. An interesting aspect is that, in contrast to group 5B, Hedda and Rut actually talk about age difference. The girls do not think that the age differences between the couples are appropriate, but they also acknowledge that it does happen in life that, for example, old motorcycle men and young girls have love relationships. The discussion below begins with my trying to summarize the previous comments to clarify what the girls' take on age differences is.

Example 3

Bianco Footwear: Group 5AB, Sweden, Focus group discussion 1
Focus group participants: Hedda (age 11), Rut (age 11), Anna (focus group leader, age 44)
Focus: Talking about two Bianco Footwear advertisements from 2003 (Figures 12.1 and 12.2)

1. ANNA: So, it's okay to have relationships like that?
2. RUT: Yes
3. HEDDA: Ehm
4. RUT: You get to decide for yourself if you want to
5. ANNA: Ehm, you get to choose for yourself
6. RUT: Ehm
7. HEDDA: It's like nothing I would want (RUT: No) I wouldn't want to be going with somebody who's maybe like seventeen years old now and I'm just eleven (ANNA: Ehm), that's a difference of six years, but like it would be strange if I was going out with a twenty-year-old, that's a lot of years different
8. ANNA: Right now
9. HEDDA: Right now
10. ANNA: But if you (looks at Hedda) were seventeen, or if you were twenty, and then you were dating someone who was thirty?
11. RUT: Noo ... or you know
12. HEDDA: My mum is dating a fifty-one-year-old, and she is only thirty-four, so there's a difference of sixteen years.

In turns two and four, Rut's way of enacting age differences between couples is somewhat more allowing than what we saw in group 5B. Rut gives a clear yes to my question (turn 1) while Hedda with her "Ehm" (turn 3) is not as overtly positive. Rut explains further that it is up to each individual "to choose for yourself" and "if you want to" (turn 4) be in an age-mixed love relationship. After this, Hedda generates a more negative statement, by testifying that she would not want, we have to assume, to be in a love relationship with a big age difference. Rut agrees with this statement ("no"). This is the first and only time in all of the focus group material that one of the children explicitly enacts her own age in relation to the age relations generated by the discussed advertisements.

Hedda argues that it would be strange if she as an eleven-year-old girl went out with a seventeen-or twenty-year-old (turn 7). By sticking the age numbers to one another (eleven and seventeen) she creates an exact numerical age difference, six years, which it would entail (turn 7). She then increases the age difference by considering her partner to be twenty years old, this time not calculating the age difference in numbers. It seems as if the age difference then is so large, "a lot of years" (turn 7), that it is unspeakable in numerical order, or beyond what is possible. When I pick up on the "now" expressed by Hedda, I suggest she does not want to have a relationship with that age difference at this moment in her life (turn 8), and she confirms this by repeating "right now" (turn 9). To make sure though that we mean the same thing with "right now," I present a future scenario to Hedda where she is seventeen or twenty years old and her partner is thirty, that is a numerical age difference of ten to thirteen years, but at a later period in life. Would that be okay? Strangely enough it is not Hedda, but Rut who responds to this question. Rut begins with an extracted "noo," but then hesitates and begins to explain herself (turn 11). However, Rut never finishes her sentence, as she is interrupted by Hedda, who introduces a new discussion about her mother who is thirty-four years old and going out with a man sixteen years her senior. This interruption leads to a discussion about how large age differences can or should be.

Hedda and Rut's discussion about their own ages raises a few questions. Why do they not want to be in relationships with big age differences? The way the two girls stick their own ages to other ages and to romance enacts the cultural reproduction of age difference in romantic relationships as unacceptable. Their argument could, however, also open up a reversed way of thinking: the way children stick and enact their own ages in social practice also has relevance for how they enact other age differences, in this particular case the age-mixed couples in the two *Bianco Footwears* ads. That is, they draw on their understandings of themselves when enacting age in the images rather than reproducing stereotypical commercial advertising norms. Their discussion (turn 7 and 9) hints towards an awareness that age differences in love relationships are not necessarily enacted in the same way throughout the life course, but rather depend on the phase in life when they take place. What is clear is that the girls enact their own age through numbers. They enact themselves as being eleven years old, and that numerical age matters to them in romantic relationships.

Conclusion

By combining cultural age studies, child (sexuality) studies, enactment theory, and the affective economy of emotions, it has been possible to explore how age is enacted through connections between material (images) and nonmaterial (words, emotions) components. This chapter has proposed a complex and practice-based framework for exploring children's enactments of age-mixed romantic relationships in visual advertisements. It has investigated in what ways age is enacted—being done and made—in and through social practice, and how it entangles notions of sexuality and feelings like disgust.

The analyses emphasize how age is enacted between the characters in the images, between the characters and the consumer products depicted, in the relation between the images and the interpreting children, between the children and the group leader in the focus groups, and between the children and the way they enact their own ages in practice. This practice-based approach to age, exploring how objects and subjects stick together, has made it possible to study in detail how age is being done. The analyses show a complex interlinking of different objects and subjects, which point to how age is made to be young, old, disgusting, or laughable. This chapter does not reveal how children value old and young age per se. It does tell us something, though, about how children enact young and old age in relation to each other. We cannot be certain that the older man and the older woman depicted in the images would have been called "gaffer" and "hag" if they had, as the children suggest, been placed together. Young and old age are enacted as disgusting because they are related to each other and to love and sexuality. In short, according to the children, what is old or young differs in various stages of life and is further dependent on the quality of the relationships.

Nothing in the discussions suggests that the way the children enact the age differences depicted in the advertisements is directly attributed to their own young age. Age differences between old and young couples in sexual relationships tend to be described as inappropriate. The interaction in the focus group shows that the children enact that same discourse. At the same time, it becomes clear that the children neither pity nor generally talk badly about old or young age. They enact the old people in the advertisements as resourceful and sexually active in the sense that they define them as being in a romantic relationship. Even though the older people in the ads are empowered by being sexualized, the children either laugh or express concern about sexual relationships between young and old.

Moreover, the analyses show that when age in practice intersects with bodies, looks, consumer products, sexuality, and commonly shared morals and values, the notion of age multiplies. Staying with this complexity, it becomes possible to capture how age intertwines with other aspects, and how, when and where the borders of age are being made relevant by the children. They approach age as such in different ways: age hierarchy and consumption; age differences and sexuality; age awareness; age chronology; age and normality; ageism; what age "looks" like, and age, gender and love. From this follows, for the Western World, a more unstable view on age that aligns more with how age in non-Western countries is more commonly discussed, that is in terms of functional or relational age (Morrow 2013). It is not possible to single out age as an isolated object. It gets its function through how it is used in practice. This goes also for numerical age. The same numerical age can have different values depending on when, where, by whom and to what it is related. The age eleven can, for example, be enacted as immature and problematic in a presumed love relationship between an eleven- and a seventeen-year-old, while at the same time being performed as reliable and informed when talking with a researcher. This simultaneity suggests new avenues for thinking about age and its functions in relation to both children and elderly people, and across different social and cultural settings.

Notes

1. "Elderly" is here used in accordance with Anne L. Balazas's definition as "over the age of seventy-five." Concepts like "older," "mature," and "senior" are used interchangeably with reference to people older than seventy-five.

2. "Majority World" is another term for the Third World (the developing countries of Asia, Africa, and Latin America). The former is preferred to the latter, because it makes clear that these developing countries comprise most of the world's population.

3. It was launched in English from the beginning, with no translation.

4. See *Bianco*, http://www.bianco.dk/indhold/campaigns (accessed on 24 January 2016).

5. Etiska rådet för könsdiskriminering (ERK) has since 2009 been merged with the Swedish advertising ombudsman established by the markets as a self-regulating organization. Before the merger, all ERK cases were public and could be found and read online. ERK itself could take action against advertisements, but most complaints reached the organization through private persons. One complaint was sufficient for the board to decide on actions.

6. See *International Chamber of Commerce*, http://www.iccwbo.org (accessed on 25 January 2016).

7. See ERK cases—2003: 63; 66; 70; 84; 99; 102; 106; 119; 134; 164; 170 and 2004: 04.

8. See *Bianco*, http://www.bianco.dk/indhold/campaigns (accessed on 24 January 2016).

9. Remark to ERK from Bianco Footwear Sweden AB (28 April 2003, see ERK 63,66 and 70/03).

10. This study is inspired by David Buckingham and Sara Bragg's research project *Young People, Sex and the Media: The Facts of Life?* (Palgrave, 2004) but has taken a different turn.

11. Altogether, two schools, eight classes, and 175 children were asked to participate in the project. Twenty-seven children (United States = 10, Sweden = 17) consented to participate in the study, and twenty-three of them actually attended the focus groups. In total ten girls and thirteen boys participated. Altogether, there were eleven focus group sessions. The small number of participants has been discussed by Sparrman ("Access").

12. The same material was used in the Swedish and American focus groups. Most of the ads contained texts written in English, which is why the American children were sometimes able to interpret the pictures at multiple levels, while the Swedish children at times needed help translating the English (see Sparrman, "Access").

13. All the children's names are anonymized.

14. It should be mentioned that these advertisements at times had a banner under the images showing shoes. That was, however, not the case when they were downloaded from ERK's homepage.

15. In the transcription, the following conventions are used: x = inaudible word, xxx = inaudible words, ( )= comments on body language, CAPITAL LETTERS= strong emphasis.

16. The interaction has been translated from Swedish to English by a professional proofreader.

17. We see this combination as used by female pop stars like Toni Basil, as pointed out by Walkerdine (139–163) or Baby Spice in the Spice Girls, as pointed out in Sparrman ("Barns," "Visuell kultur" 153–182).

Works Cited

Ahmed, Sara. "Affective Economies." *Social Text* 22.2 (2004): 117–139.

Ahmed, Sara. *The Cultural Politics of Emotion*. Edinburgh: Edinburgh University Press, 2004.

Balazs, Anne L. "Forever Young: The New Aging Consumer in the Marketplace." *Aging, Media, and Culture*. Eds. Lee C. Harrington, Denise D. Bielby, and Anthony R. Bardo. Lanham: Lexington Books, 2014. 25–36.

Egan, Danielle R., and Gail Hawkes. "Girls, Sexuality and the Strange Carnalities of Advertisements: Deconstructing the Discourse of Corporate Paedophilia." *Australian Feminist Studies* 23.57 (2008): 307–322.

Fineman, Stephen. *Organizing Age*. Oxford: Oxford University Press, 2011.

Hockey, Jenny, and Allison James. "Back to Our Futures: Imaging Second Childhood." *Images of Aging: Cultural Reflections on Later Life*. Eds. Mike Featherstone and Andrew Wernick. London: Routledge, 1995. 135–148.

Law, John. *After Method: Mess in Social Science Research*. London: Routledge, 2002.

Marshall, Barbara L. "Sexualizing the Third Age." *Aging, Media, and Culture*. Eds. Lee C. Harrington, Denise D. Bielby, and Anthony R. Bardo. Lanham: Lexington Books, 2014. 169–180.

Mol, Annemarie. *The Body Multiple: Ontology in Medical Practice*. Durham: Duke University Press, 2002.

Morrow, Virginia. "What's in a Number? Unsettling the Boundaries of Age." *Childhood* 20.2 (2013): 151–155.

Renold, Emma, Danielle R. Egan, and Jessica Ringrose. "Introduction." *Children, Sexuality and Sexualization*. Eds. Emma Renold, Jessica Ringrose, and Danielle R. Egan. Basingstoke: Palgrave Macmillan, 2015. 1–17.

Schweitzer, Marlis. "Accessible Feelings, Modern Looks: Irene Castle, Ira L. Hill, and Broadway's Affective Economy." *Feeling Photography*. Eds. Elspeth H. Brown and Thy Phu. Durham: Duke University Press, 2014. 204–236.

Solberg, Anne. "Negotiating Childhood: Changing Constructions of Age for Norwegian Children." *Constructing and Reconstructing Childhood*. Eds. Allison James and Allan Prout. London: Falmer Press, 2007. 123–140.

Sparrman, Anna. "Access and Gatekeeping in Researching Children's Sexuality: Mess in Ethics and Methods." *Sexuality & Culture* 18.2 (2014): 291–309.

Sparrman, Anna. *Barns visuella kulturer—skolplanscher och idolbilder*. Lund: Studentlitteratur, 2006.

Sparrman, Anna. "Seeing (with) the 'Sexy' Body: Young Children's Visual Enactment of Sexuality." *Children, Sexuality and Sexualization*. Eds. Emma Renold, Jessica Ringrose, and R. Danielle Egan. Basingstoke: Palgrave Macmillan. 123–140.

Sparrman, Anna. *Visuell kultur i barns vardagsliv—bilder, medier och praktiker*. Linköping: Univ, 2002.

Walkerdine, Valerie. *Daddy's Girl: Young Girls and Popular Culture*. Cambridge: Harvard University Press, 1998.

NOTES ON CONTRIBUTORS

GÖKÇE ELIF BAYKAL is a PhD candidate and research assistant in the design, technology and society program at Koç University in Istanbul, Turkey. She currently carries out research on evidence-driven content development in children's media to facilitate preschoolers' spatial skills. Baykal has worked as a freelance screenwriter for TRT Çocuk (the national TV channel in Turkey for children), contributing to series for children such as *Nane ile Limon* (Mint and lemon) and *Bulmaca Kulesi* (Riddle tower).

LINCOLN GERAGHTY is reader in popular media cultures in the School of Media & Performing Arts at the University of Portsmouth. He serves as editorial advisor for the *Journal of Popular Culture*, *Reconstruction*, *Journal of Fandom Studies*, and *Journal of Popular Television*, with interests in science fiction film and television, fandom, and collecting in popular culture. He is senior editor for the online open access journal (from Taylor Francis) *Cogent Arts and Humanities*. Major publications include *Living with* Star Trek: *American Culture and the* Star Trek *Universe* (I. B. Tauris, 2007), *American Science Fiction Film and Television* (Berg, 2009), and *Cult Collectors: Nostalgia, Fandom and Collecting Popular Culture* (Routledge, 2014).

VERÓNICA GOTTAU is research assistant at the Universidad Torcuato Di Tella in Argentina, where she obtained her master's degree in educational policies in 2014. She is a doctoral candidate in the School of Education at the University of San Andrés in Buenos Aires. Her research interests include educational policies and the sociology of education. She is currently working on a research project on school choice from the perspective of symbolic interactionism.

VANESSA JOOSEN is professor of English literature and children's literature at the University of Antwerp. She is the author of *Critical and Creative Perspectives on Fairy Tales* (2011), which was given a Choice Award for Outstanding Academic Research by the American Library Association, and coeditor of *Grimms' Tales around the Globe* (together with Gillian Lathey, 2014), which won the Children's Literature Association Honor Award for Edited Book 2014.

SUNG-AE LEE is lecturer in Asian studies in the Department of International Studies at Macquarie University, Sydney. Her major research focus is on fiction, film, and television drama of East Asia, with particular attention to Korea. Her research centers on relationships between cultural ideologies in Asian societies and representational strategies. She is interested in cognitive and imagological approaches to adaptation studies, Asian popular culture, Asian cinema, the impact of colonization in Asia, trauma studies, fiction and film produced in the aftermath of the Korean War, and the literature and popular media of the Korean diaspora.

CECILIA LINDGREN is associate professor at the Department of Thematic Studies at Linköping University, Sweden. Her research concerns family, childhood, and parenthood, and she has a special interest in legislative processes, family and welfare politics, and professional practices in social work. She specializes in child adoption law, policy, and practice in the 1900s and today. Her publications include studies of domestic and intercountry adoption, with a focus on definitions of "the child's best interest," parent capacity assessment, and adoptees' perspectives on background and roots.

MAYAKO MURAI is professor in the English department at Kanagawa University, Japan. Her latest book, *From Dog Bridegroom to Wolf Girl: Contemporary Japanese Fairy-Tale Adaptations in Conversation with the West*, was published by Wayne State University Press in 2015. Her other recent writings appeared in *Grimms' Tales around the Globe: The Dynamics of Their International Reception* (Wayne State University Press, 2014), edited by Vanessa Joosen and Gillian Lathey, *Angela Carter traductrice—Angela Carter en traduction* (Centre de Traduction Littéraire, 2014), edited by Martine Hennard Dutheil de la Rochère, and *Marvels & Tales: Journal of Fairy-Tale Studies*. Her current research aims to reconsider the human–animal relationship by bringing together ecocriticism and fairy-tale studies.

EMILY MURPHY is lecturer in children's literature at Newcastle University. Before accepting her current post, she lived and worked in Shanghai, China, for two years. She has published several essays on children's literature in, among others, *The Lion and the Unicorn* and *Children's Literature Association*

Quarterly. She is currently finishing her monograph *Growing Up with America: Myth, Childhood, and National Identity from Postwar to Present* (under contract with the University of Georgia Press).

MARIANO NARODOWSKI is professor of education at the Universidad Di Tella in Argentina. His research is focused on education and the history and future of childhood. He served as president of the Argentine Society of History of Education and as Minister of Education of the City of Buenos Aires. He was a John Simon Guggenheim Fellow and Harvard Visiting Scholar, and he has delivered seminars, conferences, and public lectures in numerous universities around the world. He has published twenty books and papers in several journals, including *Discourse*, *Pedagogica Historica*, and *Compare*. In 2016 he was awarded the Lasig-CIES Oustanding Scholar Award.

JOHANNA SJÖBERG holds a PhD in child studies. She is senior lecturer at the Department of Thematic Studies at Linköping University, Sweden. Her research focuses on children's role in consumer culture, with a particular interest in visuality and age relations. She has worked with advertising, Internet clothing stores, and laws and regulations surrounding children's consumption.

ANNA SPARRMAN is professor at the interdisciplinary Department of Thematic Studies—Child Studies at Linköping University, Sweden. Her work is carried out at the intersection between visual culture, children's consumer culture, child culture, and child sexuality. Her primary areas of interest are norms and values of children and childhood, as well as ethnographic research with children. She also has a special interest in visual research methods. Her latest collaborative publications "The Ontological Practice of Child Culture" and *Doing Good Parenthood: Ideal and Practices of Parental Involvement* are theoretical advancements of childhood concepts.

INGRID TOMKOWIAK is professor of popular literature and media at the Institute of Social Anthropology and Popular Culture Studies at the University of Zurich. Also a specialist in children's and youth's media, she has written articles on children's classics and their film adaptations, as well as on bestsellers and blockbusters. She is the editor of the series *Populäre Literaturen und Medien* and coeditor of the journals *Interjuli* and *kids+media*. Current research projects deal with material poetics in picture books and popular animation films.

HELMA VAN LIEROP-DEBRAUWER is full professor of children's literature and the coordinator of the MA in children's and young adult literature at Tilburg University. Her research interests are literary socialization, the history of children's literature, adolescent novels, and life writing for children and young adults. She acts on the advisory board of *International Research in Children's Literature* and on the editorial board of the *European Studies on Children's and Young Adult Literature Series*. In 2014 she coedited *Een land van waan en wijs*, a new history on Dutch children's literature (together with Rita Ghesquiere and Vanessa Joosen).

ILGIM VERYERİ ALACA is assistant professor at Koç University, in the Department of Media and Visual Arts. Prior to this position she taught at Bilkent University and the University of Richmond. She holds a bachelor of fine arts degree from Mimar Sinan University, a master's degree from California State University, a master of fine arts degree from the University of Illinois at Urbana-Champaign, and a PhD from Hacettepe University. She has contributed chapters to *The Routledge Companion to International Children's Literature*, *The Routledge Companion to Picturebooks*, and *The Routledge International Handbook of Early Literacy Education*.

ELISABETH WESSELING is director of the Centre for Gender and Diversity at Maastricht University. She studies the intersections between gender and age, more specifically, the cultural construction of childhood. She is the editor of two volumes within the field of childhood studies: *The Child Savage: From Comics to Games* (Ashgate, 2016) and *Reinventing Childhood Studies in Contemporary Convergence Culture* (Taylor & Francis, 2017). Wesseling is President of the International Research Association for Children's Literature and directs the international research network PLACIM (Platform for a Cultural History of Children's Media).

INDEX

abandonment: of children, 128, 129, 131, 133–37, 143; of the elderly, 20, 33, 128, 134
abuse, 6, 129
adaptations, 44, 48, 49, 51, 54, 56, 58, 49, 62, 94, 108, 109, 130, 147, 148, 152, 155, 157, 210, 212, 215
adolescence, 13, 76, 84, 122, 169, 170
adoption, 133
advertising, 228–44
adulthood, 13, 15, 17–19, 45, 64, 88, 95, 109, 115, 117, 122, 124, 134, 143, 165, 169, 189, 192, 203, 215, 216
adults, 14–16, 18–20, 26, 29, 33, 35, 50, 58, 65, 66, 74, 76, 80, 82–84, 88, 89, 93–95, 97, 98, 102, 104, 105, 110, 113, 114, 117, 125, 129, 137, 140, 146, 149–54, 156–58, 164, 165, 170, 171, 175, 176, 181, 185–89, 191, 192, 194, 195, 198, 200–202, 208, 209, 211, 214–16, 233
affinity between childhood and old age, 14–17, 22, 65, 69, 70, 137
age, 45, 60, 54, 78–80, 87, 88, 109, 113, 117, 118, 186, 209, 210, 220, 225, 232
age difference, 69, 228–44
age discrimination, 79
ageism, 3, 6, 18, 22, 76–89, 96, 100, 101, 109, 113, 114, 176, 244
age-mixed relationships, 232; and children, 235–40
age studies, 11, 14, 61, 98, 108, 109, 125, 208, 270, 243
Agewise, 5, 22, 76, 86, 89. See also Gullette, Margaret Morganroth
Ahmed, Sara, 230, 231, 235, 237, 240
Americans, 85, 110, 113, 115, 152, 172, 189, 234

Andersen, Hans Christian, 44, 45
Ansello, Edward, 76, 77
archetype, 10, 50, 52, 53
asexuality, 229
audience, 12, 21, 22, 44, 55, 58, 63, 67, 68, 70, 73, 93, 97, 100, 108, 147, 148, 150, 151, 153, 155, 159–63, 187, 189, 208–10, 212, 216–18, 225

baby boomers, 4
Balazs, Anne L., 230, 232
Basting, Ann Davis, 207
*batteries not included, 153
Batty, Nancy, 185, 188
Bazalgette, Cary, 151, 159
Beail, Linda, 185
Beckett, Sandra, 208
Benz-Conzen, Jana and Andreas, 33
Bhattacharya, Sharika, 208
Bianco Footwear, 229, 231–34, 236, 237, 241, 243
Big Head Spring series, 112
Bildungsroman, 45
Blakeborough, David, 180
Bond, Michael, 152, 160
Boston, Lucy, 104
Boy in the Striped Pyjamas, 147
Boym, Svetlana, 172
"Brave Little Tailor," 45
"Bremen Town Musicians," 48, 49
Brexit, 3, 4, 17
Brown, Noel, 150, 152, 155, 159
Buckingham, David, 209, 210, 218
Buddhist ascetics, 15, 52, 57, 141
Bunke, Simon, 29

Burton, Tim, 16, 155–59
Butler, Robert, 79

Callister, Mark, 212, 219
Can, 214, 215
Cantor, Paul, 171, 172
Capaldi, Peter, 160, 162
cartoons, 12, 21, 22, 180, 208–20
Chambers, Aidan, 77–78
Chang, Ta-Chun, 108, 109, 112, 113, 115, 117, 119, 121, 124
Charlie and the Chocolate Factory, 146–57
Chen, Yen-Jen, 118
Cherry Tomato, 22, 129, 132, 134, 135, 137, 140, 142, 143
childhood, 5, 6, 8–17, 19–22, 29–32, 35, 45, 53–55, 58–74, 78, 78, 84, 86, 93–106, 108–10, 115–25, 136, 137, 146, 147, 149, 150, 152–55, 157, 158, 161, 164, 165, 168, 184, 186–90, 192, 194, 195, 198, 200–203, 210, 211, 214, 220, 224, 228, 229
Children's and Household Tales, 49
Children of Green Knowe, 104
children's books, 9, 2, 16, 18, 21, 33, 76–89, 95, 97, 101, 104, 105, 118, 124, 153, 154, 160, 187. See also individual titles
children's films, 150–54. See also individual titles; family films
children's media, 43, 148, 163, 207, 209, 210, 212, 213, 216, 218, 224, 225
Cille, 213
"Cinderella," 45–47, 50
Classic of Filial Piety, The, 114
Close Encounters of the Third Kind, 154
Cocoon, 14, 153, 154
Cocoon: The Return, 153
coming of age, 43, 45, 47, 58, 116
competence, 128, 129, 136, 169
complementarity, 14, 15, 22, 65, 66
conflict, 14, 15, 17, 20, 56, 59, 65–66, 105, 115, 150, 220
Confucian society, 49–50
Confucius, 114, 115
Crawford, Patricia, 77, 208
Culture and Commitment, 168, 169

Dahl, Roald, 152, 155
Davies, Máire Messenger, 152, 208
decline narrative, 7, 12, 15, 19, 37, 39, 98, 186, 203
Depp, Johnny, 155, 158, 159
depression, 80, 85, 89
Depression, the, 148, 151
DiSalvo, Carl, 207
Disney, 44, 51, 55–59, 148, 150
divine child, 26, 29, 30, 32
Dong-Cheol, Kim, 133
"Dragon Palace Boy, The," 52, 53
Duffy, Michael, 155
Durkheim, Émile, 169, 170

Egan, Danielle R., 230
Empire Strikes Back, The, 154
empirical research, 21
enablers, 16, 21, 22, 202
enactment, 229–31, 235, 239, 243
enlightenment, 29, 131, 142
Escher, Georg, 28
E.T. the Extra-Terrestrial, 154
euthanasia, 15, 21, 77, 78, 80, 81
Ewers, Hans-Heino, 31, 32
extended family, 214
Extremely Loud and Incredibly Close, 16, 19, 21, 93, 94, 97, 98, 101, 104, 105. See also Foer, Jonathan Safran

fairy tales: narrative, 50; and the old in Japan, 43–59; Western, 43–49, 59. See also individual titles
"Faithful Johannes," 46
family, 50, 79, 143, 171
family films, 16, 20, 21, 149, 153. See also individual titles; children's films
father, 6, 45, 57, 63, 68, 72, 78, 82, 83, 94–98, 101, 103, 113, 131, 135, 155–57, 158, 159, 171, 188
filial piety, 111, 114, 115, 118, 119, 129, 131
Fineman, Stephen, 228
Foer, Jonathan Safran, 16, 19, 21, 22, 93–106
folktales, 20, 21, 43, 46, 52–54, 130, 212
Frye, Northrop, 208
functional age, 11, 13, 228, 229

Gamble, Nikki, 215
gatekeepers, 16, 21, 22, 79, 84, 202
gender, 11, 17, 61–63, 66, 68, 69, 73, 172, 185, 186, 211, 214, 218, 220, 224, 229, 232, 234, 237, 239, 244
Gillespie, Jason, 180
globalization, 59, 124, 132, 148, 157, 172
glocalization, 148
"Goose Girl at the Spring," 45
Goren, Lilly J., 185
Goryeojang, 131, 132, 142
grandfathers, 26–28, 31–34, 40, 52, 94–96, 98, 99, 104, 105, 108, 113–15, 117, 119–23, 125, 133, 135, 137, 154, 174, 176, 189, 190, 193, 194, 214, 216, 220, 224, 239. *See also* grandparents
"Grandmother," 44
grandmothers, 14, 16, 18, 26, 27, 33–40, 48, 78, 81–84, 95, 96, 98–104, 114, 134–138, 140–43, 192, 215, 216, 220–24. *See also* grandparents
Grandpa in My Pocket, 216, 220
grandparents, 8, 14, 21, 77, 93, 105, 114, 133–35, 140, 142, 142, 155, 168, 171, 179, 181, 189, 192, 198, 201, 202, 208, 209, 213–16, 218–20, 222–25
Gray, Jonathan, 180
Grayson, James H., 131
Grimm's tales, 44–46
Gros, Christophe, 30, 35
growing up, 7, 20, 7, 116, 158
Growing Up and Growing Old, 9, 179. *See also* Hockey, Jenny; James, Allison
Gullette, Margaret Morganroth, 5, 7, 11, 19, 45, 76, 79, 80, 84–89, 98, 113, 114, 228
Gutierrez, Anna Katrina, 148

Halter, Ernst, 30
"Hansel and Gretel," 45
Härle, Gerhard, 34
Harry Potter, 147, 160
Hays Code, 150, 151
Healey, Tim, 186
Hearn, Michael, 26

Heidi, 26–40
Heilbrun, Carolyn, 80, 84, 86
Henneberg, Sylvia B., 18, 37–30, 96
Herder, Johann Gottfried, 31
Herskovic, Chantal, 180
Highmore, Freddie, 155, 158, 159
Higonnet, Anne, 187, 203
Hockey, Jenny, 9, 10, 20, 99, 137, 179, 229
Hof, Marjolijn, 14, 77, 78, 81, 82, 88, 97
Hoffmann, E. T. A., 30

Inada, Koji, 44
industrial revolution, 79
interdependence, 21, 216
intergenerational bonds, 60, 77, 83, 89, 103, 106, 128–43, 184–86, 189, 207–25
intergenerational conflict, 65–66
intergenerational contact, 83, 89, 98, 103, 106, 108–25, 158, 159, 168–81
intersectional theory, 61

James, Allison, 9, 99, 137, 179, 229
Japan, 14, 15, 17, 20, 21, 43–59, 62, 109, 113, 116, 140, 144nn1–2
Janeway, James, 115
Jensen, Helle Strandgaard, 215
Jige (A-frame) script, 130–32
Joosen, Vanessa, 9, 21, 30, 36, 37, 77, 109, 115, 118, 121, 187, 208

"Kachi Kachi Mountain," 47
Kağıtcıbaşı, Ciğdem, 216
Kaminski, Winfred, 32
Katz, Stephen, 109
Kawai, Hayao, 52, 53
Keith, Lois, 30
Kelly, David, 155
Kermode, Mark, 57
King, Paul, 16, 160
Ki-Young, Kim, 131
Klein, Hugh, 180
Klein, Norma, 78, 136
Kostebekgiller, 213, 220
Krämer, Peter, 150
Kubo, Kayo, 48, 49

Kuijer, Guus, 8, 16
Kuyper, Sjoerd, 16

Lakoff, George, and Mark Johnson, 5, 10, 130, 146
Lamb, Charles, 8
Lane, Joseph, 185, 203
Lang, Andrew, 47
Lang zal ze leven, 77, 85–89
Lee, Christopher, 157
Lee, Nick, 19–22
Leimgruber, Walter, 28
Lemish, Dafna, 185, 186
Le Pesant, Tanguy, 116
Liao, Jimmy, 20, 108, 109, 112, 119, 121, 123, 124
"Little Mermaid," 45
"Little Red Cap," 48
loneliness, 98, 99, 104
Lury, Karen, 149, 187

Mad Men, 184–203
Magoffin, Dawn, 212
Malot, Hector, 61–73, 104, 156
Mark, Geraldine, 110
Marshall, Barbara L., 229
McCallum, Robyn, 213
Mead, Margaret, 21, 168–70, 179
Meinderts, Koos, 77, 85, 88
melodrama, 12, 63–65
Metaphors We Live By. *See* Lakoff, George: and Mark Johnson
middle adulthood, 149
middle age, 6, 13, 17, 19, 124, 154, 165, 172, 178, 181
Ming-liang, Tsao, 111
Mo, Weimin, 114
Mol, Annemarie, 230
"Monkey and the Crab, The," 47
Moore, Jennifer, 212, 219
Morris, Tim, 157
Morrow, Virginia, 228, 229
mother, 14, 18, 52, 57, 63–68, 80, 81, 83, 84, 87, 94–99, 104, 105, 117–19, 131–33, 135, 142, 143, 171, 172, 186, 192, 195, 200
"Mother Holle," 47

Muhlbauer, Varda, 185, 186
Mullins, Matthew, 99, 163
Murai, Mayako, 12, 15, 20, 111–12

Nakamura, Akira, 111
naturalism, 64; literary, 69, 70, 73
natural piety, 31–32
nature, 15, 19, 26–40, 52, 54, 55, 61, 79, 87, 104, 105, 116, 142, 163, 189
Neiman, Susan, 18, 19, 116, 119, 125, 165, 207
Nelson, Claudia, 9
Nelson, Todd, 79, 81
Netherlands, the, 77–82, 90
Neumann, Erich, 52
Nikolajeva, Maria, 18, 147, 149, 208
Niloya, 213–15
Nodelman, Perry, 149, 150
nostalgia, 11, 18, 109, 147, 152, 154, 160–63

"Old Bachelor's Nightcap," 44
"Old House," 44
"Old Man Who Made Flowers Bloom," 43, 47, 48, 51
"Old Sultan," 46, 49
O'Neil, Naomi Bell Cornman, 181
Ongg, Christina, 110
Onur, Bekir, 220
oral storytelling tradition, 46, 48, 49

Paddington, 16, 21, 22, 146, 149–52, 154, 164, 165, nation and nostalgia in, 160–63
Palmore, Erdman B., 50
pastoral tradition, 140–43
"Peach Boy," 47, 48, 51
Pepee, 213, 214, 216, 220
Perrault, Charles, 46, 55
Pestalozzi, Johann Heinrich, 35
pietism, 27, 36
pluralism, 207, 215
polarities, 27
Polleke series, 16
Pomerance, Murray, 152, 153
postfigurative culture, 168–71, 174, 181
prefigurative culture, 168–75, 181; and *The Simpsons*, 172–75

prejudice, 3, 5, 17, 22, 76, 79, 86, 88, 89, 99, 153, 176, 186
Pricing the Priceless Child, 17
printing press, 79
Prout, Alan, 208
puer senex trope, 5, 6, 9, 10, 14, 15, 20, 78, 111
Pulliam, June, 155

Queer Child, The, 156

realism, 64, 94, 208
regels van drie, De, 10, 14–16, 18, 22, 77, 81–85, 87–89, 95, 97
Return of the Jedi, 154
Rigger, Shelley, 109
Ringrose, Jessica, 230
Renold, Emma, 230
Robin en God, 16
Robinson, Tom, 211, 219
romanticism, 15, 22, 29
root metaphor, 5, 10–12, 102, 146, 148, 154, 156, 157
Rosen, Michael, 3
Ross, Karen, 186
Rousseau, Jean-Jacques, 28, 31, 32, 35
Rutgers-van der Loeff, An, 77
Rutschmann, Verena, 28

Sanders, Bengt, 154, 157
Sans famille, 61–73, 104, 156
Schenda, Rudolph, 46, 47
Schiffman, Kenneth S., 176, 180
Schindler, Regine, 31, 36
Schmiesing, Ans, 49
Schoentjes, Pierre, 181
Schweitzer, Marlis, 231
seesaw effect, 17–19, 97, 98, 121
self-determination, 10, 15, 76–89
senex consciousness, 52, 53
sexuality, 122, 170, 189, 229, 230, 232, 234, 235, 243, 244
Shen, Wenju, 114, 115
Signorielli, Nancy, 214
Simpsons, The, 21, 100, 168–81
Skrine, Peter, 28, 32
"Snow White," 45, 48

social age, 12, 229
social ecology, 129, 133, 134
Solberg, Anne, 229
Someya, Yoshiko, 50
"Son Who Abandoned His Old Father in the Mountains, The," 130
South Korea, 21, 25, 116, 128–43
Spyri, Johanna, 14–16, 19, 21, 26–33, 37, 38, 95
Staples, Terry, 151, 159
Starry Starry Night, 20, 22, 108, 109, 112, 119, 121, 123, 124
Star Wars, 148, 154
Stephens, John, 18, 213
stereotypes, 12, 46, 62, 78, 80, 82, 137, 148, 163, 170, 181, 214, 216; ageist, 4, 112–19, 202; gender, 220
Stockton, Kathryn Bond, 156
Strawberry generation, 17, 21, 108–25
Studio Ghibli, 44, 54, 56, 57, 59, 148
suicide, 130; rational, 80–81, 87–89, 113
Switzerland, 40n1

Taine, Hippolyte, 64, 65, 68
Taiwan, 17, 20, 108–26
Takahata, Isao, 44, 54–58
"Tale of the Bamboo Cutter, The," 44, 53, 54, 58
"Tale of the Horse, the Dog, the Cat, and the Chicken, The," 48
Tale of the Princess Kaguya, 44, 54–58
Tales of Times Now Past, 15, 52
Taoism, 50, 52
Taylor, Albert, 179
television, 11, 12, 16, 21, 148, 150, 152, 162, 168, 178, 180, 181, 185, 186; in Turkey, 207–25
"Thumbling's Travels," 45
Tieck, Ludwig, 30
Tincknell, Estella, 154, 187, 203
Token for Children, A, 115
"Tongue-Cut Sparrow," 43, 47, 48, 51
trauma, 70, 95, 103–5, 158
Treeless Mountain, 128, 135–37, 140–43
Trites, Roberta Seelinger, 208
TRT, 210
TRT Çocuk, 211
Tufan, İsmail, 210

Turkey: and animated television, 210; children's television, 210–18; demographic shifts in, 209–10. *See also* children's literature
Twenty-Four Examples of Filial Piety, 114, 115

Ubasute-yama stories, 52
"Ugly Duckling," 45
United Kingdom/Britain, 3, 4, 58, 160, 163, 211
United States, 80, 109, 171, 184, 189, 230, 231, 234
Ürkmez, Başak, 210

Villain, Jean, 34
voluntary death, 75–89

Walkerdine, Valerie, 239
Wang, Ban, 124
Way Home, The, 128, 129, 132–34
Weekly Journal of Young Big Head Spring, The, 112
Weiner, Matthew, 184, 185
Weinstock, Jeffrey, 158, 159
Welcome to Dongmakgol, 141
Why Grow Up?, 18, 116–18, 125
Wild Child, 20, 108, 109, 112, 113, 118, 124
Wilder, Gene, 155
Wilkending, Gisela, 28
Willemsen, August, 72
Willy Wonka and the Chocolate Factory, 152
Wilson, Julia, 185, 203
wise old man image, 119–25
Wissmer, Jean-Michel, 36
"Wolf and Seven Little Goats, The," 48
women, 17, 43, 46, 62, 54, 57, 61, 66, 73, 84, 86, 117, 184, 186, 188, 189, 232, 237
Wood, Robin, 154
Wu, Andrea Mei-Ying, 112

Yazici, Suzan, 210
Yufan, Lim, 110
Yumurcak TV, 211

Zelizer, Viviana, 17, 110
Zipes, Jack, 214

www.ingramcontent.com/pod-product-compliance
Lightning Source LLC
Chambersburg PA
CBHW030616230426
43661CB00053B/2018